Margaret Heffernan is an awar[...]
and playwright and blogs fo[...]
Huffington Post.

Further praise for *Wilful Blindness*

'Entertaining and compellingly argued' *Sunday Times*

'*Wilful Blindness* makes a convincing case that while we are
supposedly better informed than ever, we are guilty of frequent
and self-destructive acts . . . Full of juicy, awkward stories . . .
Given how so many of us wander around in the warm fug of
distortion, it is good to be beaten to attention every now and
again' *Financial Times*

'Writing in clear, flowing prose, (Heffernan) draws on psychological
and neurological studies and interviews with executives, whistleblowers and white-collar criminals. The book made me think long
and hard about how the pace and priorities of our daily lives can
hinder our ability to live as decently and as truthfully as we can'
New York Times

'An engaging read, packed with cautionary tales . . . With deft
prose and page after page of keen insights, Heffernan shows why
we close our eyes to facts that threaten our families, our liveli-
hood, and our self-image – and, even better, she points the way
out of the darkness' Daniel H. Pink, author of *Drive* and *A Whole
New Mind*

'A remarkable book . . . It is a tour de force of brilliant insights,
broad span applications and written in the most engaging style'
Philip Zimbardo

'Uniquely broad in scope, insightfully analyzed, and engagingly
written. This in-depth look at wilful blindness is an excellent
read' Albert Bandura

WILFUL BLINDNESS

WHY WE IGNORE THE OBVIOUS AT OUR PERIL

MARGARET HEFFERNAN

**SIMON &
SCHUSTER**

London · New York · Sydney · Toronto · New Delhi

A CBS COMPANY

First published in Great Britain in 2011 by Simon & Schuster UK Ltd
This paperback edition published in 2012 by Simon & Schuster UK Ltd
A CBS COMPANY

1 3 5 7 9 10 8 6 4 2

Simon & Schuster UK Ltd
1st Floor
222 Gray's Inn Road
London
WC1X 8HB

www.simonandschuster.co.uk

Simon & Schuster Australia, Sydney
Simon & Schuster India, New Delhi

A CIP catalogue copy for this book
is available from the British Library.

ISBN: 978-1-84739-905-2

Typeset in Bembo by M Rules
Printed and bound by CPI Group (UK) Ltd, Croydon, CR0 4YY

For Pamela

CONTENTS

INTRODUCTION

On July 19, 2011, MP Adrian Sanders asked James and Rupert Murdoch a question that temporarily silenced them both.

'Are you familiar with the term "wilful blindness"?'

Reading from my blog on the subject, the member of the Select Committee on Culture, Media and Sport proceeded to explain what was, apparently, a highly uncomfortable idea for both Murdochs.

I had first encountered wilful blindness when reading the transcript of the trial of Jeffrey Skilling and Kenneth Lay, CEO and Chairman of Enron. In his summing up, Judge Simeon Lake gave this instruction to the jury:

> You may find that a defendant had knowledge of a fact if you find that the defendant deliberately closed his eyes to what would otherwise have been obvious to him. Knowledge can be inferred if the defendant *deliberately blinded himself to the existence of a fact*.[1]

Judge Lake was applying the legal principle of wilful blindness: you are responsible if you could have known, and should have known, something which instead you strove not to see. Skilling and Lay could have known, and had the opportunity to know, just how rotten their company was. Their claim not to know was no excuse under the law. Since they could have known, they were responsible.

Once the idea of wilful blindness lodged in my mind, I started to see it everywhere: in the Catholic Church, Nazi Germany, at BP, in Iraq and Egypt, in our continuing failure meaningfully to reform the banking system. I was struck that so many, perhaps even most, of the greatest crimes had been committed not in the dark, hidden where no one could see them, but in full view of hundreds or thousands of people who simply chose not to look and not to question.

I noticed it in domestic lives too – in failing marriages: why had she never asked about all those business trips? In hospitals: why had he skipped his check up? Why had she started smoking? At home: how could so many people have got themselves so deeply in debt? And why were skin cancers and obesity so intractable when everyone knows that suntanning and over-eating are dangerous?

When I mentioned wilful blindness to friends and colleagues from any walk of life, their eyes lit up: they knew exactly what I was talking about. Doctors described unnecessary treatments their patients demanded and got. Lawyers recounted their struggles to forget information their clients should never have shared with them. Technologists expressed their amazement that Microsoft hadn't seen the Internet coming, while Google had been blindsided by social media. Intelligence chiefs confided that they had had no insight into the Arab spring while chief executives acknowledged that the hardest part of their job, even in a small company, was knowing what was going on. Almost everyone mentioned the Iraq War and global warming: big public blunders caused or exacerbated by a reluctance to confront uncomfortable facts.

Wilful blindness had started life as a legal concept in the nineteenth century. A judge in *Regina v. Sleep* ruled that an accused could not be convicted for possession of government property unless the jury found that he either knew the goods came from government stores or had 'wilfully shut his eyes to the fact'.

Thereafter, English judicial authorities referred to the state of mind that accompanied one who 'wilfully shut his eyes' as 'connivance' or 'constructive knowledge'.[2] Over time, lots of other phrases came into play – deliberate or wilful ignorance, conscious avoidance and deliberate indifference. What they all have in common is the idea that there is an opportunity for knowledge, and a responsibility to be informed, but it is shirked. Nowadays, the law is most often applied in cases of money laundering and drug trafficking: if you've been paid a large amount of money to carry a suitcase, then you are being wilfully blind if you don't check what is inside.

The law doesn't care *why* you remain ignorant, only that you do. But I am interested in why we choose to keep ourselves in the dark. What are the forces at work that make us deny the big threats that stare us in the face? What stops us from seeing that burying knowledge only makes it more powerful, and us so much more vulnerable? Why, after any major failure or calamity, do voices always emerge saying they'd seen the danger, warned about the risk – but their warnings went unheeded? And why, as individuals, companies and countries do we so regularly look in the mirror and howl: how could we have been so blind?

As I investigated the causes and patterns of wilful blindness, from our daily lives to the boardrooms of global corporations, I could have confined myself to business alone; there's no shortage of material. But it struck me that one source of our blindness at work is the artificial divide between personal and working lives. Every workforce is a conglomeration of individuals whose behaviors and habits started well before they were hired. Individuals, singly and in groups, are equally susceptible to wilful blindness; what makes organizations different is the scale of damage they can cause.

Whether individual or collective, wilful blindness, doesn't have a single driver, but many. We can't notice and know everything: the cognitive limits of our brain simply won't let us. That means we have to filter or edit what we take in. So what we choose to let through and to leave out is crucial. We mostly admit the information that makes us feel great about ourselves, while conveniently filtering out whatever unsettles our fragile egos and most vital beliefs. It's a truism that love is blind; what's less obvious is just how much evidence it can ignore. Ideology and orthodoxies powerfully mask what, to the uncaptivated mind, is obvious, dangerous or absurd and there's much about how and even where we live that leaves us in the dark. Fear of conflict, fear of change keeps us that way: almost all employees believe their bosses do not want to hear the truth. An unconscious (and much denied) impulse to obey and conform shields us from confrontation and crowds provide friendly alibis for our inertia. And money has the power to blind us, even to our better selves.

Of course, wilful blindness it isn't always disastrous. It oils the wheels of social intercourse when we don't see the spot on a silk tie, the girlfriend's acne or a neighbor's squalor. Ignoring political differences may contribute to office calm. In times of national emergency, blindness can be positively helpful. During the London Blitz, morale was better sustained by dancing and party-going than by acknowledging a terrifying future. And it's far easier for all of us to maintain optimism and momentum by ignoring our own mortality.

Perhaps it is the sheer utility of wilful blindness that sucks us into the habit in the first place. It seems innocuous and feels efficient. But the mechanisms that make us blind to the world also put us in peril. The children who grow up among abusive parents come to maturity feeling crazy, confused and anxious because their reality has been consistently denied. Ideologues, refusing to see data and events that challenge their theories, doom themselves to irrelevance. Fraudsters only succeed when they depend on our desire to blind ourselves to the questions that would expose their schemes. Companies full of compliant employees take on levels of risk beyond their ability to recover. And all the time that these perils go unacknowledged, they grow more powerful and more dangerous.

That wilful blindness is so pervasive does not mean that it is inevitable. Some of the most inspiring people in this book are those who have had the courage to look, a fierce determination to see. That is what makes them remarkable. They aren't especially knowledgeable, powerful or talented. They're not heroes; they're human. But their courage in daring to see reveals a central truth about wilful blindness: we may think being blind makes us safer, when in fact it leaves us crippled, vulnerable and powerless. But when we confront facts and fears, we achieve real power and unleash our capacity for change.

1. AFFINITY AND BEYOND

In life one and one don't make two. One and
one make one.
And I'm looking for that free ride to me: I'm
looking for you.

'Bargain'
The Who

Meet Rebecca.

The first thing you will notice is that she is very tall – just under six foot. Mid-thirties. Healthy, wholesome and, even today when she's had to bring her two children into work with her, she has plenty of energy.

Meet Robert.

He's tall too – just over six foot. Mid-thirties. Handsome, clean-cut and, despite some looming deadlines, unfailingly polite.

If you meet Rebecca and Robert together, you will notice what all their friends comment on: they look very alike. Not the same, of course; they're not twins. They're husband and wife. And their looks are not deceptive.

'Amazing similarities,' Robert concedes. 'Similarities in background that I didn't notice, but I like more and more. Not rich, not poor. Went to the same university, both in broadcasting, both Christian. But then there are more nuanced things, like the way we both think about family and friends, and believing in hard work. And of course we work in the same industry and,' he looks over at Rachel and beams, 'wear the unofficial uniform: neat jeans, crisp shirt.' They both laugh.

Rebecca and Robert enjoy the fact that they are similar, because it makes them feel comfortable, safe, located within each other.

'It isn't that we like all the same things,' says Rebecca when she's on her own. 'I love going for walks – and Robert's had to learn to like them! But the skeleton of our lives, that's what we have in common. Very settled home lives, parents still together, parents who were always very encouraging. We didn't think consciously about these things when we started going out, but you look back and see these things, these patterns.'

Rebecca and Robert enjoy the fact that they're so similar. They have very little sense that it limits them, narrows their perspective on life or blinds them to a wide array of opinions, experiences and different ways of thinking and being. But the fundamental human preference that they exemplify – for the familiar over the alien, the known over the unknown, and the comfortable over the dissonant – has insidious but important consequences. Embedded within our self-definition, we build relationships, institutions, cities, systems and cultures that, in reaffirming our values, blind us to alternatives. This is where our wilful blindness originates: in the innate human desire for familiarity, for likeness, that is fundamental to the ways our minds work.

Because for all that their similarities are so pronounced, in fact Rebecca and Robert are typical. Most people marry other people very like themselves: similar height, weight, age, background, IQ, nationality, ethnicity. We may think that opposites attract, but they don't get married. Sociologists and psychologists, who have studied this phenomenon for decades, call it 'positive assortative mating'[1] – which really just means that we marry people like ourselves. When it comes to love, we don't scan a very broad horizon.

Gian Gonzaga used to work as a senior research scientist before leaving to join eHarmony, the online dating site. The 'science of compatibility' that the site promotes argues that 'compatibility is not enough! 29 Dimensions™ predict great relationships.'

But this is not romance, it's business. So eHarmony stands or falls on its success in finding people who really will like each other. In 2007, eHarmony claimed credit for 44,000 American weddings: 2 per cent of all the marriages in America[2] that year,[3] and today they claim to average 236 marriages a day. What were all those people looking for?

'We know that people select for appearances, which is why you upload your picture. But our questionnaire goes a lot deeper and that's really based on what we know works. So we ask lots of questions about personality – how neat you are, how punctual – and about values: do you value religion, altruism, volunteering? Values are the things you hold on to even in tough times and they are the things you most want validated by others. Of course interests count too, but they change. You can learn to love walking, but values are really sticky.'

When it comes to marriage, there are cultural differences of course. Married people in the United Kingdom consistently express greater satisfaction than in the US with the amount of consensus they experience in their marriage. They're more satisfied with their family relationship, the way they make decisions and how they take care of household chores. And this striking degree of consensus even affects their sex life: compared with the US and Australia, British couples are the least likely to report that being too tired for sex is a problem for the marriage. All couples, according to eHarmony, want to agree with each other about career decisions, friendships, leisure activities and friendships, but

British couples in particular care about family, sharing household tasks equally and about definitions of proper behaviour.

Gonzaga and his wife, Heather Setrakian, don't just practise what they preach – they *are* what they preach. They met while working as academic researchers in UCLA's marriage lab, they're both in their thirties, dark-haired and, according to their friends, both brilliant, witty and wise. The eHarmony system could have matched them, Gonzaga says, except that when his wife filled out her questionnaire she said she wanted someone two years younger.

That questionnaire certainly tests for patience and endurance. It takes at least half an hour to complete – longer if you're seriously committed to finding a mate. The questions are all designed to identify your key values and attitudes – those twenty-nine dimensions – and to match them up with someone else whose dimensions are as close to yours as possible. It may be software but it is, quite literally, matchmaking. It is not looking for opposites or quirky combinations.

'People may have an interest in people who are different from themselves,' said Gonzaga. 'But they don't marry them. They're looking for confirmation, for comfort.'

Gonzaga bases his claims on data from twenty-five million questionnaires. What these tell him is that, whether you're using the wiring in your brain or the software underneath eHarmony's site, we go through life looking for people who make us comfortable because they're so much like us. We may be intrigued by difference – but, ultimately, we reject it.

'For a while, I went out with women who looked different,' Robert told me. 'And women who really were different – sometimes very different indeed. But the turbulence of those relationships really drew me back to the centre. You'd think it would widen the circle but it really didn't. I tried but I found I really didn't love Albanian women! Clearly some Albanian women are wonderful – I have nothing against the Albanians! But

I think I learned that you're given a centre of gravity that is immutable. You've been given a set of rules that you return to almost without thinking.'

It isn't that Robert wasn't curious about other kinds of people and other cultures; he was. He wanted, more than many people, to explore beyond his own immediate knowledge and experience. But ultimately he did what most of us do most of the time: he rejected a difference that just felt too great. That puzzled him enough to make him think about it, but not enough to change his mind.

'I wonder if I might feel I am looking at myself when I look at Rebecca,' Robert said. 'Have I chosen myself?'

Robert and Rebecca are well educated and sceptical. They aren't inclined to take anything at face value. What makes them unusual is that they were prepared to analyse and talk about the powerful influence that their similarity has had on their relationship. They both acknowledge that it is a source of delight and comfort, but worry that sticking to their own kind narrows their experience of life. By choosing to live and work among people like themselves, are they restricting what they see?

These findings – that we mostly marry and live with people very like ourselves – always annoy people. Confronted by the data, the most common response is a challenge: I'm not like that, my husband's not like that. Why are we so affronted? Because we all want to feel that we have made our own choices, that they weren't predictable, that we aren't so vain as to choose ourselves, and that we are freer spirits, with a broader, more eclectic range of taste than the data imply. We don't like to feel that we're blind to the allure of those who are not like us; we don't like to see how trapped we are inside our own identity.

But our minds operate somewhat like eHarmony's software: we go through life searching for good matches and, when we find one, it feels good; the more something is like us, the more we're inclined to like it. And that habit of mind pertains equally to things that really matter (like choosing a wife) and to things that don't matter at all. So when subjects in an experiment were led to believe that they shared a birthday with Rasputin, they were far more lenient in judging the mad monk than those who had nothing in common with him. Just the thought that they shared a birthday made people like him more.

Even when it's something as trivial as our own initials, we stick to what we know best. A meta-analysis of the most severe hurricanes between 1998 and 2005 showed that people were more likely to donate to relief funds if the hurricane's name shared their first initial – so Kate and Katherine were more likely to donate to Hurricane Katrina relief than Zoe was.[4] I've always been baffled by monogrammed towels and shirts (do we really not know who owns the towels in our own homes?) but clearly these familiar letters mean a lot to us.

In other experiments, asked to choose a preferred letter from several pairs of letters, subjects tended, quite reliably, to opt for letters from their own names. What's so interesting about these findings is that the letters themselves are meaningless – nothing will happen as a result of the choices made. Yet still the participants gravitated towards letters they see, and sign, every day.

When you take this out of the lab and into the real world, the same pattern emerges. Carol, it seems, is more likely to drink Coke while Pete will choose Pepsi.[5] Leo likes Listerine but Catherine prefers Colgate. And while those choices may seem unimportant, it appears that life choices too may be influenced by those initials we love so much. Dentists are over-represented by people whose names begin with 'D' and there are more people named George than you should expect to find living in Georgia.

Familiarity, it turns out, does not breed contempt. It breeds comfort. In a series of experiments at the University of Michigan in the 1980s,[6] one group of sixty-four students were shown photographs of a male college student once a week for four weeks; the other group of sixty-four saw different faces each week. After the four weeks were up, the two groups were asked to assess how much they thought they would like the people whose faces they'd seen if they were to meet them in the future. They were also asked how far they believed those people to be similar to themselves.

The students who had seen the same face for four weeks believed more strongly that these were people they would like in real life. They also believed (on no evidence except the photograph) that those faces belonged to people who were similar to themselves. In other words, the familiar faces – with no supporting evidence – felt nicer. Women responded to the experiment in exactly the same way as men. A similar experiment, using irregular octagons, generated the same pattern of responses. The familiar makes us feel secure and comfortable.

This pertains even when we go looking for emotional experiences, as when we listen to music. It can be hard fully to enjoy a new piece the first time you listen to it; only after repeated hearings does it become a favourite. Part of that may be because if you're trying out, say, Mahler's 8th Symphony for the first time, there is a lot to take in: two orchestras, two choirs and eight soloists over eighty minutes won't create an instant impression. And listening to music is a hugely complex cognitive exercise.[7] Even the White Stripes' 'Seven Nation Army' can take some getting used to. But once we've heard it a few times, we're used to it and like it. And then we don't want something different; we want more of the same.

'We score hundreds of attributes of every song and then we find the matches between those songs – and then that's what we recommend to you. Because we know that if you liked one piece of music, you are very, very likely to like another one that shares the same characteristics.'

Tim Westergren isn't talking about dating, but about his company, Pandora Internet radio. It does for music what eHarmony does for dating. Each song is scored manually by musicians for 400 attributes; there are 30 for the voice alone, capturing everything from timbre to layers of the voice to vibrato. Then that 'score' is matched to other songs that have scores that are as closely similar as possible. Pandora software is doing to music what we do when we meet people: looking for matches. And, when it finds them, people feel very happy.

'God, I love Pandora!' said Joe Clayton, a music fan in Boston. 'I love it. I'm always finding new bands, new stuff that I just couldn't find otherwise – certainly not in any music store. And it's kinda creepy – but in a good way – because they almost never give me something I don't like. Almost never.'

In May 2007, Pandora was prohibited from operating in the UK, although many devout fans still access it via proxy servers. To date, over fifty million people around the world have tried Pandora, and its users are avid evangelists. But what Pandora can't do is come up with that serendipitous suggestion that introduces you to something completely different from anything you've ever heard before. I like Bruce Springsteen, Frank Zappa and the White Stripes – but I also adore Handel. And given my first three preferences, Pandora would never offer me Handel.

Westergren acknowledges that limitation. 'It's about broadening your selection – but narrowing your taste. If you like jazz, you like more jazz. If you like hip hop, you like more hip hop. But Pandora is never going to take you from Springsteen to Handel.'

All personalisation software, whether eHarmony, Pandora, Amazon's book recommendations or MyShape.com's clothing suggestions, does the same thing: make our lives easier by reducing overwhelming choice. And they're doing it the same way that our brain does, by searching for matches. It's as though, online and offline, our life is one gigantic game of Snap! This is immensely efficient: it means that the brain can take shortcuts because it is working with what it already knows, not having to learn everything from scratch. When we find what we like, part of our pleasure is the joy of recognition.

As Westergren says, we are narrowing our taste, reducing the music or books or people that might widen our horizons. Our brains aren't designed to draw us into experiences that are wild and different; there would be no advantage in doing something so risky. And so, by focusing in one direction and excluding others, we become blind to the experiences that don't match.

This is not to say that strange, serendipitous things never flow into our lives. Of course they do. You meet someone at work who introduces you to Handel and you develop a love of baroque music. Or – more likely – your son introduces you to Rammstein. But these encounters are random and risky. Remember Robert's problem with Albanian women.

There's a circle here: we like ourselves, not least because we are known and familiar to ourselves. So we like people similar to us – or that we just imagine might have some attributes in common with us. They feel familiar too, and safe. And those feelings of familiarity and security make us like ourselves more because we aren't anxious. We belong. Our self-esteem rises. We feel happy. Human beings want to feel good about themselves and to feel safe, and being surrounded by familiarity and similarity satisfies those needs very efficiently.

The problem with this is that everything outside that warm, safe circle is our blind spot.

We aren't just rejecting music that doesn't match; we use these same processes to make important decisions in our everyday lives. When I had my first opportunity, as a producer at the BBC, to choose my own team, I hoped to hire people who would challenge me and each other and who would invest the entire project with intellectual richness and vigour. With all that firmly in mind, I selected liberal-arts graduates who were all female, spoke several languages and had birthdays within the same week in June. In other words, they were all like me.

Did I consciously intend to do that? Of course not. Like hiring managers the world over, I intended to hire only the best and the brightest and that's what I thought I was looking for. But did I also want people I'd feel comfortable working with, enjoy spending late hours with, people who shared the values of the project? Well, yes.

I was biased, in favour of those just like me. Everyone is biased. But just as we are affronted when told that we're likely to marry and associate with those very similar to ourselves, so most people vehemently reject the idea that they are biased: others may be, but not us. 'And why beholdest thou the mote that is in thy brother's eye, but considerest not the beam that is in thine own eye?' is how the Bible puts it.[8] Of course we consider the people who disagree with us to be the most biased of all.[9]

It's recently become easier to identify and measure biases with a suite of tests called the Implicit Association Test, or IAT for short. Designed by three psychologists, the computer-based tests examine thoughts and feelings that exist outside of our conscious awareness or control.[10] These may pertain to gender, age, race or religion. In the test, participants are given two sets of images and two lists of words – one positive, one negative. Images and words appear randomly on the screen and you have to associate them with positives or negatives. You may link 'male' with 'intelligent' or 'old' with 'stupid'. When making a link that isn't comfortable for us, we take longer. And that delay, say the researchers, is telling: it takes more time to overcome bias. The longer we take to accept a match, the greater our bias.

Since 1998, over 4.5 million people have taken these tests and what the researchers have found is that bias is pervasive, among all of us, whether we think we're biased or not. White physicians are friendlier towards anonymous white patients than black ones. Seventy per cent of citizens in thirty-four different countries associate science more with men than women. More than 80 per cent of us have a bias against the elderly. Ordinary people (including the researchers who direct the project) harbour negative associations in relation to various social groups even though they say they don't and often wish, quite earnestly, not to.

We see this play out in daily life everywhere. Go into any major corporation and look around. Despite decades of diversity campaigns and millions of dollars invested in programmes to make recruitment and retention less biased and more equitable, the homogeneity of most companies is overwhelming. Look at the lists of where the graduates of Harvard Business School or London Business School go and you will see the same phenomenon: armies marching into banks, financial institutions, consulting firms, year after year.

This is one reason why, despite a great deal of goodwill and commitment and equality legislation, it has proved so hard to shift women into top roles, shovel venture capital into ethnic businesses or train more male midwives. It isn't the only reason, of course, but the fact that we like people like ourselves, are unconsciously biased in their favour, has a big impact. Stereotypes are energy-saving devices – they let us make shortcuts that feel just fine.[11] That's why they're so persistent.

The famous development of blind auditions for new symphony members provided graphic illustration of this point. Harvard economist Claudia Goldin and Princeton's Cecilia Rouse found that when musicians were allowed to audition behind screens, where their gender could not influence the evaluation of their music, women's chances of making it through the first round increased by 50 per cent – and in the final rounds by *300* per cent. Blind auditions have now become standard in the

US, with the result that the number of female players in major orchestras has increased from 5 per cent to 36 per cent.

In Europe, that practice is not ubiquitous – and many musicians argue that this perpetuates both gender and ethnic discrimination. Some of this bias isn't even implicit: the Vienna Philharmonic did not accept women until twelve years ago and even now only 2 per cent of its 137 musicians are women. Moreover, despite the recent rise to prominence of many brilliant Asian musicians, the Philharmonic has never hired a visible 'non-Aryan' because it feels that such individuals would 'destroy the ensemble's image of Austrian authenticity'.[12] Music may be a universal language but not, apparently, universally.[13]

The many voices arguing in favour of diversity in recent years have not been motivated only, or even primarily, by notions of social justice. The argument for diversity is that if you bring together lots of different kinds of people, with a wide range of education and experience, together they can identify more solutions, see more alternatives to problems, than any single person, or homogenous group, ever could. Groups have the potential, in other words, to be smarter than individuals; that's the case put forward so compellingly by James Surowiecki in his book *The Wisdom of Crowds.* But the problem is that, as our biases keep informing whom we hire and promote, we weed out that diversity and are left with corporate headquarters crammed full of people pretty much the same. They aren't exposed to other ways of seeing the world, they don't share different experiences. They can't celebrate difference because they are blind to it.

What happens at work doesn't stay at work. Just as we choose to work with people very like ourselves, we choose to live among them also. Opposites don't attract. The psychologist David Myers says that the way we move around and build neighbourhoods mirrors the way we choose our spouses.

'Mobility enables the sociological equivalent of "assortative mating"', he says. Now that we enjoy so much freedom to move around, choosing the jobs that we like, we can also choose the communities that we like. And by and large we choose 'those places and people that are comfortably akin to ourselves'.[14]

In the United States, Bill Bishop studied this pattern and found that, over the last thirty years, most Americans had been engaged in moving towards more homogenous ways of living, 'clustering in communities of like-mindedness'. He calls this 'the big sort' and what strikes him is how well defended these communities can be. When a lone Republican neighbour, living in a staunchly Democratic part of Austin, Texas, dared to articulate his political opinion in a local listserv, the response he got was unambiguous: 'I'm really not interested [in] being surprised by right-wing e-mail in my inbox, no matter what its guise. It makes me feel bad, and I don't like it.'[15] At first, I thought this was a specifically American phenomenon – until a mother at my children's school dared to send an email to other mothers during the 2010 election campaign. Criticising the local MP provoked a vociferous response: pleas for lost games kit were fine but an exchange of political views was not welcomed.

As we have either more freedom or less security in our work, we move more. Every year, some forty million Americans choose to move their home and more than a third of these are moving county or state. It's just one of the fourteen moves made in each American lifetime. And when people move, they mostly choose to live among people who like the same coffee shops, bookstores, festivals and politics. When Bill Bishop went on to map this trend across the United States, his data revealed that the preference people have for living with others like themselves made a clear impact on the political map of the country. Whereas, in 1976, only 26 per cent of people lived in landslide counties, by 2000 45.3 per cent did. This goes a long way towards explaining the stridency and polarisation that has so beset American politics in recent years. But it isn't just an American phenomenon.

'The London neighbourhood where we live,' Rebecca says, 'is lovely. The neighbours are lovely. The family on the other side of us, Paul and Juliet – they *are* us! Mid-thirties, two boys. Slightly younger but exactly parallel. Juliet doesn't work, but I'm only part time. The street is full of people like us. Each house is a carbon copy of the same kinds of people.'

When they were house-hunting, Rebecca recalls that they were driven by price, proximity to work, choice of schools. All her neighbours were using the same parameters, so perhaps it isn't so surprising that they'd all end up together.

'I guess you could say that,' Rebecca concedes. 'But there were other places that would have fit the bill. But when we came here, it was more than just functionality. We liked it here – we still like it here. It feels right for us.'

Bishop argues that we have come to demand living arrangements that won't challenge us. We seek confirmation and validation from those around us, even if it is just a matter of our pastimes. Wesleyan University in Connecticut caters to this desire, by offering twenty-eight different dorms organised around themes, including one for 'eclectic' students. (Apparently even dislike of themes is a theme.) Colgate University in New York has a dorm for the lovers of foreign films.

Living in London isn't that different either. I used to live in Stockwell, which estate agents at the time would call 'a mixed area' – meaning an ethnically mixed and sometimes volatile combination of early Victorian terraces and 1960s council housing. But you didn't see much traffic between those two architectures, not a lot of cups of sugar being borrowed. Teachers, professors, business people and TV producers lived in elegant stucco homes; single, often teenage, parents lived across from them. At least we could see each other, but that was about as far as it ever went.

Then we moved to Boston, where we chose to live in the North End, the colourful Italian district of the city. Coming from Europe, we'd chosen it because it felt less alien than other parts of the city. We were used to, and enjoyed, hearing Italian spoken on the streets and we liked the aroma of garlic in the evenings. But we didn't have any Italian friends. We had an Italian long-shoreman as a neighbour but we knew Louis only well enough to say 'ciao'. But who were we spending time with? People like us: educated white professionals with young kids.

Now we live in Somerset and I'm struck by the polarisation between city and country. My village neighbours rarely travel to London, and when they do they go as tourists, both critical and a little intimidated. But this cuts both ways. An esteemed British playwright wrinkled up her nose, telling me about her sojourn in Dorset. She had cut her time there short because, while she liked the scenery, not enough of her city friends came to visit at the weekends. What she'd aspired to was her London life but with roses around the door. She wanted to live in the country, not engage with it. And every year, as more Londoners move down to the country, I watch as they search out fellow *émigrés* who are so much easier to make friends with.

The same may be said of academic communities. The University of Chicago is not famous for the diversity of its economic theories but for the homogeneity of its monetarist doctrine. Likewise, when I attended a celebration at the retirement of a distinguished Cambridge psychologist, what was so striking after an entire day of academic papers was the total absence of any other discipline in the room. We were talking about the human mind and social behaviour – but where were the neuroscientists, the sociologists, the anthropologists? The consensus of the room was unsettling.

By following our instincts to cluster together in like-minded communities, we reduce our exposure to different people, values and experiences. We slowly but surely focus on what we know, losing sight of everything else. We may have more choices than ever before but our narrow tastes are better defended.

Media companies understand this perfectly. They know that, when we buy a newspaper or a magazine, we aren't looking for a fight. The loyal Sky News fan isn't a regular *Guardian* reader. We select our media knowingly, rejecting the programmes, news-papers and TV stations that we don't agree with, because we feel comfortable sticking to the same groove. The search for what is familiar and comfortable underlies our media-consumption habits in the same way as it makes us yearn for Mum's bread-and-butter pudding.

This is natural but it isn't neutral. In what he calls the 'group polarisation effect', legal scholar Cass Sunstein found that when groups of like-minded people get together, they do not just chal-lenge one another, they make each other's views more extreme.[16] (It is worth noting that Sunstein, a professor at Harvard, is married to Samantha Power, also a professor at Harvard, and they are both currently on leave serving the Obama Administration. Even people who write about this behaviour aren't immune to it.) Just as Pandora narrows your taste, like-minded people have the same impact on opinions.

In 2005, Sunstein and some of his colleagues brought together two groups of like-minded people: liberals from Boulder, Colo-rado, and conservatives from Colorado Springs. In their respective groups, each was asked to deliberate on three topics: civil part-nerships, affirmative action and climate change. But before the discussions began, individual participants recorded their private opinions on each topic. And then the groups were mixed up and encouraged to discuss their views.

The group deliberations were consistently respectful, engaged and substantive, but when they were finished, almost every member ended up with more extreme positions than they had held at the start. Conservatives from Colorado Springs who had been neutral on a climate-change treaty now opposed it. Boulder liberals who had felt somewhat positive about civil partnerships became firmly convinced of their merit. What small diversity each group might have had at the outset was, says Sunstein, 'squelched', while the rift between them had grown larger.

Even when presented with a wide range of data and arguments, Sunstein's work with groups demonstrated that when individuals read, they focus on the information that supports their current opinion, paying less attention to anything that challenges their views. Overall, people are about twice as likely to seek information that supports their own point of view as they are to consider an opposing idea.[17] Rather than broadening their attitudes, the very process of discussion renders them blind to alternatives. Just as Robert stopped going out with Albanian women, we stop looking at places or jobs or information or people that will prove too uncomfortable, too tumultuous for our closely held beliefs. We may think we want to be challenged, but we really don't. Our intellectual homes are just as self-selected and exclusive as our physical homes.

In theory, the Internet was going to change all of this. Access to the world's store of knowledge was supposed to liberate us from the confines of the people we knew and the institutions we belonged to. After all, online you can meet anyone from anywhere. But while it's true that all of us now have access to more information than ever before in history, for the most part we don't use it. Just like newspapers, we read the blogs that we agree with – but there we encounter a virtually infinite echo chamber, as 85 per cent of blogs link to other blogs with the same political inclination.[18] The transition of the Internet, from the PC to mobile phones, has just exacerbated this trend. Reliance on phone apps means that the information we consume becomes more

filtered than ever, as narrow perhaps as the days before the
Internet became a mass medium.

In fact, the great strength of the Internet lies in this ability to
develop and connect affinity groups. It goes beyond connecting
Tea Party members with other Tea Party members, and jihadists
with jihadists. Wherever you live, whatever your age, whether
you love orchids, aikido or ideology, you can find and connect to
like-minded enthusiasts. Why do you want to do that? Because,
in doing so, you gain access to shortcuts: information from
people like yourself that you believe to be reliable. If you don't
know how to lift and split your orchids, the community of orchid
aficionados will save you a lot of money and grief. Offline or
online, what's the advantage of clustering in strongly defined
communities of like-minded people? You believe the advice or
recommendations your neighbours give you. If they like a school
or a restaurant or a movie, well, then you will probably like it,
too; you don't have to try them all or read all the reviews. We
cling together because it feels comfortable and safe but also
because it's highly efficient. We don't have to learn everything
ourselves, the hard, slow way.

Shortcuts do make us smarter and more efficient and they
reward us in many ways – until they lead us astray. Which is what
happened when Bernie Madoff tapped into a community of
investors, all very much alike and eager to pass on what they knew.

'I inherited my account from my dad,' said Irvin Stalbe.

We spoke in Stalbe's modest apartment in Pompano Beach,
Florida. He retired there when he was fifty-five, but had
continued to work part time in a bank, just for the companion-
ship. The money he made from his Madoff account was for
extras – vacations, a little gambling – and to pay for his grand-
children's education.

'I didn't know much about it. I got it when my parents died.
They weren't wealthy, they just put a little aside every year. I'd

tried investing for myself but I wasn't that good at it, and I just thought: it's steady and it works.

'When I brought the paperwork to my accountant and he saw the income, he said he'd like to add money to it. So we worked out a way we'd issue statements to anyone who put money in. In the end, I had forty friends and family in the account.'

Did the accountant, did anyone, do any research before they joined, I wondered.

'No, not really. We were in it for twenty-five years, my parents twenty years before me! Over the years, we brought in friends, grandkids, all under my name. For many years, it was wonderful. Of course what I realise now is I should have remembered the golden rule: never put all your money in one place. But at the time, I mean, everyone was in it. We didn't have to worry.'

Madoff's was an affinity crime, preying on people like himself who knew people like themselves, who didn't ask questions because their level of comfort with each other was so high that they felt they didn't need to do research – they could take short-cuts. Sitting with Stalbe and his family in their Florida sitting room, it's clear that these aren't greedy people. They just wanted the safety of a reliable return and they believed they'd found that in an investment vehicle that they all validated for each other. It is the kind of shortcut we take every day, though few of us pay such a high price for it.

'I'm OK,' Stalbe says. 'I still have some income and I work at my son's take-out restaurant, cleaning tables, working behind the counter. I like to talk to people. But my sister, she's devastated, she has nothing. My sister-in-law, the same thing: ninety per cent of her money was in there. Because of me.'

These days, what distresses Stalbe most isn't his own loss but the fact that he drew in so many others. He's angry with himself because his confidence is what gave them confidence. Everyone felt so comfortable with each other, they all had so much in common, that no one ever asked any questions. It's that affinity too that allowed Madoff's fraud to reach such astronomic proportions. Everyone used the shortcut of someone else's validation to confirm their investment strategy.

Shortcuts can be very pragmatic but, when you take them, you miss a lot along the way: that's what shortcuts are for. Living, working and making decisions with people like ourselves brings us comfort and efficiencies, but it also makes us far narrower in how we think and what we see. The more tightly we focus, the more we leave out.

These blind spots have a reality in the brain. Robert Burton used to be chief of neurology at Mount Zion-UCSF Hospital. He has a restless mind and is always looking for ways to understand and challenge the certainty that our biases give us. He's very aware that, in its endless search for matches, our brain rejects the information that might broaden our outlook, widen our gaze or make us just a little less certain.

'Neural networks,' said Burton, 'don't give you a direct route from, say, a flash of light straight to your consciousness. There are all kinds of committees that vote along the way, whether that flash of light is going to go straight to your consciousness or not. And if there are enough "yes" votes, then yes you can see it. If there aren't, you could miss it.

'But here's the thing: what does your brain like? What gets the "yes" vote? It likes the stuff it already recognises. It likes what is familiar. So you will see the familiar stuff right away. The other stuff may take longer, or it may never impinge on your consciousness. You just won't see it.'

We were talking on a beautiful morning in Sausalito, California, overlooking the harbour. It was early, there weren't many people about, but there were a few. Even before his first coffee, Burton eagerly scanned the horizon.

'I'm aware of people moving around, the town starting to

wake up,' Burton continued. 'But it's a kind of fuzzy background, it doesn't get much attention from me. But if someone I knew walked across the street, I'd see that at once. Zip – straight in to my consciousness, yes votes all the way. A perfect match.'

Burton is very wary of our love for matches and craving for certainty. It goes right against the spirit of enquiry to which, as a scientist, he's dedicated. But mostly he's suspicious of it because he thinks it stops us seeing so much. He likens the development of the neural networks in our brain to the creation of a riverbed.

'Imagine the gradual formation of a riverbed. The initial flow of water might be completely random – there are no preferred routes in the beginning. But once a creek is formed, water is more likely to follow this newly created path of least resistance. As the water continues, the creek deepens and a river develops.'

It's a beautiful metaphor, and a useful one too. The longer we live, and the more we accumulate similar experiences, friends and ideas, the faster and more easily the water flows. There's less and less resistance. That absence of resistance gives us a sense of ease, of comfort, of certainty. Yet, at the same time, the higher the sides of the riverbed grow. As we pursue like-minded people, in like-minded communities, doing similar jobs in homogenous corporate cultures, the riverbed sinks deeper and deeper, its sides climb higher and higher. It feels good; the flow is efficient and unimpeded. You just can't see anything.

This is how wilful blindness begins, not in conscious, deliberate choices to be blind, but in a skein of decisions that slowly but surely restrict our view. We don't sense our perspective closing in and most would prefer that it stay broad and rich. But our blindness grows out of the small, daily decisions that we make, which embed us more snugly inside our affirming thoughts and values. And what's most frightening about this process is that, as we see less and less, we feel more comfort and greater certainty. We think we see more – even as the landscape shrinks.

2. LOVE IS BLIND

Love to faults is always blind,
Always is to joy inclin'd,

William Blake

The vaccine for German measles was first introduced in 1970 but, in the years before that, getting German measles when pregnant was dangerous for the mother and the baby. Michael's mother knew this – there were so many doctors in the family – but there was nothing she could do. So Michael was born in 1948 with a congenital heart defect.

Growing up, he was frail and allowed not to do sports. But, as though he knew that his future must depend on brain not brawn, he was so very clever. All his Jesuit teachers knew he was a student to cherish: bound to do well in exams and get into a top university, maybe even become a priest himself. They were disappointed in the last ambition but not the rest, as Michael grew up to be one of those individuals you knew, almost at first sight, was electrifyingly brilliant. That he was also very funny was a necessary saving grace.

Leaving university, he worked in broadcasting, first in radio and then in television. But TV was too stressful and his time there coincided with his first heart valve replacement. Typically, he confronted the event with bravura that masked fear. Open-heart

surgery wasn't something most men in their twenties had to contemplate. Afterwards, when kids in the public swimming pool
marvelled at the thick red scar that ran down his chest, he would
impress them – and intimidate them a little – by explaining he
was a bionic man, with just one little piece of clicking plastic
keeping him alive.

Like tuberculars in the nineteenth century, the closeness of
death made Michael more alive than other people. Each experience was so vivid, every encounter so vital. When the plastic
valve started to fail and another operation was needed, he wasn't
so afraid because he knew the drill. For friends, sitting by his
hospital bed being regaled by tales of the long-fingered, Porsche-
loving heart surgeon Magdi Yacoub, was one of the best social
scenes in town. But it was becoming clear that, as far as marriage
and a family went, Michael wasn't a great proposition. However
much women might find him charismatic, attentive and insight-
ful, he was a bad bet. By the third operation, his girlfriend of nine
years' standing, Leslie, decided it was time to move on. She took
him to tea to explain that, however much she might love him,
she had a long life to consider. Walking back to work after their
conversation, he thought about the different ways a heart can fail.

But a few years later, back in radio, he fell in love with a colleague, was married and for a time had everything he had ever
dreamed of: a good marriage, a stimulating job that earned him
respect and the company of writers, artists and musicians who all
enjoyed his courage and his wit. He began to think of starting a
family, but then became ill again. This time he would need a
heart transplant but, before it could be arranged, Michael died at
the age of thirty-eight.

Was I wilfully blind when I married Michael? Of course I was.
I knew about his heart condition – everyone did. But I fell in
love with him and decided it didn't matter. We were going to live
for ever, somehow. Now I know that the fact that we had the

same initials, were both expatriates, had gone to the same university, and were of medium build made the relationship highly determined. But I might have done the research and discovered his short life expectancy or talked to psychologists about the pain of grieving or read books about the sadness of widowhood. But I didn't do any of those things. I looked away from those sad certainties and pretended that they weren't there.

Love is blind, not, as in mythology, because Cupid's arrows are random but because, once struck by them, we are left blind. When we love someone, we see them as smarter, wittier, prettier, stronger than anyone else sees them. To us, a beloved parent, partner or child has endlessly more talent, potential and virtue than mere strangers can ever discern. Being loved, when we are born, keeps us alive; without a mother's love for her child, how could any new mother manage or any child survive? And if we grow up surrounded by love, we feel secure in the knowledge that others believe in us, will champion and defend us. That confidence – that we are loved and therefore lovable – is an essential building block of our identity and self-confidence. We believe in ourselves, at least in part, because others believe in us and we depend mightily on their belief.

As human beings, we are highly driven to find and to protect the relationships that make us feel good about ourselves and that make us feel safe. That's why we marry people like us, live in neighbourhoods full of people like us and work with people like us: each one of those mirrors confirms our sense of self-worth. Love does the same thing but with infinitely more passion and drive. We think well of ourselves because we are loved and we will fight fiercely to protect the key relationships on which our esteem depends. And that seems to be just as true even if our love is based on illusion. Indeed, there seems to be some evidence, not only that all love is based on illusion – but that love positively requires illusion in order to endure.

When psychologists studied young dating couples, they analysed each partner's view of their beloved, and then compared that with the beloved's own view or him- or herself. What they found was not only that there was a big disconnect – the lover thought better of her beloved than he did of himself – but the relationships were more likely to persist where that idealisation occurred. Individuals were more satisfied in their relationships when they saw virtues in their partners that their partners did not see in themselves. In other words, idealising the loved one helped the relationship endure.[1]

The beneficial effect of these positive illusions went even further. When you love someone, they may even start to adapt to your illusion of them. So there is a kind of virtuous circle: you think better of your beloved, who starts to live up to your illusions and so you love them more. It sounds a little like a fairy tale but kissing frogs may make them act like princes or princesses. It is indeed a kind of magic: illusions transforming reality. We don't have to love people for who they are but for who we think they are, or need them to be.

So I married a man whom I did not think of as an invalid, and one reason we were happy together was because we lived as though there was nothing wrong with him. This was a benign blindness, without which the relationship stood no chance. And even when it isn't a matter of life and death, this is something everyone does: overlooks the flaws, discounts the disappointments, focuses on what works. Our love for each other allows us, even compels us, to see the best in each other.

This doesn't mean we don't have doubts; of course we do. But such doubts tend to surface only after we have already invested a great deal in a relationship. And that investment – although it sounds very cold-blooded to say so – is like our other investments: as the behavioural economists Kahneman and Tversky found, losses loom very much larger than corresponding gains.[2] What that means when you apply it to love life (instead of the stock market) is that when a relationship starts to sour, our fear of losing it may far outweigh any hopes we might cherish of freedom and release. If things go wrong in a relationship, we hang on, trying hard to adapt, or we try to trivialise our worries. We find excuses (he's had a horrible day, or a horrible childhood), we weave alternative interpretations (she didn't really mean it, I must have misunderstood) or we may just trivialise the disappointment (it's not a big birthday). We use considerable ingenuity to sustain our illusions, blind ourselves to inconvenient or painful facts. We protect our life with our illusions.

Because our identity and security depend so much on our loved ones, we don't want to see anything that threatens them. So, most of the time that I was married to Michael, I didn't think about his frailty or his heart. We went on walking trips and swam a great deal. I might rationalise that, in keeping him fit, I was keeping him healthy, and perhaps I was. But I was also acting as though my husband were just as strong and fit as anyone else my age. I had to believe that.

Mine was perhaps an extreme case of love masking all physical realities. But even the most educated and rational can be amazed by how little impact rational understanding makes when love is involved.

'I remember my mother calling me up and explaining about the pains she was having in her arm and her stomach that had lasted about twenty minutes,' Dick told me one evening. Dick is a highly experienced, level-headed physician not known for pulling his punches. Like many doctors, he loves the intellectual puzzle of diagnosis and isn't easily second-guessed. 'And she said to me perhaps it was something she ate. And I said, instantly, yes, it must have been something you ate. And I put the phone down.'

As he tells this story, Dick's wife, Lindsey, looks on, bemused. She is also a doctor, but it isn't her parents we're talking about.

'So I hung up the phone and told Lindsey about the conversation and she looks at me and says, "No, it isn't what she ate. She's having a heart attack." And of course she was right! So I was straight back on the phone to her.'

Dick tells his story with wry amusement that he could have got something so simple so wrong. But of course that is why physicians aren't supposed to treat family members – because love blinds them to the realities of the case. This doesn't, unfortunately, stop family members from asking for advice and even, on occasion, free care. And it has proved impossible for professional organisations to prevent doctors treating their own families. The dangers are twofold: either a tendency to under-play the problem (I love you and can't bear for you to be ill) or to over-play the problem (I couldn't bear to lose you so will treat the tiniest symptom). Every doctor I've met has experienced one of those responses; they know they can't do a proper diagnosis and they also know that that isn't a reflection of their clinical expertise.

Our identity depends critically on the people we love, and a central function of family life is to preserve our positive illusions about one another. That is what families are for. The fictional poster child for love blindness in families must be Carmela Soprano, who hovers between knowing and not knowing that her husband is a murderous, adulterous gangster. How can she acknowledge the truth? It would destroy everything she loves: her family, her home, her children, her sense of herself as a good person. For the children, Meadow and Anthony Jr, facing facts is easier; they did not choose their father and don't feel their identity wholly depends on his. But Carmela chose Tony, so for her the cost of facing what she has condoned is too high: not just Catholic guilt but responsibility for 'terrible acts' that she cannot bring herself to imagine. She so desperately wants Tony to be a good father, for her family to be the archetypal American happy family, that most of her physical and psychic energy is devoted to maintaining the illusions that make her life worth living. She is blind to Tony's criminal activity because she has to be.

Carmela's dilemma is extreme but it is also something everyone can relate to; that's why it's great television. So many couples find themselves in predicaments where they fear something bad is happening but prefer not to know. Like Carmela, it feels easier to turn a blind eye and act as if everything is normal. In this respect, fiction is not so different from fact. Although far from the glamorous and affluent wife that Carmela struggles to represent, Primrose Shipman appears, by all accounts, to have denied that her husband Harold was the worst serial killer in British criminal history. She has always maintained his innocence, despite the overwhelming evidence that found him guilty. At the inquiry that followed her husband's conviction, she answered 'I don't know' over a hundred times. Yet no one thought she was being disingenuous. Dame Janet Smith, who chaired the inquiry, described Primrose as 'honest and straightforward'. She had been present at, or immediately after, the death of three of Shipman's patients and had stood by one – Irene Chapman – while her husband went to see another patient. Yet all indications are that she did not see what was going on.

While neighbours were surprised and disgusted by her loyalty, other observers were not. The only psychiatrist to have interviewed Shipman, Dr Richard Badcock, described his tremendous need for control and in his wife he had found a perfectly subservient subject. Primrose Shipman was, after all, entirely dependent on her husband. Cut off by her parents when she became pregnant by Shipman when she was seventeen, the hasty wedding was the last time she ever saw her father; her mother did not even attend. Barely literate, she earned a little money as a childminder and running a sandwich shop, but, with four children to look after, she was emotionally and financially dependent on Shipman. There's no evidence she had close friendships or other relationships that could have given her the sense of role and place that her marriage, however abusive, provided. At no point in her life does she appear to have had the strength or the independence to be able to see what was happening in front of her eyes.

Most of us will never have to deal with the scale of denial Primrose Shipman needed to survive. The secret we are more likely to uncover is infidelity. Although rates of couples having affairs are notoriously difficult to pin down (for obvious reasons) estimates run between 30 and 60 per cent of marriages.[3] At the time of divorce, 24 per cent of divorces cite infidelity as a proven fact.

'In couples when someone is having an affair, nobody really wants to know,' says Emily Brown. Brown is a marriage therapist whose deep knowledge and study of marital infidelity doesn't seem to have damaged her optimism. In her mid-fifties, she dresses in warm but vibrant colours. In an office crammed with books and artwork, only a pottery jar labelled 'Cognitive Overload' hints that sometimes knowledge can be a burden.

In her professional practice, Brown works with couples and individuals whose marriages are threatened by affairs. By the time her clients come to her, the affair has usually been discovered and part of what she sees is the rage that betrayed spouses feel at not having noticed what was going on.

'They may have had their suspicions,' says Brown. 'But even in marriages where one spouse has suspicions, how can you ask and have things remain the same? If the other partner is not having an affair, you've created doubt and hostility. If the other partner is having an affair and denies it, now he or she has been rumbled. If the other partner is having an affair and admits it, everything starts to fall apart. So there is no way to ask and have things remain the same.'

That state – of knowing and not knowing – is extremely painful and can last for months or for years. The sheer routine of daily life makes blindness easier, less dramatic, less traumatic.

'So I see people thinking: I should ask. I won't ask. It's self-protection. Many of my clients have grown up in families where no one ever talked about risky topics – there's plenty of polite conversation but nothing meaningful – so they don't know how to have the conversation in the first place. But then they think: if we're talking about it that means it could be real. So they try to make it disappear by not saying anything.'

In Brown's experience, the blindness is on both sides: the unfaithful spouse is blind to the possibility of being found out, refusing to see what the consequences might be and preferring to maintain the illusion that no one will get hurt. This isn't stupidity; it's a genuine desire that the affair and the family can peacefully co-exist. And on the other side, the betrayed spouse resolutely refuses to connect the dots because, as long as they're just dots, nothing is happening, nothing has to change, and love remains.

'I had one case,' Brown recalled, 'where the husband had had an affair and his wife hadn't guessed. And his wife had got a sexually transmitted disease and had gone to the doctor about it. When she told her husband, he just brushed it off, saying, "You must have got that when you were camping with the kids." So she thought no more about it.

'Ten years later, she's at the hairdresser's and she's reading a magazine article about STDs and she figures it out! And only then did she confront her husband. Now, in that case, there was a double blindness: he was blind to being caught and she was blind to what was going on.'

Most people, according to Brown, do intuit that something is amiss. One reason these marriages are so hard to repair is that the betrayed spouses feels so angry, not just with their partners but with themselves. 'How could I not have known?' each asks, feeling so stupid, so naïve. Suddenly they feel like they are watching a jigsaw puzzle self-assemble: all the pieces snap together, creating a hideous picture that no one wants to see. Self-esteem, that precious self-worth that has been fed by the illusions that sustain love, is destroyed as the truth emerges.

That we will fight so hard to protect our self-esteem is a universal. It doesn't matter how successful or wealthy people are. They all need to feel that they're good people, even – or especially – when they're bad.

'I knew my actions were wrong but I convinced myself normal rules didn't apply. I thought I could get away with whatever I wanted to.' Even Tiger Woods was wilfully blind when it came to his own marriage.[4]

'Success confers its own blindness,' says Brown. 'Successful people believe they can get away with it. I talked once to a group of men who'd all become millionaires before the age of forty and who'd had affairs. They don't even see the danger! It isn't a love of risk. They think: the wives will never know, so where's the harm? Everything else in their lives has worked out, so they think they have some kind of magic, that their success has meant that they can have everything they want and they're invulnerable. And they were completely blind to the harm that they had done. They just couldn't conceive that, as good men, they'd done something bad.'

Talking with Brown, she feels like a veteran, her consulting room a battlefield where wives and husbands have waged titanic battles to preserve their self-respect. Blindness helps them do that, she says. And where children are involved, adulterous spouses can be especially blind. They convince themselves that kids, of any age, know nothing, notice nothing, that just by dint of being children they couldn't have any insight into the lives of grown-ups. It's a comforting fallacy often bolstered by the kids themselves, who say nothing because they are trying so hard to keep the family together. Everyone colludes in the collective fantasy that the family is fine.

'One couple I've worked with, they're semi-separated,' Brown recalls. 'They had a lot of fights in front of their kids and the husband moved out into an apartment that was above the garage. And they got together for one of the kids' birthdays. But both the husband and the wife said they thought the kids didn't suspect a thing. Well, their kids are thirteen and ten and Dad isn't living at home any more . . .'

Talking to Brown, it's clear that this kind of blindness is so common that it no longer surprises her. But she also thinks that the blindness that accompanies affairs often started very much earlier. One of the many downsides of living in communities where we are always surrounded by people like ourselves is that we experience very little conflict. That means we don't develop the tools we need to manage it and we lack confidence in our ability to do so. We persuade ourselves that the absence of conflict is the same as happiness, but that trade-off leaves us strangely powerless.

'In many cases, affairs start because people are conflict-averse or intimacy-averse. People stay away from stuff that needs to be dealt with; they think that they mustn't ever say anything negative – they don't know how to articulate criticism or doubts in a way that won't feel like an attack. So then when they finally articulate their discomfort, via the affair, it does come out as an attack and provokes more attacks. A lot of this derives from not dealing with emotions, not understanding one's own feelings. It feels easier to be blind than to deal with uncomfortable feelings.'

Running throughout Brown's conversation, and the experience she's had in her practice, is a belief that we become blind because we are so afraid of what we might see and what we might feel. Our identity and sense of self-worth depend on the people we love, to the extent that we cling to them even though they do us harm.

'We want our parents to love us and one way to do that is to be what they want us to be,' recalled Louise Miller.

Miller was a client of Brown's, coming to her for advice and therapy after years of an abusive marriage in which she had worked hard not to notice what was going on around her. Miller was so eager to please the people she loved, she says, that she never really dared to question anything.

'I got married in my early twenties – I really didn't want to but I thought that was what you do. I was dating, I was the right age to get married, I got married. Then, in my thirties, I had kids and I thought: I'll have this perfect life according to my parents' thinking. I had a beautiful huge home with a big garden in a nice neighbourhood and I thought: now I will have my nice life. I didn't see *me* until I was forty. All those years I was trying to do what my parents wanted, what my husband wanted. I thought, if they were happy, I'd be happy. But I was just blind to myself!'

So desperate was Louise to secure the approval and love of her parents and her husband, by sticking to her 'cookie cutter' idea of what happiness and family life should look like, that she never dared to ask any serious questions about what was going on around her.

'When I was growing up, there was never any alcohol in the house – not even for cooking. So when I met my husband, I had no way of knowing he was an alcoholic. I met him in university, and when he was a little wild, I just thought that was party behaviour and he'd grow out of it. But he never did. And I'd complain but he couldn't stop. Then one day his father said to me, "Do you know you're married to an alcoholic?" I was in my forties! How can you be in a relationship with an alcoholic and never even see it?'

In a desperate attempt to break free from everyone else's expectations for her, Louise had an affair with a colleague at work.

'I never thought anything would happen. I became very depressed and guilty and one night I told my husband. I thought that, once I told him, we could reconnect and fall in love again! And that's when we went to see Emily. And I really hoped she would know the end of the story and everything would be all right. It took me a long time to see that I had choices. And that it was my life.'

As Louise tells me her story, it feels as though layers upon layers of blinders are being removed, one at a time – the love for her parents, the love she had for her husband, the love she has for her children. She had struggled so hard to cling on to these because for years she simply did not believe that she was anybody without them. Emily says how amazed she is how far Louise has come. But her journey is one she could never have made without daring to confront the truth about herself and her marriage.

Tales of marital blindness are legion, the stuff of high drama and low comedy alike. From Othello to Pierre Bezukhov to *Mad Men*'s Betty Draper, we can identify with characters who won't see the truth, because they let us explore our deepest fears, that we might be wrong about each other or wrong about ourselves. We laugh with relief because it isn't us, and we weep because it so easily could be.

Nowhere is that drama more intense or more threatening than in families damaged by child abuse. Although we are all so conscious of 'stranger danger' and go to great lengths to ensure that our children keep well away from anyone unknown or suspicious, it remains the case that most child abuse occurs within families or involves perpetrators known to the children. According to the NSPCC, fully 16 per cent of children experience sexual abuse before they reach sixteen years old. With numbers like those, you have to wonder: how can it be that, within such a small unit as a family, abuse goes unnoticed?

'In the majority of cases of child abuse, it is family members or friends who are responsible,' says Chris Cloke, Head of Child Protection Awareness for the NSPCC. 'It's often very hard to see because there's often a great deal of love – for the family, for the child – which just doesn't want to acknowledge what's going on. Lots of people don't even want to acknowledge that child abuse exists at all – and they'd far prefer to think of stranger danger than of the fact that it mostly occurs within families.'

One of the many people on the frontline at the NSPCC is Felicity Wilkinson, who mans the charity's helpline. 'You often find a situation where a mum is in a relationship with a man who is abusing her kids. That is someone she is in love with and the last thing she wants to think about is that they would do that kind of thing. It can take a long time for it to sink in, even where there are certain signs.

'One case that springs to mind is a woman who was saying that she was aware her partner had a conviction from the past for sex abuse. She was trying to convince herself that that didn't matter now because it had all happened such a long time ago, so he must have changed. She was really calling to ask for confirmation – hoping against hope that I would say it was so long ago that she need not worry. She was in love with this man and he was doing a lot for her and looking after her kids. She just didn't want to think that her kids were at risk.'

Wasn't it hard, I asked Felicity, for parents to acknowledge that there might be danger in their own family?

'It is always hard. So hard. When I worked as a social worker for a local authority, the parents always struggled with this. And it was very hard for the parents to acknowledge that their own behaviour might contribute to the problem. They loved their kids and hoped that that was enough. And it's also hard because if they give us, at the NSPCC, information that indicates the child truly is at risk, we are obliged to contact Children's Services. So they don't want to acknowledge what is going on – and they're afraid to start that whole process.'

'It isn't necessarily that they are unconscious,' says Eliana Gil, 'but that they are unable or unwilling to face up to what is happening.'

Dr Gil works for one of the largest child-welfare services in the United States, Childhelp. She has had years of experience watching families make the painful transition from being blind to finally seeing what they so much did not want to see. And she says that there is a pattern to the revelation.

'The way I think about it is this: it is as if someone has been invited to attend something. They turn up, the door is opened and they see it is a surprise birthday party for them. In that moment of shock, they suddenly understand – that's why there was a ribbon on the bed this morning and that's why my brother cancelled dinner tonight and that's why Jane's been acting so strangely. Suddenly all these little pieces of information, which have been stored in memory without meaning, get retrieved in context and have a whole new meaning.

'That is my experience with the mothers. When someone says your child has been abused by the father – suddenly they remember: that's why I found her walking around the room at night and that's why her clothes were in my bedroom . . . All those details, stored without meaning, suddenly acquire meaning.'[5]

Dr Gil works primarily with children who have been abused and their mothers. It is, she says, all too common for mothers to have been aware and yet not aware of what was going on in their own homes.

'That kind of response – of seeing and not seeing – helps to explain how these things go on for such a long time. It doesn't explain why the abuse itself happens in the first place, of course.

But it does explain how it can continue for such a long time inside the family. If you maintain an illusion, you don't have to make the hard choices. Life just goes on. But if you accept reality, it forces a huge decision and many people want to avoid that.'

According to Dr Gil, it is often several fears together that conspire to keep unwanted knowledge from their minds. If the abusing father is the major breadwinner, fear of losing support and income may suppress knowledge. Fear of shame and social exclusion are powerful forces, too. But underlying all of these threats is a more existential fear, a sense that acknowledging the abuse would destroy everything.

'It's just too dangerous to acknowledge the idea – it's the last thing anyone wants to imagine. Mothers feel that just to ask the question is to question their own reality. And especially mothers who themselves come from unhappy families. They are so idealistic that they want to shield the child. In putting together that illusion and protecting it, they just cannot break through the barrier to explore the possibility that something is wrong.'

The happy family, the happy children are so critical to the mother's sense of her own identity and worth that her doubts have to be quashed.

'For many of the mothers I've worked with, their identity is so tied into the role of being a good mother, or a good wife, that they have very little sense of self. Putting on an identity like a coat becomes very important to them. And they cannot take that coat off, it would leave them too vulnerable. It is like they've invested themselves in this role and they simply cannot afford to challenge their illusion. It is such an invested process. So when it turns out that it was an illusion, they often feel that they have absolutely nothing left.'

For someone navigating such painful issues, Dr Gil is remarkably positive, utterly determined that, out of this family wreckage, real gains can come – but only by recognising what has occurred.

She's a passionate believer that, if wilful blindness perpetuates abuse, it is only facing facts that can end it.

'I've been working with a woman who has four children. Her husband was arrested for having a lot of child pornography on his computer and I started working with the mother, and her kids, because they were just in shock when this happened. And at first, the kids seemed OK except that they'd been photographed by him in rather unusual poses.

'As I started working with the mother, helping her to learn how to get along without her husband, other things started to surface. The couple had had no sex for two years, and she thought that was odd but then she figured they were older, maybe it was not a big deal. Then she realised he did have a special relationship with their ten-year-old little girl. And a little part of her was happy for the child – that he had such a strong attachment – but she also started wondering. "I wondered if I should have been concerned" – that was just how she phrased it. "I wondered if I should have been concerned."'

After working with the mother and her children for about nine months, Dr Gil became concerned that the ten-year-old had behaviours compatible with a child who has been abused. So she asked the mother about that.

'And she says, "Well, I guess there was one time I walked in and they were in bed together cuddling and I could see he had an erection." So I asked her if she had talked to him about it and all she said was, "I mentioned it and he denied it so I thought I must have been seeing things."'

For all her experience, even Dr Gil was amazed that so much could have happened and not been seen. Over the next few months, Dr Gil was impressed as the mother gradually developed the courage to put the picture together.

'Gradually things are becoming more clear in her mind but at the time they were just too threatening to consider. Now her eyes are brighter and it is like she has a new sense of herself. But at the time, she couldn't compromise her sense of identity because she couldn't see possibilities for herself. Her daughter paid the price for that, because her mother couldn't see what was in front of her face.'

This is the true cost of blindness: as long as it feels safer to do and say nothing, as long as keeping the peace feels more benign, abuse can continue. Our desire to protect our self-worth can result in others paying a very high price.

Emerging brain science lends a physical reality to the emotional turmoil experienced by the victims of romantic and maternal love alike. A team of neuroscientists at the University of London have spent years studying brain activity in romantic couples and in mothers. They knew that love itself has an evolutionary advantage; we fall in love, mate and look after our children because that is how the species perpetuates itself. But they wanted to understand which areas of the brain are active in response to love and which areas are not.

They found, not so surprisingly, that love activates those areas of the brain associated with reward; the cells that respond to food, drink, money or cocaine respond to love too. That's why it feels so good, to love and to be loved. Moreover, there appears to be some evidence that love may even reduce our fear of death.[6] While it would be inaccurate to conclude that we are addicted to love, it is the case that we need it.[7]

Even more illuminating than the areas activated by love were the areas of the brain that were de-activated. As volunteers lay in fMRI scanners, thinking of their children or their partners, two particular parts of their brains were not engaged. The first was the area responsible for attention, memory and negative emotions; the second was associated with negative emotions and social judgement, the ability to distinguish other people's feelings and intentions. In other words, the chemical processes of our brain that are stimulated by love disable much of our critical thinking about the loved one. Our illusions persist because our brains don't challenge them. Like much neuroscience, this gives a concrete reality to what the poets have always known: love does not judge.

The neuroscience is a helpful reminder that blind love isn't stupidity or ignorance. It is a physical reality of a kind that doesn't distinguish between rich and poor, educated or otherwise. We develop and protect illusions around the people we love because we are made to do so, because we feel our very lives depend on it. What is impressive though is that when men and women who have suffered in abusive, unhappy relationships successfully overcome their blindness, and insist on facing the truth, they have surmounted very real, very daunting obstacles.

Such obstacles are even more formidable when they are reinforced by institutional, social and political support. That is what happened in the child-abuse scandals that have ripped through churches in England, Ireland, Canada, Austria, Australia and the United States. Love of church, love of parents, love of tradition all conspired to keep whole communities blind to what they somehow always knew.

'For so long, everyone pretended these things weren't happening. So sad. So ridiculous. If we acknowledge these things, we can address them. But for years, everyone knew. And no one knew. You just couldn't say anything.'

Colm O'Gorman runs Amnesty International in Ireland. He's a powerful force in the land these days, well known and highly respected, organised, efficient and bold. But he wasn't always that way. In the 1970s, growing up in Wexford, he was regularly abused for two and a half years by a local priest, Sean Fortune. O'Gorman was trapped, between his love for his father, his love for his mother and their love of the Church. At the time, he was just a child, with a very fragile sense of identity. When Fortune threatened to tell O'Gorman's father what had happened, the one thing O'Gorman knew was that that could not be allowed to happen.

'Panic raced through me and the world started to spin. I wanted to escape, jump from the car, anything to get away from that awful moment. Anything to prevent what he said he might do. My father . . . it would kill him to know what I'd done, what I was. He would die of shame . . . I knew I could not stay alive if everyone knew, especially if my father knew.'[8]

O'Gorman felt that everything his life depended on would be destroyed if anyone knew what was being done to him. So he kept silent while the abuse continued and for years afterwards. His experience, tragically, was far from unique. The 2005 Ferns Inquiry unearthed one hundred complaints against twenty-one priests in O'Gorman's diocese alone. A year later, the Murphy Report examined the history of 46 priests, picked from a sample of 102 against whom complaints had been lodged. Enquiries into just those 46 priests produced allegations from more than 320 children. 'One priest admitted to sexually abusing over 100 children, while another accepted that he had abused on a fortnightly basis during his ministry which lasted for over 25 years,' the report said. 'The total number of documented complaints recorded against those two priests is only just over 70.' The 2009 report found that 'maintenance of secrecy, the avoidance of scandal, the protection of the reputation of the church and the preservation of its assets' was more important than justice for the victims. The report concluded that the vast majority of priests turned a 'blind eye' to abuse, and strongly criticised the Garda – Irish police – for regarding priests as outside their remit; the relationship between Church and police was deemed 'inappropriate'. And that was just in Dublin.

At this level, nothing can quite be a secret. It was, O'Gorman says, the scandal that everyone knew about but no one would admit. In his own village, people talked about the priests that should be avoided when you were on your own, the ones you shouldn't go to the graveyard with. Likewise, the Garda would, informally, mention that perhaps certain priests shouldn't be left too long with children. Widespread knowledge and widespread blindness co-existed; as O'Gorman puts it, 'They'd tell you but they hadn't told you.' Everyone knew but didn't know.

Eventually, O'Gorman left home and wandered, frequently unemployed and homeless, through the streets of Dublin and London, an outcast who belonged nowhere. It was only many years later that he had the confidence he needed to acknowledge what had been done to him. When he finally confided in his parents, they did not reject him and his life could begin again. He brought a lawsuit against Sean Fortune and he established a helpline for victims of child abuse.

'What silences the child,' says O'Gorman, 'is the fear that the family will be broken up. Family is the only source of love and security that the kid knows. How can he hurt his parents, whom he loves and might also fear? What would he have left? I couldn't prevent what was happening to me and I couldn't escape it, so I just refused to allow it to be true. I would just look at a spot on the ceiling and split myself off from what was happening. In that place, denial kept me sane. I didn't go mad. Finding the spot on the wall meant I wasn't in the room.'

The fact that O'Gorman's wasn't a solitary case, and that abuse was so pervasive, meant that it wasn't only O'Gorman's family that was threatened. Ireland at the time was a highly theocratic culture. The Church ran most of the major institutions and was largely left to do so by the government. Any attack on the Church, therefore, challenged its dominance, threatened its role in the social and political life of the nation. To dare to question the moral authority of the most powerful institution in the land might make anyone hesitate.

'If one has a strong sense of connection with the Church, then the destruction of that is terrifying,' says O'Gorman. 'It really is unthinkable. Unthinkable. It is a loss of security. It makes you wonder whether any security is real. Suddenly everything is at risk. My acceptability within my institution and by God is because I am acceptable to the faith. If I name all that, accuse all that, do I lose my connection with God? Never mind the power of the institution . . .'

The blind intransigence of the institution has stunned even some of its most faithful adherents. The Pope's envoy to Ireland refused to testify before Irish lawmakers, while none of the bishops who failed to report paedophile priests has been fired. O'Gorman was appropriately daunted.

'Ireland was a country in denial,' says O'Gorman. 'If a whole society is in denial, you are really in trouble – because you believe your survival depends on turning a blind eye to the truth. So the thing that we feared most as a society – that our sense of self would come crashing down – that turned out to be valid.

'But what we didn't question at the time was whether that might be a good thing. We had had a sense of ourselves as a good pure Catholic society, where good exists and always wears a collar. But when we finally understood the cost of that illusion, then we had to let it go. The cost was just so high, the damage so great.'

Sean Fortune, O'Gorman's abuser, committed suicide before his trial concluded. Other priests and bishops retired or disappeared. The Church itself, when it learned of the scale of the abuse, did nothing to protect the victims but moved quickly to protect its assets, taking out insurance policies against the cost of future lawsuits. But some clergy felt let down by their own hierarchy, which left them ignorant and inexperienced in dealing with these cases.

'I knew of the existence of child abuse certainly but less about recidivism in the offender and the long-term effects in the life of the victim,' one churchman confided to me.

Not surprisingly, he insisted on remaining anonymous. Sitting in the lobby of an elegant Dublin hotel, he would, years ago, have been the centre of attention, a man of power, accustomed to deference. Now our conversation was muted, his presence shrunken, almost furtive. He described to me how rumours would reach him but he never quite knew what to do about them.

'What I still find quite remarkable and almost unbelievable twenty years later is that not a single person among the legal, medical and counselling profession whom I consulted on innumerable occasions advised me either to report an offence to the Gardai or to remove a priest from ministry except for a very short period of time,' he said. 'I knew that this problem had surfaced in the USA and was being dealt with by numerous US bishops but their approach offered no great insights into the problem. In fact, they seem to have made all the mistakes that we in Ireland were to make about a decade later. On the home front, we showed a marked reluctance to discuss the problem, hoping, I suppose, that, if we didn't discuss it, it would go away.'

That hope − if we don't talk about it, it will go away − persisted for decades. And the Church and police together colluded in keeping it that way. In the end, it was not the Church but the courage of victims like O'Gorman that finally brought priests into court and the clergy's disgrace out into the open. That was the moment when many priests might have sided with the abused, but instead most of them just slunk away. If the problem would not disappear, they would.

Moreover, the Church has continued to protect the identity of abusing clergy, which means they can't and won't be brought to trial. Around the world, the story has repeated itself. It is as though the Church, having been so determinedly blind, wishes to remain so, and would prefer that believers did too. For O'Gorman, this has been their ultimate failure: not to have sided with the truth once it was out there.

'For fear of the worst of ourselves, what we do or people close to us do or institutions do, is we deny the best of ourselves which is our capacity to respond,' O'Gorman says. 'We make ourselves powerless by pretending we don't know.'

As O'Gorman and I discussed the profound impact the scandals have had on the whole of Irish social and political life, I was struck by the sympathy and breadth of his argument. He seemed to be arguing that while the greatest harm was that done to children by priests, further harm still was caused by the Church's moral failure to support their victims. The crisis offered an opportunity for the Church, and its priests, to dig deep and find the best in themselves. But they lacked the vision and courage to seize it. Today, a third of the Irish population has no trust 'at all' in the Church; the police, the supermarkets and the media enjoy higher levels of public confidence.[9] When I contrast my conversation with O'Gorman and my earlier one with the priest, it is O'Gorman who, despite years of suffering, confusion, poverty and personal vilification, has led the richer life. The priest has enjoyed comfort and respect but today he is left still embroiled in a battle, between himself and the truth, trying to decide which gets the upper hand.

Some critics might dispute this interpretation, saying the priest just doesn't care, that his apologies and explanations are just an easy way of making sure he gets to live as he's always lived, without having to change. That is certainly what many said of Albert Speer, Hitler's chief architect and, after 1942, the second-most powerful man in the Reich. One of the few of the Nazi elite not to be hanged following the Nuremberg trials, he was outspoken about the criminality of Hitler's regime and determined to accept responsibility for what he had done as a member of the government. In some ways, that decision was Speer's simplest; he believed in collective responsibility. But the hard part for Speer was seeing what it was that he took responsibility for.

'Speer didn't see anything he didn't want to see,' says Gitta Sereny, Speer's biographer. 'I think he would have liked to have that capacity, but he just didn't. Speer was in fact a highly talented man, highly intelligent, but studied obliviousness was his defence. And the defence was there because he somehow knew there was something wrong.'[10]

Sereny saw Speer at Nuremberg but she got to know him when, in 1978, she began a conversation with him – almost an interrogation – that would continue right up until his death in 1981. In her book, *Albert Speer: His Battle with Truth*, she meticulously chronicles Speer's tortuous negotiation with himself, and then with her, as he tries to see, but also wriggle out of seeing, the full horror of what he did as a Nazi. Sereny's is a masterful confrontation, obsessive about detail, challenging Speer's facts and constantly blocking ethical escape routes. What makes their duel so dramatic is that Speer is even more desperate to know the truth than Sereny; she wants to know but he needs to know. The obstacle they both wrestle with is his lifetime of abnegation and blindness. That blindness, according to Sereny, was profoundly motivated by Speer's love for Hitler.

'In the early years, Speers is very hung-up on Hitler – and in a very personal way,' she said. 'It's something quite apart from politics. It is more of a father/son feeling. Speer found that difficult to give up; he depended on it. He needed it to feel whole.'[11]

Indeed, when Speer described to Sereny his first meeting with Hitler in 1933, his account comes dangerously close to the purple prose of romantic fiction.

'Can you imagine this,' said Speer. 'Here I was, young, unknown and totally unimportant, and this great man, for whose attention – just for one glance – our whole world competed, said to me, "Come and have lunch." I thought I'd faint.'

Because Speer, an architect, had visited a building site prior to his meeting with Hitler, his jacket was dusty and Hitler loaned him one of his own.

'Can you conceive what I felt?' Speer asked again. 'Here I was, twenty-eight years old, totally insignificant in my own eyes, sitting next to him at lunch, wearing his clothes and elected – at least that day – as virtually his sole conversation partner. I was dizzy with excitement.'[12]

It isn't only Hitler's power that so bedazzled Speer. Hitler saw in the young, mediocre architect far more than Speer saw in himself. Given tremendous commissions for the new Reich, it was clear that Hitler believed him to be talented, important and artistic – all those things Speer longed to be and that his own parents had signally failed to see in him. Hitler, as Speer said later, became his life.[13]

'He saw himself as Hitler's son,' said Sereny. 'All his chances, his opportunities came to him through Hitler. He liked Hitler and he loved Hitler – and it was reciprocated. Hitler really loved Speer and Speer grew to love Hitler.'[14]

Speer's reciprocated love for Hitler, and the political climate around the Fuhrer, was for Speer a deadly combination. With his own identity so entirely dependent, nothing critical of Hitler could ever be allowed to impinge on Speer's consciousness. He saw pools of blood near one of his building sites. One of the architects in his practice resigned after Kristallnacht. But, says Speer, 'my mind was on other things'.[15] When the evacuation of Jews from Berlin began in 1941, Speer wrote about 'a feeling of unease, a foreboding of dark events' but Sereny challenged him, thinking him evasive. How, she wondered, could he be uneasy if he knew nothing?

'By that time,' Sereny wrote, 'I was very familiar with that sudden sharp look from under those thick black eyebrows when he sensed disbelief. It was not only his look which became both hooded and guarded; his voice on the whole invariably quiet could also suddenly change. "I was blind by choice," he said coldly, "but I was not ignorant."'

In 1942, when Speer was made Minister of Armaments and War Production, blindness and ignorance became increasingly difficult to preserve. Speer was no longer designing rallies and memorials for the thousand-year Reich; now he was in charge of arming Germany and ensuring that the war machine had the labour it needed. In appointing him to this position, Hitler had identified Speer's true genius, which was not as an architect but as a manager and administrator. But just as Speer discovered his true talents, they embroiled him in atrocities. Now he was spending more time with Hitler's inner circle, privy to conversations about the Jews.

'This is when I should have begun to realise what was happening,' Speer said. 'This was the point, I now think, when, had I *wanted* to, I could have detected hints.'

Sereny asked Speer what he would have done if he had known about the Final Solution.

'Don't you know that this is the question I have asked myself a million times, continuously hoping that I would be able to give myself an answer I could live with?' He rested his head in his hands. 'My answer to myself is always the same,' he said, his voice dark and a little hoarse. 'I would somehow have gone on trying to help that man win his war.'

Speer's moral corruption, Sereny says, 'had its seed in his emotional attachment to Hitler – he likened it to Faust's fatal bargain with Mephistopheles. Achievement and success rooting it ever deeper over the years, he lived – almost addictively – in an increasingly vicious cycle of need and dependence.'[16]

He carefully avoided visiting any labour or concentration camps. His one visit – to Mauthausen – carefully protected him, and other visitors, from anything they might find shocking. But Speer's new role brought him closer and closer to the evil that his

Ministry perpetrated. In August 1943, he visited Dora, the underground labour camp deep in the Harz Mountains where Wernher von Braun's V-2 rockets were being produced. There, slave labourers worked eighteen hours a day with their bare hands, sleeping in tunnels they had hollowed out, over a thousand prisoners on four levels that stretched for a hundred yards. Without heat, ventilation or water to drink or wash with, the cold and filth and dysentery killed 30,000 men.

'I was entirely unprepared,' Speer told Sereny. 'It was the worst place I have ever seen . . . I saw dead men . . . they couldn't hide the truth. And those that were alive were skeletons.'[17]

Three months later, the regional Nazi Party leaders and paramilitaries (*Reichsleiter*) were assembled at Posen to learn about the Final Solution in order that they all be implicated. An unresolved debate still rages over whether Speer was still there for Himmler's speech about the extermination of the Jews. Speer believed he had left before Himmler spoke, but both Sereny and Speer himself doubted his memory. But, whether or not he was actually present for Himmler's speech, he would undoubtedly have learned of its contents.

In January 1944, Speer was losing ground in power struggles with others in Hitler's circle. He also now had unavoidable knowledge of Hitler's genocidal programme. It was too much. Everything on which his identity depended was undermined. Speer's love of Hitler, and Speer's love for the Speer that Hitler had created, became untenable. Studied obliviousness failed and Speer had a breakdown. The bond between them had snapped. When he returned to work three months later, everything had changed.

'Meeting Hitler again was a shock. I stood up as he entered the room. He came up to me very quickly holding out his hand. But even as I stretched out mine, I had an extraordinary sense of unfamiliarity. Of course I hadn't seen him for almost ten weeks, but that wasn't it. It was his face: I looked at it and thought: "My God, how could I have not seen how ugly he is? This broad nose, this sallow skin. Who is this man?"'

The spell was broken. Speer could see the evidence of Hitler's criminality all around. He started secretly to ignore orders, to undermine command, to resist Hitler's scorched-earth plan. When he was arrested and tried, Speer accepted 'co-responsibility' – but not guilt. In prison and after his release, Speer waged a titanic battle with himself, not wanting to believe he was a bad man, but well aware he wasn't stupid either. Like a lover awakening from a dream, he could not quite make sense of what had happened or of what he had become.

'He had loved Hitler, he thought Hitler loved Germany and that was enough,' Sereny told me. 'But once he had seen that his ambitions were wrong, he couldn't feel the same way, about Hitler, about Germany, about himself. Speer's tragedy was that, after Posen and Dora, he really wanted to die. But his will to live was too strong. And so he really spent the rest of his life struggling, trying to become a different man.'

Sereny's account of Speer's life after the war describes an epic struggle between what Speer knew and what he must have known. That debate continues to this day, with some historians still sceptical of what they see as Speer's disingenuousness. Sereny, although she clearly liked Speer, is no apologist for him. She was impressed not by what he had done but by how hard he was finally prepared to work in order to see clearly. She is drawn to his battle because it is so intensely human.

'Not knowing, that's fine. Ignorance is easy. Knowing can be hard but at least it is real, it is the truth. The worst is when you don't want to know – because then it must be something very bad. Otherwise you wouldn't have so much difficulty knowing.'

To some degree, Speer's post-war struggle with the truth was Germany's: the desire not to know, coupled with an awareness that confronting the truth was the only way to construct a meaningful future. While he still loved the image of himself that Hitler had constructed, Speer could not become a different man, just as, while it was still in love with the past, Germany could not become a different nation. The pain of that struggle is in all of us, particularly when we are in love and there are truths we don't want to acknowledge. You don't have to be a war criminal to have closets you would prefer not to open.

Nations, institutions, individuals can all be blinded by love, by the need to believe themselves good and worthy and valued. We simply could not function if we believed ourselves to be otherwise. But when we are blind to the flaws and failings of what we love, we aren't effective either. As Colm O'Gorman said, we make ourselves powerless when we pretend we don't know. That's the paradox of wilful blindness: we think it will make us safe even as it puts us in danger.

3. DANGEROUS CONVICTIONS

> Ideology is a conceptual framework, it's the way people
> deal with reality. Everyone has one. You have to. To exist,
> you need an ideology.
>
> *Alan Greenspan, 23 October 2008*

It's as easy to fall in love with an idea as with a person. Big
ideas are especially alluring. They bring order to the world,
give meaning to life. When we join political parties or
churches or governments, we find soulmates with the same
worldview, the same values, and life feels complete. We may
even talk of being 'wedded' to our ideas. Much of our identity is defined by what we believe and we actively seek
confirmation of those beliefs. Actually, we go even further: our
brain treats differently any information that might challenge
our closely held beliefs.

In 2004, a team of cognitive neuroscientists set out to see what
this process actually looks like. Drew Westen, at Emory University, was interested in what psychologists call 'motivated
reasoning' and what Freud called defence mechanisms: the
processes by which people adjust what they know to avoid bad
feelings like anxiety and guilt. He theorised that the brain's neural
networks would try to satisfy two kinds of constraints: cognitive
constraints – we want to put information together in a way that

feels rational – and emotional constraints, meaning we want to feel good about the information we take in.

To test his theories, Westen and his team recruited fifteen committed Democrats and fifteen committed Republicans to submit to fMRI scans of their brains while reading political material. As they lay in the scanner, they read pairs of quotes attributed either to President Bush or presidential candidate John Kerry. In each pair, one statement was entirely compatible with the candidate's position, but one statement was contradictory. What Westen wanted to find out was: would the brain treat the contradictions of the preferred candidate in the same way as it would treat the contradictions of a disliked candidate?

What the experiment found was that the partisan participants gave a far rougher ride to the contradictions that came from the candidate they opposed.

'They had no trouble seeing the contradictions for the opposition candidate,' Westen wrote. 'But when confronted with potentially troubling political information, a network of neurons becomes active that produces distress. Not only did the brain manage to shut down distress through faulty reasoning – but it did so quickly. The neural circuits charged with regulation of emotional states seemed to recruit beliefs that eliminated the distress and conflict.'[1]

But, said Westen, the brain didn't stop at eliminating the uncomfortable contradictions. It worked overtime 'to feel good, activating reward circuits that give partisans a jolt of positive reinforcement for their biased "reasoning"'.[2]

In Westen's experiment, the reward circuits the brain was using were the same that are activated when a junkie gets a fix. In other words, when we find the thoughts we agree with, or are able to eliminate the ones that make us uncomfortable, we feel that same kind of euphoria and reassurance that an addict feels when reunited with his drug of choice: all is right with the world. At least for a while.

The brain doesn't like conflict and works hard to resolve it. This may be one reason why, when we gather with like-minded people, we are more likely to seek out common ground than areas of difference: quite literally, it feels better. But it also feels rational, even when it isn't. Which means that when we work hard to defend our core beliefs, we risk becoming blind to the evidence that could tell us we're wrong.

In 1942, the physician Alice Stewart had come to Oxford to work as a resident physician at the Radcliffe Infirmary. She was, by all accounts, an outstanding doctor, the youngest woman at the time to enter the Royal College of Physicians. Her colleagues considered her to be a wonderful teacher and an outstanding diagnostician, full of boundless energy, with an appetite for big challenges and hard problems. Doctors were much needed during the war and the fact that, as a mother with two small children, she couldn't be called up for military service made her even more valuable, while her failing marriage meant she was willing and able to go wherever she was needed.

While in Oxford, Stewart treated patients but also led a number of research projects into problematic, puzzling disease patterns. One of them involved trying to figure out why munitions workers filling shells with TNT seemed so susceptible to jaundice and anaemia. In wartime, the factory was staffed by 'the ragtag of the population'[3] which posed the question: were they getting ill because they were vulnerable anyway, or was TNT the culprit? What originally started as a laboratory study soon became a field study: by persuading her healthy medical students to work in the plant and emulate the lives of the factory workers, Alice was able to prove that the diseases were not a consequence of the workers' weaker health but of their exposure to TNT. Subsequent projects – investigating high turnover in labourers using carbon tetrachloride, and another into miners suffering from lung disease – meant that, without having deliberately chosen to do so, Alice found herself working in the field of social medicine and epidemiology. It was an emerging discipline awash with hard problems.

Growing concern about the connection between high rates of illness and low social status led to the creation in 1942 of Oxford's Institute of Social Medicine. Why did poorer people suffer approximately twice the rate of infant mortality, ear, mastoid and respiratory illnesses, ulcers and heart disease? What was the relationship between poverty and illness and what, in the light of the soon to be formed National Health Service, could be done about it? Stewart was recruited to the Institute by one of the founding fathers of epidemiology, John Ryle, and she brought to her work all the indignant energy that was her hallmark.

'Practising medicine without asking these larger questions is like selling groceries across the counter,' she said. 'You go in with an illness; the doctor sells you a pill. It's no more responsible than that. Nobody goes out and asks, "who didn't come in because he was too sick to come? Why are so many people coming in with this, and so few with that?"'[4] But when Ryle died in 1950, Stewart's progress ground to a halt. Ryle's institute was demoted to the 'Social Medicine Unit' and Stewart lost her mentor and her status.

Abandoned by the Oxford establishment, and left with a tiny salary but no building, no funding and no work, in a field that commanded little respect or kudos, the only way that Alice could make her mark was by identifying – and solving – a hard problem. The burning issues of the day – lung cancer, cardiovascular disease and polio – were crowded. This left just one: leukaemia. Incidence of the disease was on the increase, at a rate that made it look like an epidemic, but the number of patients was still so small that the field was difficult to study using statistics, the traditional tool of epidemiology. Two anomalies caught Alice Stewart's eye. Leukaemia was affecting children aged two to four. That was odd because typically by that age children are healthy: they've survived infancy and haven't yet started school. And the children dying from leukaemia weren't poor: in fact, they came from countries with better medical care and lower overall death rates. How could that be? Stewart decided to interview the mothers of leukaemia victims to see if she could find anything in their lives that might account for this pattern. She didn't know what she was looking for, so her questions started with conception.

'It was a needle-in-a-haystack search,' says Gayle Greene, who first met Alice Stewart in 1992. Even at the age of eighty-six, Stewart was so dazzling that Greene was inspired to write her biography.

'Alice didn't know what she was looking for, so she asked questions about everything: exposure to infection, inoculation, cats, dogs, hens, shop-fried fish and chips, highly coloured drinks, coloured sweets and have you had an x-ray?'[5]

Stewart proposed interviewing all of the mothers of children who had died of leukaemia and other forms of cancer between 1953 and 1955. But she couldn't get mainstream funding for her work. A mere £1,000 was found, from the Lady Tata Memorial Fund for Leukaemia Research, to pay for Alice's pioneering study. With such minimal resources, she had to be inventive. So she designed her questionnaire and took it in person to all the medical officers in 203 county health departments in the country. With characteristic tenacity, she persuaded them to use their own people and local records to answer all the questions on her survey. Her tiny grant was all spent on train fares as she went up and down the country, laden with carbon paper and brown envelopes.

'When the Americans tried to do a study like ours,' Alice later recalled, 'They gave up because it cost too much. But it cost us so little because I was making use of existing records.'[6]

Her study matched 500 leukaemia deaths, plus 500 deaths from other forms of cancer, with 1,000 live children of the same age, sex and region. When the surveys started to come back, the results leapt out. The culprit wasn't the coloured sweets, the pets or even the fish and chips.

'"Yes" was turning up three times for every dead child to one for every live child, for the question: "had you had an obstetric x-ray?" *Yes was running three to one.* It was a shocker. They were as like as two peas in a pod, the living and the dead. They were alike in all respects except on that one score. And the dose was very small, very brief, a single diagnostic x-ray, a tiny fraction of the radiation exposure considered safe. And it was enough to almost double risk of an early cancer death.'

The recognition that x-raying pregnant mothers so dramatically increased the chances of childhood cancer was the kind of finding epidemiologists dream of: a hard problem with good data pointing to a clear solution. But, like the thorough scientist she was, when her excitement died down, Stewart questioned her results over and over again and she asked colleagues to check them before she published them. When her article 'Preliminary Communication: Malignant Diseases in Childhood and Diagnostic Irradiation *in utero*' appeared in the *Lancet* in 1956, it caused a stir. The Nobel Prize was mentioned and Alice was asked to repeat her survey in Scotland. Over the next eighteen months, Stewart and her team continued to collect data. Within a three-year period they had traced 80 per cent of *all* childhood cancer deaths in England between 1953 and 1955. Publishing a full report in the *British Medical Journal* in 1958, they were able to conclude definitively that a foetus exposed to an x-ray was twice as likely to develop cancer within the next ten years as a foetus that had not been exposed.

'We reckoned that a child a week was dying from this practice. We thought that doctors would stop x-raying on the mere suspicion that we were right and we felt that we must hurry to cover all the deaths that occurred in the next ten years, because, once they stopped x-raying, there would be no further cases.'

Alice's fears were unfounded; doctors carried on x-raying pregnant mothers for the next twenty-five years. Not until 1980 did major American medical organisations finally recommend that the practice be abandoned. The place that held out longest was England.

Why did it take so long? How could so many doctors, the world over, have been so blind? Stewart's findings were clear, her data voluminous and, initially, greeted with acclaim. To us now, and to Alice at the time, it seemed obvious that the practice of x-raying pregnant women should stop immediately. What happened?

Many like to lay the blame on a personality clash with fellow epidemiologist, Richard Doll.

'Doll was really influential and he was on the Medical Research Council and he truly did not want to let her into the story,' argues Stewart's biographer, Gayle Greene. 'I think he knew that she was a better scientist than he and I think she had principles that he did not have and he could not forgive her for that.'

Doll rushed out a paper refuting Stewart's paper – a tiny, quick study which he later acknowledged was 'not very good' and whose results he later described as 'unreliable'. But Doll was a dominant figure in the British medical establishment and his voice carried a long way. Alice Stewart's daughter, Anne Marshall, remembered the impact Doll's opposition had on her mother.

'I don't know if Mum was upset by Doll but he certainly made her think again and again. And then she'd settle down and do the work – and she knew she was right. She didn't enjoy a fight but, if she felt strongly about something, she was very good at having one.'[7]

It didn't help that Stewart was an unconventional scientist; she was a divorced mother with two children, at a time when there were few women in science, fewer mothers and when divorce was still not entirely respectable. Looking after her children alone didn't leave Alice much time to network, build alliances or seek out support.

'She wasn't a political person,' says Gayle Greene. 'She was doing her research, raising her family and that took thirty-two hours of the day! Compare that to Doll, who was such a schmoozer, such a political creature. So smooth! When I met him, I thought: this is a guy who's done a lot of PR! You would never say that meeting Alice. She was authentic, genuine, a very disarming person – I mean everybody loved her – but she was not playing the game.'

Doll was a major obstacle. But personality alone doesn't explain why, worldwide, the practice of x-raying unborn children persisted. At the Harvard University School of Public Health, Brian MacMahon also set out to refute Stewart's findings – but he found exactly what she had found: cancer mortality was 40 per cent higher among children whose mothers had been x-rayed. In the early 1960s, one of the largest radiation studies examined six million x-ray subjects in New York, Maryland and Minnesota; that confirmed Alice's findings, too. New statistical methods, the advent of computers, all served to make collecting and analysing data easier and more accurate – but all they did, over and over again, was to show that Alice Stewart, with her paper surveys and carbon paper, had been right all along. So why did doctors continue a practice that study after study showed to be so dangerous? How could they be so blind to all the data?

In part, the sexiness of x-rays was to blame. Ever since their discovery in 1895, x-rays had developed an aura of mastery and mystique. They were used as an exquisite and expensive form of portraiture in the 1890s and even used as the ultimate tool for finding a ring that had been mistakenly baked into a cake.[8] Shoe stores boasted of x-ray machines that ensured a perfect fit: 'the salesman, the purchaser and even a purchaser's advisory friend can visually know exactly how well a shoe is fitting, both under pressure and otherwise,' claimed the 1927 patent for the 'shoe fluoroscope'. 'With this apparatus in his shop, a shoe merchant can positively assure his customers that they need never wear ill-fitting boots and shoes . . . parents can visually assure themselves as to whether they are buying shoes for their boys and girls which will not injure and deform the sensitive bone joints.'[9]

With so much investment in it, neither shoe salesmen nor doctors wanted to hear that there might be any risks associated with the new technology. They were wedded to it.

'No one likes to be told they've been doing something wrong all their lives!' That's how Anne Marshall explains the reaction to her mother's findings. 'That's what the radiologists and obstetricians took from Mum's work– that they'd been doing something wrong. There were lots of them and they liked what they were doing and wanted to keep on doing it.'

'Doctors had enthusiasm about radiology that was so enormous that medical centres had invested in all kinds of x-ray equipment,' explains Gayle Greene. 'They didn't like being told that they were not only *not* helping their patients – but they were actually killing them! I think people are very resistant to changing what they know how to do, what they have expertise in and certainly what they have economic investment in.'

But Alice Stewart's survey of childhood cancers did something even more radical and provocative than question standard medical practice. Her findings struck at the heart of a big idea central to scientific thinking at the time. Threshold theory maintained that, while a large dose of something like radiation would be dangerous, there was always a point – a threshold – beyond which it was safe. (That point is what, today, we might call a tipping point.) But Alice Stewart was arguing that in this case, there was *no* acceptable level of radiation that was safe for foetuses. It wasn't just shoe shops and medical centres; a cornerstone of scientific orthodoxy was under attack.

She had to be wrong. If she was right, too many other assumptions had to be re-examined. What Alice Stewart had provoked in her scientific colleagues was cognitive dissonance: the mental turmoil that is evoked when the mind tries to hold two entirely incompatible views. It could not be true that threshold theory was right – but also that such tiny doses of radiation caused cancers. It could not be true that radiation was both a new wonder tool – that also killed children. It could not be true that doctors cured patients – and made them sick. The dissonance produced by mutually exclusive beliefs is tremendously painful, even unbearable. The easiest way to reduce the pain – the dissonance – is to eliminate one of the beliefs, rendering dissonance consonant. It was easier for scientists to cling to their beliefs: Threshold theory and x-rays both worked; doctors remained authoritative, smart, good people. Alice Stewart and her findings were sacrificed to preserve the big idea. Dissonance is eliminated when we blind ourselves to contradictory propositions. And we are prepared to pay a very high price to preserve our most cherished ideas.

The theory of cognitive dissonance was initially developed by Leon Festinger around the same time that Alice Stewart was studying childhood cancers. He had developed much of his theory studying the religious millenarian movements of the nineteenth century, but he yearned for a live, contemporary case study to test his ideas. In September 1954, he found his opportunity in a newspaper story.

PROPHECY FROM PLANET CLARION. CALL TO CITY: FLEE THAT FLOOD. IT'LL SWAMP US ON DEC. 21, OUTER SPACE TELLS SUBORDINATE.

The story described a suburban housewife, Marian Keech, who believed, on the basis of automatic writing, that the earth would be flooded on 21 December. The fact that the group held such a specific belief about an event destined to occur on a specific date made this a perfect test case for Festinger's research: what would happen when a deeply held belief – a big idea – was disconfirmed by events? That the end of the world was due in months, and not years, made it practical too. When, as Festinger predicted, the flood failed to take place, would Mrs Keech surrender her belief in the light of experience? Festinger's theory suggested that she would continue in her faith but also, crucially, that it would become stronger than ever.

Even more unconventional in his research methods than Alice Stewart, Festinger and a few of his colleagues from the University of Minnesota set out to infiltrate Mrs Keech's community. For two months, they monitored the beliefs and varying levels of commitment among a small group with whom Mrs Keech had shared the automatic writing that she believed came to her via extraterrestrial messengers. Dr Thomas Armstrong, a physician at Eastern Teachers College in Collegeville, and his wife Daisy became Keech's devoted followers and they, in turn, recruited numerous students until there was a core of some fifteen devotees.

Mrs Keech's messages described an apocalyptic vision, according to which Lucifer had returned to earth in disguise and was leading scientists to build ever greater weapons of destruction. Their work would culminate in the earth falling apart and the disruption of the entire solar system. While forces of Light struggled to reclaim humanity, man's only hope was that enough people were open to the light to escape another explosion.

Festinger went out of his way to point out that Keech and the Armstrongs weren't crazy and they weren't psychotic. 'True, Mrs Keech put together a rather unusual combination of ideas – a combination peculiarly well adapted to our contemporary, anxious age,' Festinger wrote. 'But scarcely a single one of her ideas can be said to be unique, novel or lacking in popular support.'[10] There was nothing in her belief system that people haven't believed before – or since.

Central to these beliefs was the prediction Mrs Keech received that the world would end with an enormous flood on 21 December. Only true believers would be saved. 'The Supreme Being is going to clean house by sinking all of the land masses as we know them now and raising the land masses now under the sea. There will be a washing of the world with water. Some will be saved by being taken off the earth in spacecraft.'[11]

The messages were so bizarre and the belief system so open to ridicule that Festinger took pains to document just how serious and how real the group's commitment was. These were not a bunch of kids pretending. One particularly devout member, Kitty O'Donnell, quit her job, quit school, lived off her small savings and moved into an expensive apartment because she did not expect to need what little remained of her cash. Two members – Fred Burden and Laura Brooks – gave up their college studies; Laura threw away many of her personal possessions. Dr Armstrong was eventually asked to resign his college position; the amount of time he spent talking to students about flying saucers had caused a flurry of parental complaints. But he was not dismayed, considering this merely 'part of the plan'.[12] His wife chose not to bother getting her dishwasher repaired: 'It isn't worth it, because the time is so short now.'[13] And when Mrs Keech received a call from a salesman of cemetery lots, she calmly explained that burial was 'the least of my worries'.[14] However ludicrous the prophecies may seem to us, this group lived their lives in the sincere belief that the flood was imminent.

Mrs Keech and her followers confidently expected flying saucers to transport them to other planets before the cataclysm occurred. Several false alarms, when messages seemed to promise the arrival of spacemen who failed to arrive, tested their faith. But on each occasion, the group either reinterpreted the messages to fit events or blamed themselves for faulty understanding. On the eve of the promised flood, the group spent the day together in 'peaceful idleness', confidently awaiting their rescue. Arthur Bergen, a teenage member of the group, complained that his mother had threatened to call the police if he wasn't home by two a.m. the next morning. 'The believers smilingly assured him that he need not worry – by that time they would all be aboard a saucer.'[15] Warned not to wear metal of any kind, they fastidiously eliminated it from their clothing – zippers, snaps, belt buckles, bra clips – and removed foil from chewing gum, watches from wrists.

The last ten minutes were tense. When one clock said 12.05, a chorus of people pointed out that a slower clock was more accurate. But even when the slower clock confirmed midnight, no one appeared and nothing happened. No flood, no flying saucers. Mrs Keech continued to receive long, confusing messages from 'the Creator' but by two a.m. Arthur Bergen had to take a cab home to his mother. By 4.30 a.m., the group was distraught, close to tears and some were beginning to show signs of doubt. How would they handle the discomfirmation of their passionately held beliefs? This was the gist of Festinger's two-month study.

At 4.45 Mrs Keech received a new message. 'Not since the beginning of time upon this Earth has there been such a force of Good and light as now floods this room and that which has been loosed within this room now floods the entire Earth.'[16] The goodness of the group had saved the world from flood.

The group was jubilant: the belief system was intact. But a greater change overcame Mrs Keech. Previously highly reticent, now she was more eager than ever to call the local newspaper and share her good news. Another member of the group insisted the news go further, to the Associated Press; the Creator surely wouldn't want the story to be an exclusive. Despite – or because of – the initial challenge to their belief, their faith now was stronger than ever and the believers more energetic in their pros- elytising. Evidence had not upset belief. Just as Festinger had hypothesised, disconfirmation had actually made their belief stronger.

And they never lost it. While Mrs Keech eventually left Lake City, she continued to receive automatic messages that she relayed to the faithful. The Armstrongs were as devout as ever, their faith 'boundless and their resistance to disconfirmation sublime'. Of the eleven members of the Lake City group, each of whom had witnessed unequivocal disconfirmation first hand, only two com- pletely gave up their belief in Mrs Keech's writings – and they were the two who had been least committed from the outset.

Festinger's academic account of this episode can't resist some of the humour implicit in it, but the thrust of his argument is deadly serious. What he and subsequent psychologists argued was that we all strive to preserve an image of ourselves as consistent, stable, competent and good. Our most cherished beliefs are a vital and central part of who we are – in our own eyes and the eyes of our friends and colleagues. Anything or anyone that threatens that sense of self produces pain that feels just as dan- gerous and unpleasant as hunger or thirst. A challenge to our big ideas feels life-threatening. And so we strive mightily to reduce the pain, either by ignoring the evidence that proves we are wrong, or by reinterpreting evidence to support us.

Psychologist Anthony Greenwald called this phenomenon the 'totalitarian ego',[17] which, he said, operates just like a police state: locking away threatening or incompatible ideas, suppressing evidence and re-writing history, all in the service of a central idea or self-image. Marian Keech's followers would re-interpret events to fit their expectations, because not to have done so threatened to destroy their sense of who they were in the world. If doctors and scientists who read Alice Stewart's research believed it, and acted upon it, then they would have had to accept that they had harmed patients. But doctors don't like to think of themselves as sources of harm: they go into medicine to be, and do, good. Scientists embracing Alice's findings would have had at least to question the big idea of threshold theory. But scientists like big ideas, organising principles, perhaps more than the rest of us. They're what hold the data together, in just the same way that our beliefs and values hold our sense of self together. Acknowledging error, in these areas that are so vital for our self-definition, feels far too costly. Even as late as 1977, the National Council of Radiation Protection argued doctors must have x-rayed only those foetuses that were destined to get cancer. Quite how they could have known which these were, the Council never explained. But that scientists should have developed so convoluted an argument illustrates how hard the mind will work to defend its most cherished and defining beliefs.

Festinger argued that, as individuals, we are all highly driven to make sense of the world and of our place in it. And we do so by gathering around us the ideas but also the people that verify our story, so to speak. The work that Drew Westen and other scientists have done more recently has served to illustrate that cognitive dissonance is not just a theory; it has a physical reality in the way that the brain handles information that we like – and the way that it handles the information that causes us distress. The fact that, as we already know, we're drawn to people similar to ourselves, merely reinforces this process. Mrs Keech and her followers would have had difficulty maintaining their faith if they had been isolated and alone: confirmation of each other by each other kept their commitment secure. In just the same way, the medical profession stuck together, led by the socially adroit Richard Doll, holding out against Alice Stewart's findings.

Social support makes it easier to do things, or believe in ideas, that would feel a lot more uncomfortable if we were on our own. That social support always comes in the form of family, friends or colleagues who share, and act on, the big ideas that bring them together. But institutional power is a particularly seductive form of social support. After all, if you are in a position of tremendous institutional or political power, then not only are you hugely confirmed by the colleagues who share your beliefs, but questioning them would threaten everything: job, position, reputation, future career.

In Errol Morris's film about Robert McNamara, *The Fog of War*, there's an exquisite moment when McNamara talks about meeting North Vietnamese former Foreign Minister Thach years after the end of the Vietnam War. As US Secretary of State for Defense in the 1960s, McNamara had been as convinced a Cold Warrior as any of his Cabinet colleagues. His job, as he saw it then, was not to question the war but to prosecute it effectively. His passion, both for the ideology of the Administration and for the success of his career, he later saw, blinded him to any understanding of his enemy.

'Mr McNamara, you must never have read a history book,' McNamara recalled Thach saying to him. 'If you had, you'd know we weren't pawns of the Chinese or the Russians. McNamara, didn't you know that? Don't you understand that we have been fighting the Chinese for one thousand years? We were fighting for our independence. And we would fight to the last man. And we were determined to do so. And no amount of bombing, no amount of US pressure would ever have stopped us.'

Cold War ideology had blinded McNamara and his colleagues to the fundamental, primary motivation of the Vietnamese. They weren't fighting to become part of a greater communist bloc. They were fighting to become free from *all* imperial powers. For anyone to have questioned Cold War orthodoxy within the Johnson administration at the time would have jeopardised status, reputation and position. McNamara's blindness doomed him to failure; he could not win the war because he did not understand his opponent. Far from making sense of events, the big idea left him powerless to understand them.

Economic models work in ways very similar to such ideologies: pulling in and integrating the information that fits the model, leaving out what can't be accommodated. The economist and Nobel laureate Paul Krugman compared such models to ancient maps. At first, they were wildly misleading but incorporated a lot of information: second-hand travellers' reports, guesses and anecdotes. But as the standard for accuracy rose, much of that information wasn't deemed good enough, so it got left out – with the result that, by the eighteenth century, most of Africa went blank. But Krugman, whose reputation for beautiful models has brought him such fame, recognises how incomplete they can be.

'I think there's a pretty good case to be made that the stuff that I stressed in the models is a less important story than the things I left out because I couldn't model them, like spillovers of infor-mation and social networks.'[18]

The problem with models, in other words, is that they imply that whatever does not fit into them isn't relevant – when it could be the most relevant information of all. But we treasure our

models and personal big ideas, because they help us to make decisions, about what to do with our lives, who to befriend, and
what we stand for. A profound and innate part of who we are,
they become so deeply entwined in all aspects of our lives that we
may forget how profoundly they filter what we see, remember
and absorb. As our brains give our preferred ideas a smooth, easy
flow, impeding distressing contradictions, the riverbed of our
beliefs gets deeper and its sides grow higher.

In the case of someone like Mrs Keech, it was very obvious (to
everyone but her and her followers) just how peculiar her ideas
were. But when ideas are widely shared, they don't attract so
much scepticism. We may not see them as ideology and we don't
see their proponents as zealots. They may even come to seem
normal. But appearances can be deceptive.

'Greenspan's wilful blindness was incredible,' says Frank
Partnoy. 'He had a highly simplistic view of how markets
behaved. He believed in the core of his soul that markets would
self-correct and that financial models could forecast risk effectively.' Partnoy doesn't criticise the former Chairman of the
Federal Reserve Bank lightly or from the lofty perch of
someone observing financial shenanigans from a safe distance.
He sold derivatives on Wall Street from 1993 to 1995 and
knew, first hand, in gritty detail, just how convoluted, disingenuous, obscure and risky they were. He eventually left the
industry, utterly disillusioned by how fraudulent it was. But his
years on Wall Street had shown him, up close and personal,
what the derivatives market was all about. Now Professor of
Law and Finance at the University of San Diego, Partnoy has
been watching the derivatives market develop ever since he left
it. And he's watched with mounting frustration and disbelief as
the so-called 'Maestro', Greenspan, failed to do anything about
it.

'There was just so much happening in markets that

Greenspan didn't understand – because it was inconsistent with his worldview,' says Partnoy. 'It really illustrates the dangers of having a particular fixed view of the world and not being open to evidence that your worldview is wrong until it is too late.'

Greenspan's worldview was significantly developed in his late twenties and early thirties, when he became a devoted acolyte of the American novelist and economic libertarian Ayn Rand. At this time, Greenspan had given up on his career playing bebop with a big touring band and turned to economics. He dropped out of Columbia's PhD programme to form a consulting firm while developing a close personal relationship, and passionate intellectual relationship, with Rand and her fellow Objectivists. Rand's attraction to men remains somewhat mysterious: an adulterous, failed screenwriter who'd emigrated from revolutionary Russia, she seems an unlikely muse for corporate titans and economic gurus. Her understanding of how markets worked derived from the traumatic experience of having lived through the Russian Revolution, in which her family lost everything. But she never trained as an economist, had never run a business and wrote extraordinarily hideous, often impenetrable prose that purported to be philosophy. Nevertheless, Greenspan was smitten, springing to Rand's defence when her novel, *Atlas Shrugged*, received a critical notice. Reviewing the book, Greenspan wrote, 'Justice is unrelenting. Creative individuals and undeviating purpose and rationality achieve joy and fulfillment. Parasites who persistently avoid either purpose or reason perish as they should.' Greenspan could not conceive that a book with such properties might have its flaws.

What Greenspan admired in Rand, and which he embraced with evangelical fervour, was the belief that, if he were only liberated from the regulations and constraints imposed by government, man would attain ever greater heights of freedom, creativity and wealth.

'I am opposed,' said Rand, 'to all forms of control. I am for an absolute *laissez-faire* free unregulated economy. I am for the separation of state and economics.'[19]

In Rand's world, those who could do well would be freed from all constraint to express and articulate the full capacity of their talents; they would achieve joy and fulfilment. Those who weren't up to it – parasites – would fail and get out of the way. It's a touchingly romantic idea, as long as you assume that you will be one of the successful ones.

Greenspan wasn't in love with Ayn Rand, but he was in love with her ideas and they framed everything he did. In his autobiography, *The Age of Turbulence*, he describes her as a 'stabilising force' in his life.[20] Identifying himself as a convert, Greenspan was clearly in awe of her, proud when he could 'keep up with her most of the time'. Ayn Rand was right there, standing next to him, when, in 1974, he was sworn in as chairman of Gerald Ford's Council of Economic Advisors. And his ideas hadn't changed a bit when he took over the Federal Reserve in August 1987. The man with a religious belief in the evils of regulation was now in charge of money supply.

'I do have an ideology,' Greenspan told Congress. 'My judgement is that free, competitive markets are by far the unrivalled way to organise economies.'[21]

'He wanted to do whatever he could to deregulate the market,' says Partnoy, who has studied Greenspan's career critically for many years. 'But he was very clever about it. Rather than lobby upfront for the repeal of Glass–Steagal, he pressed for a series of small incremental changes. I think of it as Swiss cheese: put a few holes in, then a few more – and eventually there's no cheese left! He honestly believed that we would all be better off if regulated markets got smaller and smaller, and the deregulated markets got bigger and bigger. That's how you get to the promised land.'

What's so striking, however, is that all the time Greenspan was nibbling away at regulation, the market was being rocked by a whole series of warning tremors that offered strong evidence that its most deregulated sectors – the sector Greenspan was so eager to help grow – threatened to blow everything up.

In 1994, when Greenspan raised interest rates from 3 per cent to 3.25 per cent, the marketplace was full of derivatives that assumed interest rates would stay low. When interest rates rose instead, all hell broke loose. David Askin, one of the most active traders in complex mortgage derivatives, ran a $600 million fund that went up in smoke in a matter of weeks, filing for bankruptcy on 7 April. Five days later, Gibson Greetings, Air Products, Dell Computer, Mead Corporation and Procter & Gamble admitted to billions of dollars in losses from derivatives, many of which even their internal financiers did not understand. Congressional hearings were held, in which George Soros testified that 'There are so many of them and some are so esoteric, that the risks involved may not be properly understood even by the most sophisticated investors.'[22]

In May, Greenspan's Federal Reserve Bank raised the interest rate another 0.5 per cent – and there was a bloodbath on Wall Street. Property and casualty insurers lost more than they had paid out on Hurricane Andrew; hedge funds, banks, securities firms and the life-insurance industry lost billions. According to Frank Partnoy, virtually every kind of institution, from every sector of the economy, suffered massive losses.

In Orange County, California, the seventy-year-old treasurer and college dropout, Robert Citron, bet twenty billion dollars of public money on derivatives sold to him by Merrill Lynch; in December 1994, the county filed for bankruptcy. And it wasn't alone. Dozens of smaller municipalities, from San Diego to

Georgia to Maine and Montana, along with public utilities, city colleges and pension funds, invested in collateralised mortgage obligations and other derivatives, losing millions.

In 1994, Procter & Gamble sued Bankers Trust for the huge losses they'd suffered from derivatives. The prosecution used taped phone calls that demonstrated just how deliberately and knowingly the bankers had misled the firm. For once, there was some chink of light on the 'dark market' of derivatives and what it showed wasn't pretty – and wasn't regulated. At the same time, the financial-services firm Kidder, Peabody discovered losses of $350 million. Part of General Electric at the time, under the legendary Jack Welch, it turned out that no one really understood what traders in the firm were up to. The quarter that the losses were reported was the first time in fifty-two quarters that earnings were less than the previous year. But after all this mayhem, the only legislation that emerged actually made life far harder for would-be plaintiffs when Congress restricted securities lawsuits in 1995.

Frank Partnoy has chronicled each of these debacles, from what he calls 'Patient Zero' in 1987 through to Enron in 2002 and the banking crisis twenty years later. 'It was foolish,' he wrote, 'to deregulate markets simply because large institutions instead of individuals were involved. It was a well-established economic principle that markets with large sophistication and information gaps did not function well. The more they carved up markets, the harder it was for anyone to keep tabs on risk.'[23]

Each one of these debacles reinforced the same lesson: derivatives were a 'dark market'. No one knew what went on in these deals and, because there was no statutory requirement to report anything, even the parties to the deals often did not know what they had. Had there been any reporting requirement, at least those with most at stake might have gained some insight into their own exposure. Instead, the freedom to report nothing meant that not only did the government not really know what was going on – no one did. They were all equally blind.

That this could continue was possible only because so many people shared Greenspan's ideology. The *Financial Times* journalist Gillian Tett compares such blind faith to the medieval Church.

'If this was a religion, Alan Greenspan was the Pope,' says Tett. 'He blessed derivatives. Then you had the high priests up at the altar, passing out blessings in the financial Latin that the congregation don't understand. The Pope is saying it's all miraculous and wonderful and the blessings come in the form of cheap mortgages.'[24]

A few dissenting voices had the temerity to stand up to Greenspan and argue that derivatives posed a major risk and required oversight. In 1988, Muriel Siebert testified before the subcommittee on Telecommunications and Finance, in the wake of the 1987 market crash. The major problem with the market, she said, was derivatives.

'Program trades and index arbitrage end up bringing the volatility and rampant speculation of the futures pits to the floor of the Big Board. Futures have become the tail wagging the dog.'

In 1996, Brooksley Born was appointed to head up the Commodity Futures Trading Commission, the regulator uniquely tasked with regulating the \$27 trillion derivatives market. And after the string of catastrophes in 1994, she was one of the few eager to impose some oversight. But Greenspan was having none of it. When Born's CFTC issued a 'Concept Release' outlining how regulation might work, Greenspan instantly issued a statement condemning it.

'It seemed totally inexplicable to me,' Born recalled later. 'It was as though the other regulators were saying, "We don't want to know."'[25]

Six weeks later, the hedge fund Long-Term Capital Management, which included Greenspan's former deputy at the Fed,

David Mullins, became insolvent. The size of the failure threat-ened the entire US economy.

'Long-Term Capital Management was exactly what I'd been worried about,' Born said. 'No regulators knew it was on the verge of collapse. Why? Because we didn't have any information about the market.'[26]

At last, the LTCM crisis provoked some support in Congress for regulation. But Greenspan once again moved quickly to quash it.

'I know of no set of supervisory actions we can take that can prevent people from making dumb mistakes. I think it is very important for us not to introduce regulation for regulation's sake.'

And Greenspan and his friends won the day: no regulation for over-the-counter derivatives was introduced. They could con-tinue to trade without any capital requirements or rules against manipulation or even fraud. Greenspan's free market was allowed to get bigger and bigger, and Brooksley Born resigned.

Three years later, in 2001, the sixth-largest corporation in America, Enron, went bust. Inside an intricate web of malfea-sance lay deadly derivatives, tied to the company's stock price, which left its investors with nothing. They weren't all Enron employees; many were small investors, like Mary Pearson, a Latin teacher who testified before Congress after the company failed.

I am just a pebble in the stream, a little bitty shareholder. I did not lose billions but what I did lose seems like a billion to me. I was going to use my Enron stock as my long-term health care. I was disappointed in the people that I put my trust in years ago. And after a little time passed on, bitter-ness came into being, and bitterness will eat you alive if you let it. But sometimes at night I do feel real bitter over what

I have lost, because it was a big part of my future, and I do not know how I am going to handle the future now. All I can do is hope and pray I do not get sick.[28]

This was not a narrative Greenspan could see. From his perspective, 'creative individuals and undeviating purpose and rationality' went on to 'achieve joy and fulfilment' and the parasites perished. Until, that is, the banking crisis of 2008.

'This was my worst nightmare coming true,' said Brooksley Born. 'Nobody really knew what was going on in the market. The toxic assets of our biggest banks were in over-the-counter derivatives and caused the economic downturn that made us lose our savings, lose our jobs, lose our homes.'

Just as Rand had wished, the state and economics had been separated; Greenspan had proved true to the big idea of his life, but blind to the realities of it. Even after the biggest financial catastrophe of his lifetime, when Greenpan came to testify to Congress about what had gone wrong, he held fast to his big idea. It wasn't wrong; it was just flawed.

Chairman Waxman: You had an ideology. 'My judgment is that free, competitive markets are by far the unrivaled way to organize economies. We have tried regulation, none meaningfully worked.' That was your quote. Now our whole economy is paying its price. Do you feel that your ideology pushed you to make decisions that you wish you had not made?

Mr Greenspan: Well, remember, though, whether or not ideology is a conceptual framework with the way people deal with reality, everyone has one. You have to. To exist, you need an ideology. The question is whether it exists, is accurate or not. What I am saying to you is yes, I found a flaw, I don't know how significant or permanent it is, but I have been very distressed by that fact. I found a flaw in the model that I perceived is the critical functioning structure of how the world works.

Chairman Waxman: In other words, you found that your view of the world, your ideology, was not right, it was not working?

Mr Greenspan: Precisely. That's precisely the reason I was shocked, because I had been going for forty years or more with very considerable evidence that it was working exceptionally well.[29]

Greenspan's performance was mesmerising drama: a proud, old man wriggling to protect himself from the sharp, hard prongs of fact. His adversaries had prepared long and hard for this inquisition and neither they, nor the nation as a whole, were prepared to offer him room to manoeuvre. They demanded his recantation but he fought hard to evade the cognitive dissonance implicit in events that would not change shape just to fit into his ideology. Despite failure after failure, he still could not deny his big idea. He could admit a flaw, not that he was wrong. Eerily reminiscent of Mrs Keech, he was prepared only to see that he had got a slight detail wrong. He couldn't see, or wouldn't see, the financial wreckage strewn right across his career, but instead insisted that his big idea worked just fine for forty years. The free-market economist Friedrich von Hayek once said that 'without a theory, the facts are silent'. But for Greenspan, with his theory, the facts became invisible.

'Greenspan was blind to two things,' says Partnoy. 'He missed the fact that in the modern regulated state, you can't have a truly free market. There are always partially regulated markets and therefore there are opportunities for people to exploit information traps. And he didn't understand that even to the extent that the market isn't regulated, there are serious potential downsides to a free-for-all. That's why in the US and UK we have common law. Because if those things are absent, you have problems. Not just unfairness and injustice – but also just this kind of volatility and destabilisation.'

Of course, Greenspan did not act alone. He had the support of the powerful, he had the support of the crowd – as long as the economy was doing fine. You could say that he was blind, but he operated within a collective myopia that reinforced his ideology. And he hasn't recanted.

'Greenspan isn't atoning,' says Partnoy. 'It would be very hard for him to do that. He'd be escaping from a long tunnel.'

Much the same might be said of Tony Blair, who, despite the vociferous opposition of millions before the Iraq War, and the utterly unexpected chaos that characterised the war, remained steadfast in his belief that going to war had been an appropriate, necessary and correct decision. Although Saddam's weapons of mass destruction were never found, Blair even, when testifying before the Chilcot Inquiry, appeared to imply it was the war that had stopped them being produced:

'Don't ask the March 2003 question, but ask the 2010 question. Suppose we backed off? What we now know is that he retained absolutely the intent and intellectual know-how to restart a nuclear and chemical weapons programme when weapons inspectors were out and the sanctions were changed.'

In this, Blair – like Greenspan – sounds strangely reminiscent of Marian Keech, hanging on to the old, big idea. Blair certainly remained more convinced of his big idea than Richard Doll. Eight years before Doll died, his reputation secured by proving the connection between smoking and lung cancer, he did recant, although with the most modest of *mea culpa*s. In 1997, he published a paper, 'Risk of childhood cancer from fetal irradiation', in which he quietly announced the death of threshold theory.

'The association between the low dose of ionising radiation received by the foetus *in utero* from diagnostic radiography, particularly in the last trimester of pregnancy, and the subsequent risk of cancer in childhood provides direct evidence against the existence of a threshold dose below which no excess risk arises, and has led to changes in medical practice.'

But by the time Doll changed his mind, millions of pregnant women had been x-rayed.

4. THE LIMITS OF YOUR MIND

On 23 March 2005, Warren Briggs got into his car and set off for work. The commute to the BP refinery in Texas City usually took thirty to forty-five minutes, but today it felt longer. When he got to the plant, just before six a.m., he could scarcely remember driving there. Warren had been working twelve-hour shifts, seven days a week, for twenty-nine days in a row. He couldn't remember the last time he'd had time off. He had mixed feelings about his shifts. Twelve hours off meant more time with the kids. But he still wasn't getting much sleep.

He spoke briefly to the departing night-shift operator and then read the log book to prepare for the start-up. There was just a one-line log-book entry: 'isom brought in some raff to unit, to pack raff with.' That told him more or less nothing, he thought, grumpy as he started to work.

In front of him sat the control board for the ISOM/NDU/ AU2 complex: twelve monitors divided into twenty-four screens. Some screens had pages and pages of information behind them; others were pretty simple alarms. Visitors said it looked like something from NASA; Warren wished it was that exciting.

Warren's boss was late and, when he got in, he was busy. He was always busy because he had a pile of paperwork and a bunch of contracting crews to look after. A lot of the men hated contractors, said they were unsafe and cut corners. Warren didn't mind. Those guys needed to feed their families the same as he did. It wasn't their fault BP brought them in with fewer benefits, less pay. There weren't that many jobs around Texas City to choose from.

We're running so thin. That was the phrase everybody used. At first it just meant the pipes were wearing thin but now the whole place was wearing out. The plant and the people. So much cost-cutting, you could do the form-filling but not the repairs. Warren's supervisor was buried in paperwork and he had two new operators to train. He probably wouldn't be around much today.

With no one to relieve him, Warren ate his lunch at his desk in front of the control board. Some weird pressure spikes caught his attention and he wanted to keep an eye on them. It was boring, lonely work, cooped up in a darkened room. The equipment he was supposed to be controlling stood outside in the Texas sunshine, one small part of the vast refinery. When people first saw it, they'd say it looked like something on the moon, a space-age settlement full of towers and spheres that went on for miles. Warren didn't share their romance. It was just a refinery, making 3 per cent of America's gasoline. That would fuel a lot of cars.

The isomerisation unit Warren looked after boosted octane levels in the gasoline produced at the plant. Flammable hydrocarbons, or raffinate – the 'raff' in the log book – went into a 170-foot tower to distil and separate gas components. Higher octane meant higher performance and higher prices. That was the name of the game. Starting the unit was always a tricky time, when it would have been nice to have an extra pair of eyes. In the old days, there had been two operators, but cost-cutting changed all that. Then they'd added a third unit – the NDU – and said it was so easy to operate you didn't need an extra person. So instead of two people for two refinery units, now it was just Warren, on his own, looking after all three.

Around 12.40, an alarm went off but Warren still couldn't figure out where the high pressure was coming from. He decided to open a manual chain valve to vent some of the gases to the emergency relief system and to turn off two burners in the furnace. Just after one p.m., Warren's boss called in to see how things were going. When Warren mentioned the weird pressure spikes, he suggested opening a bypass valve to the blowdown drum to relieve some of the pressure. What neither of them knew was that the isomerisation tower was too full, fifteen times more than it was meant to be. But Warren's control panel wasn't configured to display flows into and out of the tower on the same screen and nowhere did it calculate total liquid in the tower. Running thin.

An adventure, one of the guys had called it. An adventure? Sure, he said: each morning when I walk into this place, I wonder if today's the day I'm gonna die. That wasn't Warren's idea of an adventure.

At 1.14 p.m., three emergency valves opened in the tower, sending nearly 52,000 gallons of hot, flammable liquid to the blowdown drum. When the liquid overflowed into a process sewer it set off alarms in the control room. But the high-level alarm didn't go off. While Warren sat in front of his twenty-four screens, a geyser of liquid and vapour erupted from the top of the stack, propelling nearly a tanker full of hot gasoline up into the air and then down to the ground like a tall, ungainly fountain. Within ninety seconds the whole unit and all the contractors' trailers were engulfed in a vast flammable vapour cloud.[1] Then a nearby car backfired.

A mile away, Joe Bilancich was negotiating for a new apprentice scheme. He felt one concussion in the room, then another. Everybody moved to the window. Flames and smoke filled their view while pieces of pipe and metal rained down on the ground.

Forty-five minutes from the site, Eva Rowe heard the blast.

Both her parents worked at the site; she called them at once. No answer.

Fifteen people died that day at BP's Texas City site, killed by the 'blunt force trauma' of the explosion. Eva Rowe lost both of her parents. It was one of the worst industrial accidents in American history.

When investigators, lawyers and executives came to unpick the tragedy that occurred at Texas City, everybody talked about blind spots: problems, processes and warnings that everybody could see but somehow managed not to see. Some of the causes were complex and technical, but some were not. What happened to Warren was simple and obvious and not unique to oil refineries. As we know from the banking crisis, companies don't have to kill people to be dangerous.

According to the US Chemical Safety Board, which spent two years investigating the accident, Warren was one of the most rested members of his team. The Night Lead Operator, who had filled the tower from the control room before John had come on duty, had worked thirty-three consecutive days, while the Day Lead Operator – who was training two new operators, dealing with contractors, and working to get a replacement part to finish the ISOM turnaround work – had been on duty for thirty-seven consecutive days. In other words, they were all dog-tired. The CSB estimated that John was getting 5.5 hours of sleep per night, and therefore was suffering from what they call an accumulated 'sleep debt' of about a month and a half. That didn't just mean that he felt lousy. 'It is common for a person experiencing fatigue to be more rigid in thinking, have greater difficulty responding to changing or abnormal circumstances, and take longer to reason correctly,' said the CSB. Focused attention on one thing, to the exclusion of everything else – often referred to as cognitive fixation or cognitive tunnel vision – is a typical performance effect of fatigue.[2]

Warren and his operators could not see the problem. They were simply too tired. The UK Health and Safety Executive found that subjective levels of fatigue increase with consecutive early shifts (those starting around six a.m.) The third day of working an early-morning shift results, it said, in a 30 per cent increase in fatigue, while the fifth consecutive day of working early-morning shifts results in a 60 per cent increase in fatigue, and the seventh consecutive day results in a 75 per cent increase compared to the first day. The study doesn't even contemplate what happens to people's minds when they've been working like this for thirty days non-stop.

Fatigue, overwork, burnout are not unique to the oil and gas industries. On 11 November 2004, the computer-games company Electronic Arts was shellshocked to find itself the target of a blogger called 'EA Spouse' who complained with shocking eloquence about the hours EA expected its programmers to work. Addressing herself to then-CEO (now chairman) Larry Probst, the spouse asked: 'You do realise what you're doing to your people, right? And you do realise that they ARE people, with physical limits, emotional lives, and families, right? Voices and talents and senses of humour and all that? That when you keep our husbands and wives and children in the office for ninety hours a week, sending them home exhausted and numb and frustrated with their lives, it's not just them you're hurting, but everyone around them, everyone who loves them? When you make your profit calculations and your cost analyses, you know that a great measure of that cost is being paid in raw human dignity, right?'

Electronic Arts is the world's leading producer of computer games. 2004 was a good year for the company. *The Sims*, *Lord of the Rings*, *FIFA* and *Medal of Honor* generated record revenues ($3 billion) and record profits ($776 million).[3] The year was particularly noteworthy because technology breakthroughs − faster processors and improved screen resolution – resulted in a boom for handheld game devices. The introduction of Sony's PSP promised even greater opportunity. But writing about the challenges the company faced going into 2005, Probst made no mention of a workforce that was fried, or an engineering team whose turnover ran at nearly 50 per cent.

When EA Spouse's essay, 'EA: The Human Story'[4] came out, it tore through the computer-game community like wildfire. 'I was so angry and in such pain, I thought: either I get a response to this or there's something seriously wrong with the world!' Erin Hoffman, the blog's author, recalled. 'It was students and gamers who propelled the thing. Within forty-eight hours, everyone read it. But it was students who were most angry! They dreamed of working in this industry – and were desperately disappointed to learn how awful it was.'

Today, Hoffman is in less pain, but she's still angry. The gist of her complaint then was that EA routinely scheduled engineers to work 85-hour weeks. When her fiancé Lan had interviewed for a job at EA, neither of them was naïve. Computer-games veterans, they knew that, just before a product shipped, most teams went into crunch mode, which involved long hours.

'They asked Lan in one of the interviews: "How do you feel about working long hours?" It's just a part of the game industry – few studios can avoid a crunch as deadlines loom, so we thought nothing of it. When asked for specifics about what "working long hours" meant, the interviewers coughed and glossed on to the next question; now we know why.'

Crunch is only supposed to be the mode of working at the tail end of a project. At EA, the team started by doing eight-hour, days, six days a week. But that quickly turned into twelve hours, six days a week and then into eleven hours a day, seven days a week. Crunch wasn't an emergency; it was a standard. Watching what was happening to her fiancé horrified Erin. 'After a certain number of hours, the eyes start to lose focus; after a certain number of weeks with only one day off, fatigue starts to accrue and accumulate exponentially. Bad things happen to one's physical, emotional, and mental health. The team is rapidly beginning to introduce as many flaws as they are removing. The bug rate soared in crunch.'

As the debate inspired by Erin's essay continued, she and her friends became better informed about the iron laws of human productivity. The forty-hour week is there for a reason; it gets the best work from people. The first four hours are the most productive and, as the day wears on, everyone becomes less alert, less focused and prone to more mistakes. In 1908, the first known study by Ernst Abbe,[5] one of the founders of the Zeiss lens laboratory, concluded that *reducing* the working day from nine to eight hours actually *increased* output. Henry Ford, who studied productivity issues obsessively, reached the same conclusion and infuriated his manufacturing colleagues when, in 1926, he had the audacity to introduce a forty-hour working week. Subsequent studies by Foster Wheeler (1968), Proctor & Gamble (1980) and the construction industry and many, many more show that, as the days get longer, productivity declines. No study has ever convincingly argued otherwise.[6]

Once you are doing sixty hours a week or more, you don't just get tired, you make mistakes; the time you spend rectifying errors consumes all the extra hours you work. The classic, and comic, example of this was Frank Gilbreth, the efficiency-obsessed father in *Cheaper by the Dozen*. He found he could shave faster if he used two razors – but then he wasted all his saved time covering the cuts with Band-Aids.

In software companies, a lot of developers like working late; they relish the silence that comes when the sales and marketing folk go home. But that means they need to start later too. Otherwise, the extra hours produce only errors. Software bugs or accidental file deletions can have knock-on effects that take much longer to repair than did writing original code. EA's working patterns weren't just inhumane; they were counter-productive.

Then there is the sleep factor. Missing just one night's sleep has a noticeable impact on the brain's ability to function, as Dardo Tomasi[7] and his colleagues at the Brookhaven National Laboratory discovered when they took fourteen healthy, non-smoking right-handed men and made half of them stay awake through the night. In the morning, both rested and groggy subjects were put through a serious of tests that involved tracking ten balls on a screen. As they completed the tests, an fMRI scanner took pictures of their brains, to see how the rested brain differed from the one that was deprived of sleep. They found, not so surprisingly, that the sleepier the subjects, the lower their accuracy in the tests. But it was the detail that was most interesting.

What the scientists found was that two key areas of the brain – the parietal lobe and the occipital lobe – were less active in the sleep-deprived participants. The parietal lobe in the brain integrates information from the senses and is also involved in our knowledge of numbers and manipulation of objects. The occipital lobe is involved in visual processing. So both areas are highly involved in processing visual information and numbers. What was Warren looking at on his twenty-four screens? Visual information and numbers. What do computer-game engineers work with all the time? Visual information and numbers. The higher-order brain activity that was most needed in those jobs was the first thing to go.

While the parietal and occipital lobes were less active, the thalamus, on the other hand, was very busy in the sleepy subjects. Scientists hypothesise that it attempts to compensate for the reduced activity in the parietal and occipital lobes. The thalamus sits at the centre of the brain, and is responsible for the regulation of consciousness, sleep and alertness. It was, in other words, working extra hard to stay alert. All the energy you might want

to use to concentrate on solving a hard problem is devoted to the
challenge of staying awake.

In evolutionary terms, this makes sense. If you're driven to find
food, you need to stay awake and search, not contemplate recipes.
But now that, for most of us, work isn't primarily about physical endurance, mere wakefulness is not enough. What these and
other studies indicate is that, yes, we can work for long periods
of time with little sleep – but what we lose, progressively, is the
ability to think. 'A tired worker tends to perform like an unskilled
worker.'[8] Or you could say: a smart worker starts to work like a
mindless one.

Moreover, sleep deprivation starts to starve the brain. There is
a reason why we start to eat comfort food – doughnuts, sweets –
when we're tired: our brains crave sugar. After twenty-four hours
of sleep deprivation, there is an overall reduction of 6 per cent in
glucose reaching the brain.[9] But the loss isn't shared equally; the
parietal lobe and the prefrontal cortex lose 12–14 per cent of
their glucose. And those are the areas we need most for thinking:
for distinguishing between ideas, for social control and to be able
to tell the difference between good and bad.[10]

To Charles Czeisler, Professor of Sleep Medicine at Harvard
Medical School, encouraging a culture of sleepless machismo is
downright dangerous.[11] He's amazed by today's work cultures
that glorify sleeplessness, the way the age of *Mad Men* once glo-
rified people who could hold their drink.

'We now know,' says Czeisler, 'that twenty-four hours without sleep or a week of sleeping four or five hours a night induces
an impairment equivalent to a blood alcohol level of 0.1 per cent.
We would never say, "This person is a great worker! He's drunk
all the time!" Yet we continue to celebrate people who sacrifice
sleep.'[12]

A blood–alcohol level of 0.1 per cent is over all legal limits for
alcohol while driving. The UK limit is 0.08 per cent. At 0.1 per

cent, you are liable to be prone to mood swings, emotional over-expression, loss of peripheral vision, depth perception and distance acuity, and poor reasoning.

Czeisler's research team found that hospital interns scheduled to work for twenty-four hours increased their chances of stabbing themselves with a needle or scalpel by 61 per cent, their risk of crashing a car by 168 per cent and their risk of a near miss by 460 per cent. Twenty per cent of car crashes are attributed to nothing more complex than lack of sleep. Since companies vigorously prosecute alcohol policies, Czeisler argues they should do the same with corporate sleep policies.

But they do just the opposite.

Erin's fiancé Lan joined a successful class-action suit against EA's working practices and he left the company. The 'spouse' turned out to be a little premature: they never married and have since split up. Erin sits on the board of the International Games Developers Association (IGDA) but says the industry hasn't learned much: engineers are still too tired to see straight and the executives who manage them are too tired to see the problem.

'EA changed for a while, but only really because one group saw this as an opportunity to get rid of the guys responsible for the crazy hours. So there was a big political bloodbath and a new regime. Everything got better for six months and then it started all again. They're destroying people who should become our top developers! A lot of studios now won't hire EA former employees because they're so burned out, they say there's just too much work involved in rehabbing them.'

Even rested and alert, you may not be able to see what's right in front of you. In one of psychology's most famous and stupefying experiments, Dan Simons made a video at Harvard that set out to test just how much our mind can see when it's busy.

'It started as a lark,' Dan recalled.[13] 'There had been earlier experiments into visual cognition but in all of them the display was so weird that it didn't feel like real life. So I thought: what if we make this whole thing live? This was quite a lot of fun – I'm a big fan of doing fun research. I do the boring stuff too, but the purpose here was to ask: how extreme can you make this and illustrate the point?'

(Before you read further, you might want to try the experiment for yourself at www.theinvisiblegorilla.com.)

Together with Chris Chabris, Simons made a short film of Harvard students moving around and passing basketballs. One team wore white shirts, the other wore black. Simons himself is in the film but you won't recognise him, he says, because back then he had hair. When they finished making the film, Chabris and Simons asked volunteers to watch it and count the number of passes made by players wearing white. Less than a minute later, when the video ended, they asked viewers if they'd seen anything else. About half said no, they'd seen nothing.[14]

What they had missed was a female student wearing a full-body gorilla suit who walks into the scene, stops in the middle of the frame, faces the camera, thumps her chest and walks off. She is on screen for approximately nine seconds.

The experiment has been shown repeatedly, around the world, in front of diverse audiences. I first saw it in Dublin, in an audience full of executives. Like them, I was so focused on counting the passes I never saw the gorilla.

Simons was so stunned by the result that he says that for several years afterwards, he still kept expecting people to spot the gorilla. But results were always the same. In 1999, Simons and his colleagues published an account of the experiment entitled 'Gorillas in our Midst' and in 2004 they won an Ig Nobel Prize for 'achievements that first make people laugh and then make them think'. Simons has since gone on to make an academic career studying how we pay attention.

'We experience far less of our visual world than we think we do. We feel like we are going to take in what's around us. But we don't. We pay attention to what we are told to attend to, or what we're looking for, or what we already know. Top-down factors play a big role. Fashion designers will notice clothes. Engineers will notice mechanics. But what we see is amazingly limited.'

We see what we expect to see, what we're looking for. And we can't see all that much. I asked Simons whether some people saw more than others.

'There is really limited evidence for that. People who are experienced basketball players are slightly better at seeing what's happening in the video – but that's probably because they're more accustomed to watching passes; it isn't so hard for them to read what's going on. You can train yourself to focus on more than one spot. You might improve your eye muscles somewhat. But the limits are pretty fixed. There's a physical and an evolutionary barrier. You can't change the limits of your mind.'

Simons' video is used for all kinds of safety training. 'The airport security people, you know – they can find what they're looking for but they won't find what they're not looking for, no matter how dangerous it is.' Trained baggage screeners are better than Simons' respondents at spotting weapons, but not much: a third of the time, they will fail to spot weapons of any kind.[15]

Simons is often bemused by the relevance different organisations find in his work. 'The video gets talked about a lot in relation to national security forces and why they didn't see terrorists in their midst. My favourite one is a Baptist preacher who was giving a sermon in which he referred to the gorilla and said that's why the Jews didn't spot Jesus for what he was! But it is most commonly used for safety training – in power plants, for example – where people will focus on procedures and not notice anything that isn't part of the procedure.'

After a decade of experiments by himself and others,[16] Simons concludes that we see what we expect to see and are blind to the unexpected. And there are absolute hard limits to how much we can take in at any given time.

'For the human brain,' says Simons, 'attention is a zero-sum game: if we pay more attention to one place, object or event, we *necessarily* pay less attention to others.'

Simons now researches and teaches at the University of Illinois in Urbana-Champaign. On 6 September 2006, a graduate of the university, Matt Wilhelm, was riding his bicycle when Jennifer Stark hit him from behind with her car and killed him. In the subsequent investigation, it turned out that Stark had been downloading ringtones at the time she hit Matt – it was a tragic reminder of the realities behind Simons' experiments.

'There was a huge debate, when radios were introduced into cars,' says Simons. 'I'm still not sure I buy the argument but I suppose we can tune out a radio. But driving a car while talking on a mobile phone, or texting, is different. They can seem really effortless but they both use your mind's limited attention resources. You can't do it. Your brain can't do it.'

It isn't about the phone – which is why hands-free sets won't help you. It's about the mental resources that are available to you at any one time. In what sounds like another piece of fun research, Frank Drews, an assistant professor of psychology at the University of Utah, divided forty students into three teams.[17] The first team operated a driving simulator; the second team drove on the simulator while talking on mobile phones. The third team got to operate the simulator after drinking enough orange and vodka to take their blood-alcohol limit to 0.08 per cent, the legal limit for driving in the US and UK.

Comparing the three teams yielded surprises. The team using mobile phones had more rear-end collisions and their braking time was slower. The intoxicated participants exhibited a more aggressive driving style, following the vehicle in front more closely and braking with greater force, but they had no accidents. You should not take from this that it is better to drive drunk than while using a mobile phone! What Drews and his colleagues concluded was that the drivers using mobile phones were dangerous because they simply did not have enough attention to devote to their driving.

Shortly after running the experiment, Drews himself experienced the phenomenon first hand when a driver next to him on the highway drifted into his lane, forcing the psychologist on to the shoulder. Both drivers took the next exit and Drews got out of his car, very upset. 'I knocked on his window. He was still on his mobile phone!' Drews recalled. But when he finally stopped talking, the chatty driver had 'no clue' about the disruption he'd caused. He hadn't seen a thing.

The Royal Society for the Prevention of Accidents (ROSPA) estimates that approximately one-third of drivers use mobile phones while driving, while 55 per cent of drivers think that this is dangerous – even when using a hands-free set.[18] The Department for Transport is very wary of its own statistics, because it is up to police officers who attend accidents to decide the cause – and many accidents are never attended by a police officer. What the Department does note, however, is that mobile-phone use, while driving, is on the increase: between 2008 and 2009, the number of car drivers using a phone while driving went from 1.1 per cent to 1.4 per cent – and the number of van and lorry drivers was virtually twice those figures.[19]

Meanwhile, technology whiz-kids are busy inventing yet more forms of distraction for us as they bring the riches of personal computing to the car. Soon album covers, email and Wikipedia entries will all be available to us as we drive.[20]

'Cars are going to become probably the most immersive

consumer electronics device we have,' according to Michael
Rayfield, a general manager at NVIDIA, the chip company that
works with automotive manufacturers on visual displays.[21]

For Audi cars, NVIDIA's Vibrante multimedia software will
provide passengers with 'dual zone' entertainment enabling them
'to simultaneously enjoy two different movies on two different
screens in the backseat monitors'.[22] This travelling picture palace
will give drivers access to photos of their destination, reviews of
nearby restaurants and background information along with nav-
igational advice. USB ports and wi-fi capability will allow them
to plug in keyboards too, although, if they want further online
access, a notice pops up reading 'Please only use the online services when traffic conditions allow you to do so safely'. We already
know what a great safeguard that is. We know but we do not
want to know. Humans do not have enough mental capacity to
do all the things that we think we can do. As attentional load
increases, attentional capacity gradually diminishes.[23] One frustrated psychologist has argued that the case for multitasking is on
a par with 'urban legend':[24] a stupid story we like the sound of
but that is really nonsense.

What's particularly important is that the intellectual capacity
we appear to lose first may be what we need most: the ability to
discriminate, to make good judgements. Remember Warren
sitting in front of his twenty-four screens, so tired that he suffered
from tunnel vision? He worried about how to get rid of the
pressure spikes because he was too tired to contemplate the
harder issue: what was causing these spikes to appear in the first
place?

The bottleneck[25] that characterises our ability to receive
information explains why we cannot intelligently absorb all
the information presented to us on TV screens by Sky News,
Bloomberg or the BBC News Channel. The scrolling text, side
bars and stock prices don't make us smarter or better informed;

they make us stupid. What we can't do while we are watching such a busy array is think, discriminate, make critical judgements.

When we are tired or preoccupied – what psychologists call 'resource-depleted' – we start to economise, to conserve those resources. Higher-order thinking is more expensive. So too is doubt, scepticism, argument. 'Resource depletion specifically disables cognitive elaboration,' wrote Harvard psychologist Daniel Gilbert.[26] 'Not only does doubt seem to be the last to emerge, but it also seems to be the first to disappear.' Because it takes less brain power to believe than to doubt, we are, when tired or distracted, gullible.[27] Because we are all biased, and biases are quick and effortless, exhaustion tends to make us prefer the information we know and are comfortable with. We're too tired to do the heavier lifting of examining new or contradictory information, so we fall back on our biases, the opinions and the people we already trust.

This higher-order functioning that we lose when overloaded or exhausted is important – and not just in oil refineries. In the late 1990s, I worked for a company, CMGI, that, in the heat of the Internet boom, bought large numbers of companies. Regularly on a Monday morning, I would walk into the boardroom, where I would find bleary-eyed executives hung over with exhaustion, having pulled an all-nighter or two in order to complete the latest acquisition. They were fried but triumphant; they were heroes: the deal was done! But I lost count of the number of transactions that were, even at the time, strategically mindless and ultimately wasteful. Why had we bought these businesses? Too much tunnel vision, too little sleep: no one thought – quite literally – to ask: why are we doing this in the first place?

Although CMGI was a remarkable environment to work in, it wasn't – and isn't – unusual for companies to pour vast resources into deals that bring armies of lawyers and bankers into panelled boardrooms to work through the night, completing the latest acquisition. The leading investment banks require long hours and weekend work from any employee who wishes to be considered for partner, or even to be taken seriously. Many leading investment bankers tell me that, however much they hate it, these are the rules of client service. When I point out that they could solve their problem by having more employees, each doing fewer hours, they look abashed by the simplicity of the arithmetic. The truth is, many of the participants love it: the thrill of the deadline, the mountains of documents, the legal, financial and regulatory complexity of the task.[28]

Yet most of these deals achieve worse than nothing. A study by KPMG found that 83 per cent of the mergers and acquisitions they studied didn't boost shareholder value; 53 per cent actually reduced it. Another study by A.T. Kearney found that total return to shareholders on 115 global mergers was a *negative* 58 per cent![29] And while business-school professors dissect the corpse of each dead deal, it might be wiser to remember the fried executives who signed off on the strategy. Tunnel vision blinds us to the wider consequences of our decisions. It isn't just control-room operators who are dangerous.

Many psychologists have studied these phenomena, often (like Kahneman and Tversky) to understand why we make mistakes, others more tactically to devise guidelines for safer instrument panels. But one of the earliest was Stanley Milgram, who is more famous for his experiments in obedience (see chapter 6). Although Milgram himself was a native of New York City, he was fascinated by the way urbanites behaved. In 'The Experience of Living in Cities' he reflected that the very large number of people who live in the city, together with their heterogeneity, meant that 'city life, as we experience it, constitutes a continuous set of encounters with overload, and of resultant adaptations'. He wondered what the effects of living with so many people, so many impressions, so much information might be. 'Overload characteristically deforms daily life on several levels, impinging on role performance, the evolution of social norms, cognitive functioning and the use of facilities.'[30]

A natural, as well as a professional, observer of human life, Milgram noted that the country shopkeeper might engage his customers in conversations whereas the city supermarket cashier barely had time to complete one checkout before starting on the next. 'The urbanite disregards the drunk sick on the street as he purposefully navigates through the crowd,' Milgram argued, not because he was less friendly or warmhearted, but because city dwellers had learned to manage the demands made on them by a crowded city. They adapted by reducing the amount of information they took in. If a city was a system that yielded more 'inputs' than anyone could handle, inhabitants responded by taking in less. It was Milgram's unique insight to see that the city is a system, just as the brain is a system. And Milgram's fellow New Yorkers were managing themselves in just the same way that our brain manages information: letting some impressions in and leaving many behind.

Milgram's argument was provocative because he argued that what got lost wasn't random but precise: when people felt overloaded, he said, they restricted their social and moral involvement. 'Overload is made more manageable by limiting the "span of sympathy".' Milgram wasn't out to enrage city lovers the world over. He was concerned that the load-balancing trade-offs weren't just operational; they were moral. If it is hard to doubt when you're tired, it may be even harder to care.

What is true for cities may equally be true for any large organisation in which individuals operate under tremendous 'resource depletion'. Jack Kaminsky[31] worked at the largest US mortgage brokers, Countrywide, for four and a half years.

'I loved my job. I'd usually do a fifteen-, sixteen-hour day – I loved it! When business was booming, I'd be getting up at five a.m., logging in to check emails and plan my day. It was like a high, the whole day.'

Didn't you, I asked, get tired?

'Sure! Our office was a sweatshop. But the longer you worked, the more you made. We built a very successful team – out of fifty-four offices, we were near the top every year I was there. If you couldn't handle it, we'd find someone else. Countrywide was a well-respected lender, everyone wanted to be part of it. It was easy to replace people.'

Jack's job was to package up mortgages to sell on to banks.

'Everybody turned a blind eye to fraud. They're still uncovering fraud from four years ago! The frauds were so obvious. You'd have seven files from seven different brokers. In each one, the same buyer was going to be the owner occupier; I'd have the same owner buying *seven* properties from seven different banks! And I'd tell the banks but they'd just turn a blind eye. We knew it was fraud but what can you do? We packaged them up and sold them on.'

When the mortgage market collapsed, Jack was laid off – on a conference call.

Propagandists and brainwashers know what managers and corporate leaders choose to forget: the human mind, overloaded and starved of sleep, becomes morally blind. This would appear to be part of the explanation of what took place at Abu Ghraib.

'Not only did this soldier work half around the clock [from four a.m. to four p.m.], he did so seven days a week with not a single day off for a full forty days! I can't imagine any job where such a work schedule would not be seen as inhumane.'[32]

The psychologist Philip Zimbardo served as an expert witness for one of the Abu Ghraib reservists, Chip Frederick. Although his sympathies lay more with Joe Darby, who had handed in the shocking photographs of the prison, Zimbardo understood better than anyone the impact that the situational influences of a prison environment could have on young men. In 1971, he had designed and run the Stanford Prison Experiment, in which twenty-four mentally and physically healthy young men endured a prison simulation for six days. Zimbardo's detailed account of the experiment is hair-raising, but it taught him volumes about the ways in which a situation dramatically transforms behaviour.[33] A landmark in the study of power and environment, the experiment eerily presaged many of the abuses committed at Abu Ghraib by Chip Frederick and his colleagues.

'There is absolutely nothing in his record that I was able to uncover that would predict that Chip Frederick would engage in any form of abusive, sadistic, behaviour,' Zimbardo wrote. 'On the contrary, there is much in his record to suggest that had he not been forced to work and live in such an abnormal situation, he might have been the military's all-American poster soldier on its recruitment ads. He could have been the best of apples in their good barrel.'[34]

Many forces – fear, corruption, inadequate resources, absence of supervision, written procedures, formal policies or guidelines and an absolute lack of training – conspired to erode those all-American qualities. But, as Zimbardo observes, that was just the beginning. Frederick not only did a twelve-hour shift, seven days a week. After working for forty days, he got just one day off, followed by two more solid weeks on. Even when his shifts were over, he wasn't able to leave the prison but went to sleep in a six-by-nine-foot prison cell that was dirty and noisy.

That Frederick was surrounded by colleagues just as ill-trained and just as exhausted meant no one was awake enough to have any moral sensibility left. Of course other factors contributed to the abuse of prisoners but what is so striking about Zimbardo's analysis is that, at the simplest level, frightened, untrained guards were left with so little cognitive capacity.

Working hours seems such a small issue – but, by the same

token, such a small thing to get right. There's a great deal of bravura attached to overwork. For men especially, complaining of tiredness can look and sound weak. And there's no bio-feedback: if you don't eat, you starve and everyone can see there's a problem. But when we don't sleep, or when we work too hard, often even we can't see there's a problem. Sure, we don't feel great but what we can't see is what we are losing: the capacity to reason, to judge, to make good and humane decisions, to see consequences and complexity.

The allure of exhaustion is baffling. I've lost count of the number of corporations I've worked with which positively boast about the number of all-nighters they pull. Investment banking may not be the absolute worst, but it's up there, full of pride when they describe their requirement to work three weekends out of five. Client service, they say, just demands it. But I wonder how thrilled their clients would be if they knew how braindead the service they were getting often is.

'You can't change the limits of your mind,' says Dan Simon. But we keep trying. Why? Is it the last vestige of a physical model of heroism for which we lack any intellectual corollary? If so, then we'd better find that new model fast, before more reputations and lives are ruined. At the very least, as Western democracies struggle to define some kind of regulatory framework that could protect the economy from future disaster, we could do worse than demand that, after forty hours of work, everybody just goes home.

5. The Ostrich Instruction

> Lie to me just a little bit longer
> Lie to me until I'm stronger . . .
> I'm not ready yet
> To accept
> The truth.
> So lie to me.

from Heartless (Ridley/Bicat)

'Quite often when people come in here, they don't really lie – they just, what shall I say, underestimate the truth. Some deny it. They're all embarrassed. No one ever quite tells the truth.'

John Hawk isn't a priest, he's Professor of Dermatology at King's College, London. When he sees skin that has been sun-damaged, he asks his patients whether they've been sunbathing.

'You get the most extraordinary vehemence from people who've been using sunbeds constantly. They're prepared to shout at me, insisting they are not harmful. There was one lady – we'd been quite friendly – she said, "I use sunbeds all the time and I love it and you aren't going to stop me. I don't want to know!"'

Professor Hawk's angry patient isn't alone. Thousands of people don't want to know that tanning is bad for them and that sunbeds can kill them. Hawk has heard all the arguments. 'You get people saying it boosts their vitamin D levels – but you don't need to boost your vitamin D levels; food and homeostasis will take care of that. Or people saying it produces endorphins and relieves pain. It's all nonsense. I've been campaigning against tanning and tanning salons now for decades and the evidence just grows. What's so sad about these patients is that they do know tanning is bad for you – that's why they're embarrassed – but they choose not to know.'

That refusal runs very deep, even outliving its victim.

'You can go around in circles, asking yourself why this happened,' said Penny Birch, talking about the death of her daughter Hayley. A flight attendant for Virgin Airlines, Hayley loved the sun and used her freedom to travel to maintain a good tan. 'She did enjoy sunbathing and would often top up her tan on rest days between flights,' her mother recalled. 'But she was naturally dark and never overdid it.'[1]

But at the age of twenty-five, Hayley died of skin cancer. By anyone's measure, that is overdoing it. It's hard to know now why it was so important to Hayley to stay perfectly tanned – but it clearly did matter, or she wouldn't have devoted so much of her free time to it. Described as a 'girly girl who always liked to look her best', Hayley was perhaps no different from any of us who want to feel good about ourselves.

Her story was tragic but it wasn't unique. In Britain, someone dies of skin cancer every four hours.[2] While most people now recognise that overexposure to the sun is unhealthy, the fact remains that most do not protect their skin from the sun's harmful rays.[3]

'I know I shouldn't – but you feel so great, you look slimmer and everybody always says I look so fit,' a tanned mother of three told me on her return from a beach vacation.

Defenders of suntans argue that sunlight feels so good that it's counterintuitive to see it as dangerous. Or that the risks of melanoma are relatively new – linked to the depletion of the ozone layer – and not everyone's caught up yet. But the research shows that, for the most part, we all know how dangerous over-exposure to the sun is. And none of those arguments explains one of the most cognitively dissonant industries of the modern age: the tanning salon.

The 'incandescent light bath' was invented by John Harvey Kellogg. A physician and Seventh Day Adventist, Kellogg ran a sanatorium where he attacked a range of ills, using exercise, veg-etarianism and sunshine. (His other claim to fame was the invention of granola and corn flakes.) Kellogg was a passionate believer in the moral and physical benefits of sunlight and, at the end of the nineteenth century, sun baths and sun lamps were used for a wide range of therapies. In 1900, Niels Finsen won the Nobel Prize for using sun lamps in the treatment of lupus. As natural suntans became more popular, sun lamps and sunbeds did too, supplementing tans in the winter or 'preparing' the skin prior to summer vacations. The early association of tanning machinery with health has proved very persistent.

'The tanning industry likes to emphasise beneficial health effects from tanning salons, saying things like "Come to our tan-ning salon and protect yourself against cancer!"' says Mona Saraiya. She is an expert in melanoma at the Center for Disease Control in Atlanta, Georgia. Coolly discussing the latest research, she's at pains to be as objective and fastidious as she can, never-theless manifesting the scientist's utter bewilderment at irrational human behaviour.

'Or they say sunbeds are good for vitamin D deficiency or Seasonal Affect Disorder. I do wonder why they're legal.'[4]

The focus of Dr Saraiya's bafflement isn't just the individuals who use tanning salons but the companies that run them, and the disinformation they disseminate. The Sunbed Association web-site, for example, says: 'The main benefit of being tanned is seen as looking and feeling healthier. The main reason for using a sunbed is for a pre-holiday tan. Whilst the sun protection factor from a sunbed tan does not provide total protection, people having a base tan are less likely to over-expose themselves during the initial days of a holiday.' There is no explicit claim that tanning is good for you – there can't be – just the gentle implication that it is somehow more responsible.

'I disagree,' Dr Saraiya rejoined. 'Although tanning beds say they emit only UVA rays, many emit UVB rays – and anyway, UVA rays can also cause skin cancer. And many studies show that teens don't adhere to the regulations concerning exposure.'

Because skin damage early in life is more likely to develop into skin cancer, a bid to ban under-eighteens from tanning salons in the UK cleared its Commons stages in March 2010. But if the American example is anything to go by, it's unlikely that this will be rigorously enforced. The UK Sunbed Association already has a voluntary code prohibiting anyone under sixteen from tanning but there's no evidence it has much effect. It certainly didn't stop a ten-year-old girl, Kelly Thompson, from tanning for just sixteen minutes and suffering 70 per cent burns. Within hours of leaving the tanning salon in South Wales, she was taken to hospital, where she was told she would have required skin grafts had she remained on the sunbed for another two minutes. Nobody is prepared to give her a prognosis. When the British Association of Dermatologists studied 322 tanning salons in Northern Ireland, they found that only half vetted clients with regard to age and, where premises allowed minors to use sunbeds, 71 per cent did not require parents or guardians to sign a consent form. Furthermore, over 15 per cent of staff received no age-awareness training. 'Staggeringly, over a quarter of premises used "type 4" sunbeds which are designed for medical use and not for cosmetic tanning,' the study said. 'It is possible that many others are using sunbeds that emit high levels of UV, as almost two thirds (62 per cent) of salons did not know what level of ultraviolet (UV) radiation their sunbeds produced.' Moreover, 30 per cent of the population, which in Northern Ireland is overwhelmingly white, described themselves as having type V or VI skin – dark Asian or black. In other words, they were persuading themselves that a little extra sunlight wouldn't hurt them.

What is particularly extraordinary is to find that many tanning salons are, in effect, subsidised by the UK taxpayer. For example – and it is just one example – the Shenley Leisure Centre in Milton Keynes was originally managed by Buckinghamshire County Council. When the region was reorganised and it fell under the authority of Milton Keynes Council, the leisure centre was hived off and is now run as a charity, one of whose trustees remains the Milton Keynes Council, which provides the centre with an annual grant. The Shenley Leisure Centre offers a full range of tanning 'treatments', including vertical tanning units. This is a fairly typical arrangement whereby local taxpayers' money goes towards providing tanning facilities. What it means is that there is a significant risk that in some cases taxpayers may end up paying for tanning treatments which can result in cancer which the taxpayer, through the NHS, may also have to pay for.

In an argument eerily reminiscent of the 1950s love affair with radiation, many tanning *aficionados* claim that tanning must be better for you than sunshine, because it is a sophisticated technology. It is this argument that finally dents the veneer of Dr Saraiya's dispassionate professionalism.

'They just are unsafe. Unsafe at any level. It is very frustrating. They are producing more and more cancers!'

The regular use of sunbeds is now known to double the risk of skin cancer and doctors now agree that there is no such thing as a safe tan. But we keep on tanning.

'I see young girls coming out of tanning salons burned and

looking like lobsters,' Tina Farrelly exclaims. 'I feel like grabbing them and telling them what can happen.' Her niece, a mother of three, died at the age of twenty-nine after repeated sunbed use. For seven years, she had tanning sessions twice a week. When her mother tried to stop her, she just borrowed a friend's.[5]

The International Agency for Research on Cancer has defined tanning beds and sun lamps as 'known carcinogens' but the use of tanning salons persists because there is widespread social support for a tanned body.[6] The number of privately operated sunbeds in the UK has increased by 30 per cent since 1998; according to the Sunbed Association, over three million people in the UK use one. Rates of malignant melanoma in the UK have more than quadrupled in the last three decades, with 10,410 cases reported in Britain in 2006, an increase of almost 7 per cent on the previous year. By 2024, Cancer Research UK expects that figure to rise to 15,500, making the cancer the fourth most common type among men and women. That's a lot of cognitive dissonance, dependent on a lot of social support.

In their desire to reduce the dissonance they experience, tanning *aficionados* come up with some peculiar arguments. Surely, consumers argue, tanning salons wouldn't be allowed if they were harmful – would they? The very fact that they are viable, profitable businesses and that they are *regulated* is taken as proof that they must be safe – because otherwise they would be prohibited. That is as powerful a form of social validation as it is possible to find. The very existence of tanning salons – 25,000 in the US alone – provides the confirmation salon customers need to overcome conclusive data. They're blind, of course, but what keeps them confirmed in their blindness is the fact that the salons are flourishing.

'It's incredible, the arguments people come up with to perpetuate something that they know, deep down inside, is bad for them,' says Professor Hawk. 'They think a tan shows that they have leisure and wealth and people like to look like they're wealthy with lots of free time. The sad reality is they've become creatures of habit. They don't want to change. So they just pretend they don't know.'

Pliny the Elder is thought to be the earliest naturalist to write about the ostrich. In his *Historia Naturalis* he is rather rude about the bird, decrying its stupidity: 'they imagine, when they have thrust their head and neck into a bush, that the whole of the body is concealed.' Today, natural scientists say that the bird lays its head and neck flat on the ground in an effort to elude its predators. But however you describe ostrich behaviour, the one thing everyone agrees on is that they absolutely do not bury their heads in the sand.

It's a shame, really, because we need ostriches as a metaphor for the way we all behave. Judges certainly need the bird. When they apply the legal concept of wilful blindness in court cases, they are said to be issuing 'the ostrich instruction'. Scientifically accurate or not, we all recognise the human desire at times to prefer ignorance to knowledge, and to deal with conflict and change by imagining it out of existence.

All of us want to bury our heads in the sand when taxes are due, when we have bad habits we know we should change, or when the car starts to make that strange sound. Ignore it and it will go away – that's what we think and hope. It's more than just wishful thinking. In burying our heads in the sand, we are trying to pretend the threat doesn't exist and that we don't have to change. We are also trying hard to avoid conflict: if the threat's not there, I don't have to fight it. A preference for the status quo, combined with an aversion to conflict, compel us to turn a blind eye to problems and conflicts we just don't want to deal with.

So my children walk straight past the laundry basket on the

stairs because they don't want to stop what they're doing and attend to it. And I might not chastise them for it because I can't face another fight. And when I ignore the recycling, I'm hoping my husband will get the message – without a fight – that it needs to be put outside. Of course part of this is just laziness, but a big part of it is refusing to see anything that makes us uncomfortable.

An intriguing study in 1965 showed that our eyes focus on what appeals to us, and avoid what does not.[7] In the experiment, a number of people – men and women, students, housewives and secretaries – were asked to look at ten different pictures, some of which were sexual in content. A camera photographed their eye movements and later mapped these on to the pictures, to show the path of the viewer's gaze. Later, each participant was asked what they recalled of the pictures. Not surprisingly, each gave very different accounts of the same picture.

Ten minutes after the experiment, 'Mrs R' could remember six out of the ten pictures. Prompted, she could eventually recall them all but seemed to have difficulty with Picture 7.

EXPERIMENTER: It is a man reading, near a nude woman. Do you remember that one?

MRS R: No, I don't remember that one at all.

EXPERIMENTER: Take a moment. A man reading near a nude woman. You don't remember that one at all?

MRS R: I don't remember that one at all.

EXPERIMENTER: A man sat reading a paper.

MRS R: I remember the window.

EXPERIMENTER: And you could see her profile. You could see her breast.

MRS R: Yes. Now I remember. Just the top. The girl's face turned around, no waistline, that man reading the paper, and that's all I saw.

That was all Mrs R recalled because it was practically all she looked at. Photographs of her eye movement show her eyes stuck pretty firmly to the newspaper.

'Miss I', however, had a different experience.

'This is a man reading a newspaper. There's a woman by the table with her naked bosom. I thought it was very humorous because he wasn't looking at her at all.'

And the photographs of Miss I's eye movements confirm that they roved far more widely across the entire picture.

Many psychologists argue about why we behave like this: how could we know where *not* to look without looking first? But nobody denies that we do do this: we studiously avoid seeing, and remembering, those things that may cause us discomfort. In the same way that we tend to gravitate towards people who are like us, our eyes – and our minds – focus on information, objects, ideas that confirm our sense of self.

This phenomenon isn't quite as extreme as the tunnel vision in the Texas City control room, but it is similar. Both are stress responses. For Mrs R, who is described as timorous and vague, the picture posed a threat of embarrassment and potentially of conflict: why was she being made to look at this picture? For Miss I, an attractive young woman trained in the arts, the picture posed no threat at all.

Fear of change and fear of conflict have the same effect. It isn't just dermatologists who have to deal with patients embarrassed by their own habits. Doctors' offices witness a parade of patients who knew they should have come in earlier, who missed appointments or scans or check-ups. Debt-counselling services too witness the same ostrich-like behaviour.

'We have people who come in with Sainsbury carrier bags full of unopened letters,' says Andrew Steward. He works at the

Citizens Advice Bureau in Bristol. 'I had one gentleman in here. He had been a financial adviser; his job was to manage other people's money! But when he got into trouble, he couldn't bring himself to open the letters from the bank and the credit-card companies. It wasn't until he was facing a court hearing for repossession that he came to us for help. We managed to persuade the court to hold off in this case. But it was striking that this professional man had become completely disempowered by his debt problems. We see this ostrich phenomenon all the time. A kind of inertia sets in. People live with chronic debt for a long time until a trigger event – often something as bad as a visit from the bailiffs or not being able to withdraw cash – drives them to seek help. But they will still go to the wire.'

In the last quarter of 2009, 35,574 individuals were declared insolvent in England and Wales, an increase of 24.9 per cent on the same period a year earlier. Of those that weren't insolvent, however, many were in debt: on average, every adult owes £30,252, which represents 129 per cent of average earnings. Much of this, of course, is house debt, with average outstanding mortgages standing at £111,132. The banking crisis has gone some way to slowing our addiction to debt but of course it has done little to erase the vast amount of debt that the housing bubble created in the first place.

'People signed up for mortgages that they couldn't afford,' says Steward, 'because they were at the receiving end of a lot of intense selling techniques, salesmen on quotas, leaflets saying "Congratulations! You have been selected for a special rate loan." They believed it. People airbrush the terms and conditions – they only really look at them when things go wrong. A lot of people sign up for a secured loan without really understanding what that means or believing that it says what it means – that the bank will take their home. They just don't want to know.

'Very few of them ever worked out their income versus their

expenditure. It's a Mr Micawber attitude – if they can squeak by, then everything will be OK. There's a kind of fatal optimism.'

'I think my moment of wilful blindness was when I decided I needed a mortgage holiday,' Paula Daly told me. Although she'd enjoyed a successful career working as a freelance editor for public-sector publications and as a consultant in marketing and design, Daly had always felt that she was not making the most of her creative potential. When she began to make good money, she decided to follow her dream and launch the fashion brand Mouse to Minx: Where Burlesque meets Miss Marple. She researched her idea extensively and conducted a highly successful pilot inside a friend's store. She admits she 'got seduced by retail' and gambled with opening a shop on Bristol's Christmas Steps and living upstairs.

'I knew I'd made a mistake almost the moment I opened the shop. There wasn't enough passing trade. But I just kept going.'

When her business loan ran out, she signed up for a mortage.

'I got what was effectively a hundred per cent at a high-rate mortgage with a firm called Commercial First. When I started to default, Commercial First were completely inflexible and began charging punitive fees for the missed payments – up to £125 per month.'

Eventually the property was repossessed and Daly now lives on benefits, with a pile of envelopes that she hasn't opened because she knows they contain demands for money she doesn't have.

Debt counsellors say that this isn't a matter of intelligence or education; sometimes it's the most educated who have been most blind because they believed they knew what they were doing.

'People say: those people should have known better,' says Warrick. 'But those same critical people are coming in now and they're unemployed and they suddenly are in trouble, too. It crosses racial lines, socio-economic lines. And it's not like their situation is completely hopeless – sometimes there are things we can do so they won't lose their home. But they left it so late! They come to us after months and months and . . .'

'I think people live very close to the wire financially in this country,' says Steward. 'There's no typical debt client – we see everyone from people with no English to very sophisticated people. They all share the ostrich complex. Once they get into trouble, their horizons narrow. They look to the next month, day, even hours and work out a way of keeping afloat for that long. Many just can't face the fact that the deal they've worked out cannot hold.'

In business circles, this is known as the 'status quo trap':[8] the preference for everything to stay the same. The gravitational pull of the status quo is strong – it feels easier, less risky, and requires less mental and emotional energy to 'leave well alone'. Nobody likes change because the status quo feels safer, it's familiar, we're used to it. Change feels like re-directing the riverbed: effortful and risky. It's so much easier to imagine that what we don't know won't hurt us.

One reason business executives worry so much about the status-quo trap is because inertia exerts an inordinate pull within organisations. Every change carries with it the possibility of conflict, uncertainty, danger. The business environment is dynamic and difficult enough without going to look for trouble.

Nowhere was this more true than in the financial-services industry in the years leading up to the global banking crisis of 2008. Well before that, anyone breathing knew property prices and mortgage lending were out of control. By August 2006, Nouriel Roubini described the market as being in 'free fall'.[9] At the end of that year, the collapse had such momentum that a far more humble observer, Aaron Krowne, who had no expertise in economics or finance, started his website, Implode-O-Meter, to track the daily demise of sub-prime lenders.[10] That a huge and fundamental part of the American economy was going bust was not hard to see. Nor was it a state secret that all of those loans and mortgages came from – and went back to – banks. So how could banks not have known about their own risk?

To be fair, of course, some did. Goldman Sachs did, J.P. Morgan did. Cantor Fitzgerald, at the beginning of 2007, quietly shrank its mortgage book. But most of the major banks did not. One reason – and there are many – is that they did not see the risk because they did not want to. As long as everyone was making money, many CEOs either didn't see a reason to change, or lacked the courage to do so.

Pat Lewis discovered this, first hand. An engineer by training, Lewis is a straight-shooting MidWesterner, well liked and highly regarded. His friends and colleagues are never effusive about him, they just say he's a 'stand-up guy'. He joined Bear Stearns in 1998, working in Treasury where he eventually became Deputy Treasurer. Along the way, he tried to devise a means of capturing the risk carried by each business unit, relative to its returns. He hoped, and assumed, that if the risk and return were wildly out of proportion, this would identify risk that had been underestimated. What Lewis was after was a way of shining a light into areas where risks in the firm were greatest. You'd think that would be helpful – but Lewis couldn't get much help.

'So my discussions with the business units would go like this: "We want to understand the risks in your business." And they'd say, "Why?" And if you said, "Well, it will drive a portion of your compensation and it's another way – besides just net revenue – to evaluate your business," then they'd say, "Any number you have is too high." Because, of course, they knew that a high-risk number would impact their compensation. And if, instead, you said, "Well, we're just curious and want to gain another insight into your business," they'd think you weren't worth the time of day. So what do you do?'

Lewis is a long–distance runner; he didn't give up easily. For three full years, he plugged away at the project, building a mathematical model that could give ongoing visibility to the risk in each business unit relative to the capital it employed. Finally, when it was sufficiently well honed, Lewis and his boss Sam Molinaro presented a simplified version of their model to their CEO, Jimmy Cayne. He dismissed it as just too complicated.

'The CEO didn't understand it so he didn't want it used internally. It was too political. I was too old to do something useless so I quit doing it. Nobody else wanted to take it on.'

Cayne didn't reject Lewis's risk-based capital–allocation project just because it was complicated. He understood it well enough to know that, if it worked, the project threatened to produce huge amounts of change and conflict within a highly political organisation: people might lose money, they might lose bonuses, they might lose status.

Lacking the courage to confront that conflict, Cayne's decision left his bank structurally blind, without the capacity to see what it was doing. Bankers at Bear Stearns (who loved risking other people's money) were as averse to examining their own risk as dear old 'Mrs R' was to looking at the naked breast.

At the time that Bear Stearns collapsed, Pat Lewis was already interviewing; he is now managing director at Cantor Fitzgerald, with no nostalgia for the frustrating inertia of his old employer.

'At Bear,' Pat Lewis recalls, 'you'd have threats of anarchy and people quitting if anyone interfered in a business unit. No one wanted to be the instigator of that. The surest way to get fired was to be a troublemaker.'[11]

The only 'trouble' Pat made, of course, was to try to get a clear view of the business. And he was prepared to put up with quite a lot of resistance to do so. But most of us don't persevere as Pat did; most of us stay silent, and silence is the language of inertia. In a groundbreaking study, two Stern School of Business

professors studied what they call 'employee silence': the unwill-
ingness of employees to articulate or discuss problems they see
around them. Elizabeth Morrison and Frances Milliken are quite
the antithesis of the academic cliché: they're neither stuffy, nor
pedantic, but bring to their work and to their working lives
tremendous humour and engagement. So of course they found
their subject not in a textbook but right inside their own academic institutions.

'There was a new initiative coming up and a big meeting to
discuss it,' Morrison recalled. 'And everyone was talking about it
and how awful it was.'

'It inspired a lot of bad feeling and talk and a lot of anxiety,'
Milliken added.

'And then we got to the meeting and the subject came up –
and nobody said a word! Silence. Nothing. *Nada*. No one raised
a word of complaint. Just sailed on through. And that's when we
thought: that was interesting. I wonder if that happens everywhere?'

They designed a study to try to understand silence in organisations and what they found was pretty shocking. Interviewing a
cross-section of executives, fully 85 per cent said that they had, at
some point, felt unable to raise an issue or concern with their boss.
Only 51 per cent said that they felt truly comfortable raising issues
or spotlighting problems and a mere 15 per cent said that they had
never felt unable to express themselves openly.[12]

'When there are holes in the research process, we generally
don't say anything to the directors of the projects,' said one
respondent working for a not-for-profit organisation.

'I raised a concern about some policies,' replied another, 'and
was told to shut up and that I was becoming a troublemaker. This
made me go into detached mode, making me a "yes man".'

One particularly compelling interviewee tells of a co-worker
in financial services who was being phased out, he felt unfairly.

'I felt it was a moral imperative to act,' he recalled. 'But in the end, I did nothing.'

The recurrent theme in Milliken and Morrison's research is that people stay silent at work – bury their heads in the sand – because they don't want to provoke conflict, be (or be labelled) troublemakers. They may not like the status quo but, in their silence, they maintain it, believing (but also ensuring) the status quo can't be shifted.

'Everybody knew there was a problem,' said one young woman, working for an Internet consulting firm. 'But people didn't speak up. A lot of people quit. They didn't think speaking up would make a difference.'

When I replicated Morisson and Milliken's study with British employees, the results overall were roughly the same. What stood out however was the reason respondents gave for their silence. Whereas American executives were silent for fear of being branded troublemakers, their UK counterparts felt that speaking up would not make any difference. Their silence, and the experiences they recounted, articulated a deep sense of futility.

Reading these studies is a tremendously sad experience: dozens of smart, engaged, moral individuals who have, on some level, given up. They don't believe that they can change the status quo, and so they've surrendered to it. What's so awful about this is that their decision to turn a blind eye in turn renders their bosses blind. How can the boss see what the employees won't show them? The only consequence of their silence is that the blind lead the blind.

What's also so sad about this research is that it rings so true. Even as I'm writing this, I sit on the board of an organisation that has stopped in its tracks because it cannot face a single, mission-critical problem. Each board member will talk about it in private; it never comes up in meetings. Nobody can face the fight. And so the entire organisation drifts on, consuming time and resources but making no progress. For this business, the recession has come as a boon, helping everyone studiously to ignore the old, festering sore that no one wants to touch. Many board members say they don't want to raise the issue because they don't know how to solve it. But as long as it remains invisible, it is guaranteed to remain insoluble.

That is the hidden cost of ostrich behaviour: whether your head is in the sand or just lying prone along the ground, you're in no position to defend yourself. You cannot fix a problem that you refuse to acknowledge. And if the problem isn't there – how can you be held responsible for it?

CEOs like Cayne aren't all that unusual. Although most business leaders will admit privately that one of the hardest aspects of running a company is knowing what is going on inside it, many adopt leadership styles that ensure no one will ever tell them the truth. At General Motors, Roger Smith was notorious for getting rid of any executive or board member who brought difficult or dissonant information or views. At the BBC, I once had a boss whose response to adverse news was to throw telephones against the wall, a reasonable incentive to keep one's mouth shut.

Yet even in companies that are strikingly more open and that espouse a desire for honesty and transparency, silence can maintain the status quo long after the need for change has become obvious to everyone. About ten years ago, I sat on the board of a private company whose founder had recently died. Everyone in the business was in mourning, with the result that no one was prepared to assume a leadership role; it would have felt indecent, intrusive. That was fine for a week or two, but it went on for months. Routine work continued to be done as it always had been, but economic conditions changed; another bubble burst, another recession. The company had no strategy for dealing with it. Meanwhile cash reserves were falling to a dangerously low level.

'What are you doing to reduce expenses?' I asked at a board meeting. It wasn't exactly an original question but the answer stunned me.

'Nothing.'

'Nothing? Why?'

'Well, we don't want to alarm the employees,' answered one of the senior executives.

Now, the employees of this firm were smart; they could see what was happening to the economy, and they could certainly tell that the company's order book wasn't as full as it had been. When, after the meeting, I spoke with a few of them, they were seriously worried – but the economy was the least of their concerns.

'I just think the management hasn't noticed what's going on,' one confided in me. 'They are so out of touch.'

Nobody was cutting costs because everyone was afraid to talk about the parlous state of the business. Managers didn't want to alarm employees and employees felt it was a waste of time talking to managers who were clueless. Nobody wanted to make agonising choices and they were averse to the conflict those must necessarily provoke. It was a mutually assured stalemate; both sides had their heads in the sand.

We know – intellectually – that confronting an issue is the only way to resolve it. But any resolution will disrupt the status quo. Given the choice between conflict and change on the one hand, and inertia on the other, the ostrich position can seem very attractive.

Libby, Montana, is a long way from everywhere. Sixty-five miles south of Canada, a seven-hour drive from the capital, Helena. The nearest big city is Spokane, Washington – and that's a good three-and-a-half-hour drive away. But as you cross the border from Idaho, coming into Montana, the countryside becomes breathtakingly beautiful. Rising out of icy lakes, the Cabinet Mountains scream into the sky, clad in dense pine forest. This is the America of legend: big skies, bold landscapes and raw.

It says everything about the people of Libby that, when you reach the town, it doesn't feel remote. Only around 2,500 people live in the town, but they've made it a place that you want to be. The Libby welcome is warm and proud. They aren't glad to see you because they lack for company; they're glad to see you're lucky enough to share their town. The hotel guide says that Libby's assets 'include clean water, clean air, beautiful scenery and close access to nature's playground' but I'd say its assets are its people.

Stoical is the word most people use when talking about Libby. Because, while it's beautiful, it's also a tough place to live. Until the 1920s, most of the men worked in logging. Dangerous work, and seasonal, logging was a hard way to support a family. So when vermiculite was discovered in the mountains, things picked up. Year-round employment, some of it indoors. Gayla Benefield still remembers the day her father, Perley, got a job there, because it was her birthday.

'My father had been out of work prior to 1954,' Gayla recalled. 'He had had a rough year and things were tough and suddenly he came home – it was September 17, 1954 – and said he had a birthday present for me: he had a job!'

Gayla looks like she belongs in the mountains. With the blondest hair and palest complexion, her Norwegian heritage is obvious. She belongs here and knows it. Her parents moved to Libby when she was two and, after a string of disappointing jobs, the mine was a godsend. Perley loved his work, loved the men, and the sense of doing something important. But most important of all was the chance to earn a regular wage, Social Security and a pension. Starting off as a sweeper in the dry mill, he hoped he'd move on up to driving one of the big trucks. But what mattered most was that Perley had found a secure future for himself and his family.

The Universal Zonolite Company produced raw materials for housing insulation, concrete, wallboard, roofing, even soil conditioner. There seemed no end to the usefulness of the material. Ninety per cent of the country's supply came from Libby and was shipped all over America. Even though it only employed about a hundred men, it felt like an important business, helping America to grow. And working there had its privileges: in 1959, Perley boasted that the company was such a great employer they were giving everyone free x-ray check-ups.

'Dad was just so thrilled at work,' Gayla remembered. 'All the guys loved working at the mine; it was like a fraternity up there. Dad loved operating equipment and he worked his way to the top of the mountain, grading the roads. In winter, we hoped for snow because that would mean he'd get paid double time.'

What he didn't know, because no one told him, was that concerns about the safety of the mine had started three years earlier, when an engineer from the state health department, Benjamin Wake, had conducted a hygiene study measuring air quality in the mine. It was dusty: so thick with dust that the filters in his vacuum pumps kept getting clogged. And it wasn't, as the men had been told, just 'nuisance dust'.

'The asbestos in the air is of considerable toxicity,' he wrote. 'Inhalation of asbestos dust must be expected sooner or later to produce pulmonary fibrosis.'[13]

Although the toxicity of asbestos wasn't definitively established until 1964, Wake already knew that pulmonary asbestosis 'is a progressive disease with a bad prognosis'. He returned to the mine in 1958, 1960 and 1962, each time making recommendations for repairs to the ventilation systems and working conditions that might protect the workers. But levels of asbestos continued to rise, and the workforce increased to 150 men. Nobody told any of them what they were breathing or how dangerous it was; even though state authorities were monitoring the mine, they weren't sharing their findings with anyone but the company's senior management. But the company x-rays – that great free gift Perley boasted of – bore out Wake's prognosis: of the 130 workers x-rayed, 82 already showed signs of lung disease. But neither the men, nor their doctors, were told anything.

In 1961, Gayla married Gary Svenson. He was serving in the military but, when he came home, he went to work at the mine, too. But unlike Perley, he hated it.

'Gayla's dad got me a job there when I came out of the service. I didn't like it, I didn't like the dust. You'd put the ore in sacks, thump them on the ground – the stuff went up your nose. We were given respirators, but nobody used them because they got all clogged up in fifteen minutes.'

Gary lasted only four months at the mine, before leaving to go into a car dealership.

But that same year, W. R. Grace, a large American corporation traded on the New York Stock Exchange, bought the mine and production really took off. By now, the medical establishment and Grace knew that asbestos was toxic. Libby's vermiculite went all over the country. Monokote, the company's fireproofing spray, was used everywhere, even at landmark sites like the World Trade Center, where it was applied to steel support beams. The world's leading authority on asbestos estimated at the time (1969) that not one man spraying it would be alive in twenty years.[14] But no one in Libby knew that. A 1969 test showed that 24,000 pounds of dust came out of the large stack at the dry mill daily, with asbestos levels as high as 20–40 per cent. The Libby mine had several stacks and production continued to increase.

But Perley's joy in his work did not. In 1964, he went to the doctor and was told he had a heart condition, and should find some lighter work at the mine. He was only fifty-two but the management found him some easier jobs and, on the days his chest pains were worse, all his friends at the mine pitched in to help him out.

Gayla told me, 'He said: "I'm so lucky they let me work with this heart condition." He really felt so grateful. Guys would help Dad up the steps and carry his kit; they helped him all the way because he couldn't walk and step up two steps. What he wanted most of all was to be able to stay for twenty years so he could get his pension. But from 1968 onwards, he just got chest pains so bad, he got more and more ill, then he got pneumonia and started missing work.'

In 1969, the mine manager, Earl Lovick, conducted a study of his employees. With statistical precision, he noted that 'although 17 per cent of our 1 to 5 years' service group have or are suspect of lung disease, there is a marked rise (45 per cent) beginning with the 11th year of service, climbing to 92 per cent in the 21 to 25 years' service group'.

By now, Perley had been working at the mine for fifteen years. In 1971, Earl Lovick stopped smoking and had an operation to have pleural plaque removed from his lungs. But the men under him continued working at the mine, with no idea of what they were handling or how dangerous it was. At the age of fifty-nine, just five days before he was due to receive his pension, Perley died. And Gayla began to think something was wrong.

'What tipped me off was the tragic way the man died and the way the company never sent a card. I started investigating and started talking to my friends' fathers and there was another man who was forty-nine when he died. I thought perhaps Grace didn't know what was going on. And I didn't really know what it was – I didn't know it was asbestos.'

By this time, Gayla had a job reading meters for the power

company. She'd spend the daytime going from house to house, talking to people, meeting everyone. And what struck her was how many men were at home, sitting on the back porch, using oxygen tanks. The more she talked to people the more she learned how Grace was paying them off, making private settlements that no one could disclose. All the men had worked at the mine.

'Then my mom got sick. She'd gone to talk to an attorney about Dad's case and he heard Mom cough and asked to see her medical records. He called her back and said she had classic asbestosis. She had been going to hospital for years here and the doctors that had been treating her for pneumonia knew what it was, and not one of them ever told her.

'And then I remembered once, when Dad was still alive, Mom broke her leg and was in hospital for two weeks and I think the doctor took two x-rays for her leg and *nine* for her chest! Grace had an underground study going on, examining chest x-rays to understand the progression of the disease. But here's the thing: she never worked at the mine!'

Margaret had never worked at the mine, but it didn't matter. Each day, when Perley had come home from work and hugged his wife, he was covered in dust. He tracked dust all the way through the family home. There was dust in the family car. You didn't have to work with vermiculite to be contaminated by it. There was dust all over town. Everyone was at risk.

In 1990 Grace closed the mine. A fall in demand for its product, coupled with increasing and ongoing liabilities, meant the business was no longer viable. But it didn't mean that Grace's involvement in the town was over. They knew – had known for decades – that the legacy of their ownership would be decades of responsibility for their former employees and their families.

Gayla's mother had received an out-of-court settlement from W. R. Grace for $100,000, of which she ultimately received just

$67,000. Adding up the medicine receipts alone, Gayla found it cost her mother over a million dollars to die.

'She'd be fine in the mornings but by noon her lungs would be full. It was horrific because she would curse Dad, curse the company,' Gayla recalls. 'At this time her own mother was ninety-nine and getting a hip replacement – and here was my mom scarcely able to breathe. Her own brother is still alive *today*, doing ballroom dancing. This is the way our family is. We just don't quit.'

Gayla certainly didn't quit. She talked to everyone she knew – which was pretty much everyone in town. Many of them had also made private settlements with Grace that they weren't allowed to discuss. Asbestosis and mesothelioma riddled Libby and W. R. Grace had known about it ever since they bought the mine.

Just before her mother died in 1996, Gayla got her permission to sue W. R. Grace for her mother's death. Margaret Benefield hoped she'd manage to make her daughter rich and Gayla says that, in a way, she did. But it wasn't money she was after.

'Of course they tried so hard to stop me. Made offers of three hundred, four hundred, five hundred thousand dollars. But it always had to be secret and that isn't what I wanted. I wanted it to be public. I wanted everyone to know what was going on in this town. And I wanted to be able to talk about it.

'The last offer they made me was $605,000 and a letter of apology. I asked if I could publish the settlement on the Internet and they said no, so I said no. I had to have a guilty verdict. The jury came back with an award of $250,000 – but I got that guilty verdict. But you know, the local press was never there. No press at all. Just a tiny blurb in the paper. We were suing a Fortune 500 company and it was the only time there'd been a guilty verdict for secondary exposure leading to wrongful death. And it didn't make the news.'

Full of rage at what Grace had done to her family and to her community, Gayla would talk to anyone who would listen. But mostly they wouldn't listen. Local media, she's convinced, were intimidated by Grace. So too were most local politicians. Everywhere she looked, Gayla saw people dying slow, agonising and expensive deaths – and nobody wanted to know.

But in 1999, she struck lucky. Andrew Schneider, an investigative journalist from out of town – Seattle – came to Libby, researching a feature about the 1872 General Mining Act. He ran into Gayla and, with some knowledge of W. R. Grace's malfeasance in the past, he paid attention to her story. When the *Seattle Post-Intelligencer* published his front-page story, all hell broke loose.

> First it killed some miners. Then it killed wives and children, slipping into their homes on the dusty clothing of hard-working men. Now the mine is closed but in Libby the killing goes on. W. R. Grace knew, from the time it bought the mine in 1963, why the people in Libby were dying. But for the thirty years it owned the mine, the company did not stop it. Neither did the governments. Not the town of Libby, not Lincoln County. Not the state of Montana, not federal mining, health and environmental agencies, not anyone else charged with protecting the public health.[15]

The Environmental Protection Agency was called in for what would ultimately become the largest Superfund clean-up site in American history.

As Gayla had uncovered W. R. Grace's knowledge of the town's contamination, she'd discovered shocking information: not just secret x-rays but secret autopsies, doctors keeping quiet and state authorities burying information. But nothing was more shocking than Gayla's discovery that so many of her friends and neighbours did not want to know what she had uncovered.

'People would cross the street when they saw me coming,' she recalled. 'They shunned me as though I had something contagious. People said I was crazy or that the lawyers were giving me kickbacks – and these would be people whose own family members were dragging around oxygen tanks!

'One line of defence was, people would say: if the doctors thought there was something wrong, they'd tell us. But they took the secret x-rays and didn't tell anyone! The mayor said: "I know it's really bad but what can we do?" I had visions of the town jumping on the bandwagon and fixing it but instead people said nothing. They just buried their heads in the sand.'

Gayla was angry and frustrated when townspeople fought against Superfund status, and fought against getting an asbestos clinic established. She was trying to bring help, know-how and money to the town – but the town didn't want to know.

'The businessmen and townspeople were all making money from the miners! I don't understand why one didn't stand up and say: enough is enough. But they didn't. That this community would let people die – it was just incredible to me.'

Though they were now divorced, Gayla and Gary Svenson were still friends and he listened to her. 'It divided the town. People didn't want to believe it. There was real hatred between those who liked the company and those who were sick. To this day there are workers who still believe that W. R. Grace did nothing wrong. They were paid a wage to do a job and made a living for them and they are satisfied with that.'

Even among her own family, Gayla encountered opposition. 'My brother-in-law used to brag about how much money he was making – said he could buy himself a new pair of lungs. And this was after my mom and my dad had died of the disease. He died a horrible death in six months.' His sons and wife were subsequently diagnosed with asbestosis.

'We had old loggers who would say, "I could go out in the

woods and die tomorrow." But I'd say to them: that tree would-n't come back and kill your children and wife! We even had people who made bumper stickers saying "And no I don't have asbestosis!" No one had the courage to confront me face to face, they just muttered and didn't help. They just wanted to deny the whole thing.'

'I went along with that whole "it's not that bad" attitude for quite a while,' admits Leroy Thom. He's now one of Gayla's strongest allies. 'I had a friend who was on oxygen but, you know, he seemed to get along just fine – we used to go bowling together. And then, just suddenly, he just died. It really made me think: maybe I haven't appraised this as I should.'

Leroy worked at the mine for sixteen years. Today, though he's been diagnosed with asbestosis, he runs a machine shop and devotes a lot of his energies to the town's Center for Asbestos Related Diseases. He's affable and laid-back but he says himself that he's been on a steep and emotional learning curve.

'There was a lot of opposition to the clinic, and some people used to come in the back door. They didn't want to be seen coming in! But the good thing is that people trust it – especially people who have the disease. On the other side though is the fact that people are like ostriches – they don't want to acknowl-edge that the clinic even exists, because it proves that the disease is here. It divided our community. Still today even among some of the workers, they will say things like: you're not missing an arm!'

Gayla isn't the kind of person to be daunted by opposition, even the silent intransigence that she has encountered for years in Libby. Staunch support from old friends and neighbours helped her persevere in getting all the bad news out in the open. Finally, in 2000, the EPA and the Agency for Toxic Substances and Disease Registry agreed to screen all former Grace workers, their family members and anyone who had lived in Libby for at least six months up to 1990. They were expecting about 2,000 people; over 6,000 turned up. Then they extended the screening to anyone who had lived or worked in Libby. One of Gayla's oldest friends and staunchest allies, Les Skramstad, had already been diagnosed with asbestosis; so had his wife Norita and his son Brent. He knew first hand how everyone in the town felt.

'It was like waiting for your draft notice during the war,' said Les Skramstad. 'It was like going out to the mailbox – that long walk – hoping that the long white envelope from the government wasn't there.'

In December 2000, when the ATSDR released 'Mortality from asbestosis in Libby, Montana', it showed that the death rate in Libby from asbestosis was forty times higher than in the rest of the state and eighty times greater than anywhere else in America.

By now, Gayla was getting hate mail; it just made her more relentless. What kept her going was the belief that the wives and children of the miners could be, must be helped – by decent compensation and good health care. Inspired by the hope that the next generation wouldn't have to suffer as her own parents had, she hoped fervently that, the more the town knew, the more it could do for its children. That dedication received a stunning blow when she discovered that Libby's school was contaminated.

'Grace had tested the running track at Plummer School in 1983 and found that the runners were stirring up dangerous levels of asbestos. Underneath the bleachers was completely contaminated – and that is where the kids play during the game. The skating rink – where kids played in the summer when it wasn't frozen – had vermiculite trailings at its base. That is the angriest I have ever been! Angry at the town, angry at the town fathers who knew the material had been dumped there. The principal of that school loved kids – he had retired – but you'd think he'd have stepped forward to say: perhaps you should just look at the school. But he hadn't said a word! The story had broken wide open in 1999 and here we were, it was 2002 and nobody had said a thing! And for three solid years, those kids were exposed. My grandkids' first day of latency was their first day of kindergarten.'

That same summer, Gayla and her second husband were both diagnosed with lung abnormalities. Neither of them had ever worked in the mine.

As the years have gone by, the EPA has continued to find vermiculite all over Libby and to try to clean it up. In June 2009, the federal government finally declared Libby the site of a public-health emergency. An earlier attempt in 2002 had been thwarted by the previous administration's Office of Management and Budget.

Today, if you go to the centre of Libby and stop for coffee, you can sit and watch as EPA trucks drive up and down the roads, removing contaminated top soil or bringing in fresh topsoil for Libby gardens. But, to this day, not everyone has participated in the clean-up; some still don't want to know. So what does it mean if your garden is cleaned up – but your neighbours refuse to have theirs done? The EPA can't stop the wind blowing.

'There are still plenty of people who blame me for bringing this up,' says Gayla. She's at home now, mostly retired from her activism that brought help and the EPA and the clinic to the town. 'People would just have got sick and died but business would have gone on as usual. Kids would still be at risk of contamination when they played at school! But I wanted people to have everything that my parents didn't have. I didn't want them to just go home and die – die broke. I thought it was better to look this thing in the face than just pretend it wasn't there.'

How does she explain the ostrich-like behaviour of so many people in the town? With the mine closed, no jobs were at risk –

what could they hope to gain by ignoring the health crisis all around them?

'I think,' she starts, accustomed to having answers. She stops. 'I think,' she starts again, and stops. 'Maybe they thought that if you didn't talk about it, if you didn't look at it, it would go away. They didn't want a fight. It's the emperor's new clothes: if we say it's fine, maybe it is fine.'

People who've lived in Libby a long time all comment on the stoicism of its people. They don't whine and they don't want to think of themselves as victims. What Gayla understood was that they were victims of W. R. Grace when it came to lung disease but they'd be victims of their own blindness if they did nothing about it.

The story of Libby is an epic tragedy and it's important to remember that at its heart is W. R. Grace, a corporation that knowingly put its employees in danger and then concealed that danger from them. It tracked the rates and risk of asbestosis, mesothelioma and other lung abnormalities without any of its victims knowing their condition. And, in 2001, Grace declared bankruptcy as a way out of mounting, apparently endless litigation. On one level, the people of Libby refused to see what was happening around them because it simply beggared belief that a publicly traded American business could be so cavalier with the lives of its employees and their families and get away with it. But what makes the story doubly tragic is that, once the facts were known, still so many of its victims refused to see what had happened to them.

When Gayla Benefield's mother gave her permission to sue W. R. Grace, she hoped the case would make her daughter rich. The wealth that Gayla gained was in learning how powerful she was, in discovering how smart and well informed she could make herself, and in articulating her powerful passion for making Libby a stronger, healthier community. She was hungry for change and unafraid of conflict. It was only her determination, over a period of twenty-five years, that finally allowed everyone to see what had happened and how it could be different.

Pliny would have been proud of her. For although we can blame him for first creating the inaccurate image of the ostrich with its head in the sand, we can't blame him for being one. In AD 79, Mount Vesuvius erupted, covering and then preserving the city of Pompeii. While most people ran away from Vesuvius, Pliny went straight into the danger zone to look, learn and rescue survivors. He died in the attempt. But in his honour, the most violent volcanic eruptions (such as Krakatoa) are called Ultra-Plinian in honour of the man who preferred knowledge to ignorance.

6. JUST FOLLOWING ORDERS

In September 2004, the wreck of HMS *Victoria* was discovered off the coast of Tripoli. With its prow buried in the sand, it stood perfectly vertical, like a skyscraper. The 10,000-ton iron-plated leviathan served as the burial ground for 358 British sailors who had died in one of the most bizarre blunders in naval history.

At the time of the disaster, Sir George Tryon was sixty-one and at the height of his powers; vice-admiral in the British Navy, he looked every inch the Victorian gentleman. Standing six foot tall, with long sideburns, beard and moustache, it wasn't only his position as commander-in-chief of the Mediterranean fleet that gave him authority. From the time that he'd joined the navy as a cadet, aged sixteen, Tryon had enjoyed a brilliant and unimpeded career. He had served all over the world, was highly regarded, well connected and, by all accounts, affable, energetic, deeply knowledgeable, and praised for his humanity, insight and love of a prank. Contemporary portraits suggest someone rather intimidating though it is hard now to know whether that was a feature of personality or of rank.

What is clear is that Tryon was far from the Victorian archetype his picture suggests. He thought long and deeply about the traditions of the British Navy and sought to restore the verve and initiative for which it had once been famous. Under Admiral Nelson, Tryon believed, men had been inspired with a mission and entrusted to make their own decisions in the heat of battle; only that way could commanders react with the flexibility and spontaneity that intense naval warfare demanded. Just obeying orders was dangerous because too much about war at sea was unpredictable. The very fact that Nelson's own death in 1805 at the Battle of Trafalgar had not compromised Britain's victory was testament to the independent initiative Nelson had inculcated into his navy. It was that spirit Tryon longed to recapture.

Although he may not have labelled them as such, Tryon knew that his officers were capable of being ostriches – conflict-averse and eager for a friction-free career. He took the unusual step of encouraging greater openness by specifically asking all of them to tell him about any risk or threat to the British fleet that might not come to his attention in the normal course of business. He insisted that the safety of the ship and its men should always come first: mere obedience was not enough. In an age of deference and intimidation, he worked hard to inspire in his men a sense of autonomy and independence sufficient for the most threatening and unforeseeable of naval encounters. In today's terms, you might say that he preferred open-door to micro-management. His was a controversial, even radical, position; many of his contemporaries clung to the practice of sending highly detailed instructions, signalled through flags, which could be long-winded, slow and hard to see in the smoke and clutter of war. For Tryon this issue wasn't theoretical but a matter of life and death. On occasion he could be deliberately uncommunicative, believing this was the best way for his men to learn how to think for themselves in unpredictable circumstances.

June 1893 found Tryon on manoeuvres, commanding HMS *Victoria*, heading a column of six ships; his deputy, Rear-Admiral Markham, headed a second, parallel column of five ships. Orders stated that each column was to turn 180 degrees to change direction. But each ship needed at least 730 metres to turn and there wasn't space enough between them for both columns to complete their turn without colliding. With orders so ambiguous and dangerous, Markham hesitated; surely the intention was not to turn the ships into each other's paths. When no action ensued, Tryon sent a signal saying, in effect: 'What are you waiting for?' This rather public rebuke stung Markham into action; it is said that, right up to the last minute, he hoped his orders would be changed. But he did as he was told.

The orders were not rescinded or changed. Inevitably, the two vast battleships collided, causing the largest peacetime loss of life in the history of the Royal Navy. HMS *Victoria* capsized in just thirteen minutes, taking Sir George with it. His last words, apparently, were, 'It's all my fault.' How could two battleships and two experienced seamen be so blind? A court martial was never able fully to explain the incident to everyone's satisfaction. Tryon, of course, was not there to explain or defend himself; Markham did survive and was both blamed and exonerated for following orders: 'Admiral Markham might have refused to perform the revolution ordered, and the *Victoria* might have been saved,' wrote two admirals at the time. 'Admiral Markham, however, would have been tried by court martial, and no one would have sympathised with him as it would not have been realised that he had averted a catastrophe. Unconditional obedience is, in brief, the only principle on which those in service must act.'

Parodied in the Ealing comedy *Kind Hearts and Coronets* (in which Alec Guinness plays a Tryon-like figure gleefully crashing his ships), what today might strike us as absurd, to the Victorians was tragedy; certainly Tryon would have regarded it as such. For it was precisely Markham's failure to seize the initiative and *not* blindly obey which could be seen as the heart of the problem. Everything Tryon had believed in was proved by the accident – but, at the same time, his foolish death discredited everything he stood for. Whether for comedy or tragedy, the event is chiefly remembered for revealing the tension and difficulties inherent in following orders.

Such blind obedience is not, of course, the exclusive province of military men. Hierarchies, and the system of behaviours that they require, proliferate in nature and in man-made organisations. For humans, there is a clear evolutionary advantage in hierarchies: a disciplined group can achieve far more than a tumultuous and chaotic crowd. Within the group, acceptance of the differing roles and status of each member ensures internal harmony, while disobedience engenders conflict and friction. The disciplined, peaceful organisation is better able to defend itself and advance its interests than a confused, argumentative group that agrees on nothing. The traditional argument in favour of hierarchies and obedience has been that of the social contract: it is worth sacrificing some degree of individuality in order to ensure the safety and privileges achieved only by a group.

More recently, psychologists have come to understand that this social contract may be more than utilitarian. A significant component of human happiness, they say, lies in being able to contribute to a purpose larger than oneself. Because, in the developed world, most of us can satisfy our immediate, or hedonic, needs pretty easily, doing so soon ceases to feel very rewarding. Once we're warm enough and safe enough and have sufficient food, getting more heat or housing or hot dogs – the hedonic treadmill – becomes progressively less gratifying.[1] So we yearn to contribute to something beyond our own immediate self-satisfaction and, as we find our greater purpose, we become happier, healthier and may even live longer. But very few people can achieve that sense of a greater purpose in isolation. We need other people and organisations to build great art galleries or ballparks, scout teams or governments, companies or charities. We can achieve much more when we work together and therefore willingly surrender some of our autonomy in exchange for impact, achievement and evolutionary survival. We surrender to the authority of the larger purpose and, in doing so, we become responsible *to* it. This may not feel like a radical shift – indeed we may not be conscious of making it. But how we act and what we see is profoundly altered when we obey.

The great psychologist of obedience was Stanley Milgram, the social scientist who was so thoughtful about the overload of city life. Influenced by the recent experience of the Holocaust, he conducted some of the world's most famous psychology experiments in the 1960s. Milgram sought to understand whether and why individuals obey authorities even when the task is morally repugnant, there is no reward for doing it and, just as important, there is no punishment for disobedience. Using today's jargon, he would have asked: is obedience hardwired?

He did so by running a series of eighteen experiments, each of which were permutations of the first. A volunteer was invited into Milgram's basement lab at Yale and told that he (or she) was involved in an experiment to gauge whether or not punishment was effective in learning. The volunteer – or 'Teacher' – was to read word pairs to the 'Learner', who was, in reality, an actor. The Learner had to indicate which word pairs went together. If the Learner made an error, the Teacher had to administer an electric shock. Each shock would be progressively stronger, starting with 15 volts and progressing to 450 volts: a lethal dose. The Learner would simulate pain so that the Teacher would believe the electric shocks to be real. What Milgram wanted to know was: how far would the volunteer Teacher comply with a series of instructions that come increasingly into conflict with their conscience? Would the Teachers continue to deliver the shocks, even though they were clearly causing pain and even, perhaps, death? Since there was no punishment for quitting – and no reward for continuing – how far would volunteers go before refusing to obey?

Because the experiment has become so famous, it's important to reiterate a number of critical points about it that have become widely forgotten or misunderstood. The experiment was not about violence or aggression; what Milgram sought to test was obedience to authority. Participants were not being explicitly violent – though the distance between the Teacher and Learner would become germane. Nor was there any great incentive for the Teacher to continue with the experiment. Each volunteer was paid $4 plus travel expenses for their participation. It was central to the experiment that it was 'coloured by a cooperative mood',[2] conducted without any fear or threat of any kind. Any volunteer could stop, or leave, at any moment. The authority present was a well-mannered scientist in a white coat: not a boss, not a troop commander, merely an ostensibly objective observer trying to do research, which the volunteer was assisting.

Before setting out to conduct his experiments, Milgram asked three groups – psychiatrists, college students and middle-class adults – how they expected the volunteers to behave. 'They predict that virtually all subjects will refuse to obey the experimenter; only a pathological fringe, not exceeding one or two per cent, was expected to proceed to the end of the shockboard.'[3]

Although an academic experiment in a college setting, the experiment was 'vivid, intense and real' for all of the participants, and what Milgram discovered shocked and troubled him so much that it was ten years before he published a complete account of his work.[4] Sixty-five per cent of the volunteers obeyed fully. 'Of the 40 subjects, 26 obeyed the orders of the experimenter to the end, proceeding to punish the victim until they reached the most potent shock available on the generator. After the 450-volt shock was administered three times, the experimenter called a halt to the session.' What Milgram found wasn't aggression, for he observed 'there is no anger, vindictiveness or hatred in those who shocked the victim. Men do become angry; they do act hatefully and explode in rage against others. But not here. Something far more dangerous is revealed: the capacity for man to abandon his humanity, indeed the inevitability that he does so, as he merges his unique personality into larger institutional structures.'[5]

Many permutations of the experiment followed.[6] Some of Milgram's colleagues found his results so surprising that they attempted versions of their own. One of these addressed the criticism that Milgram's situation depended too much on the performance skills of an actor. Perhaps its outcome could be explained by the fact that the actor had not really been very convincing and therefore the volunteers had suspected all along that they were doing no real harm; it just wasn't real enough. To test that critique, Charles Sheridan and Richard King enlisted thirteen male and thirteen female students to participate in a similar experiment where, instead of an actor simulating pain, a cute fluffy puppy was used.[7] In this version, the level of shock was exaggerated on the display cabinet but real (albeit lower) shocks were administered to the dog. 'The first of the three actual voltage levels produced foot flexion and occasional barks, the second level produced running and vocalisation, and the final level resulted in continuous barking and howling.' There was no danger of bad acting spoiling the reality of this experiment.

Other conditions remained the same: there was no sanction or punishment for disobedience and the team adopted Milgram's script to ensure a like-for-like comparison. Like Milgram too, this team had asked a classroom of male and female students (not participants) what they expected the outcome to be. Everyone anticipated high levels of disobedience. Sheridan and King were also interested to find out whether there was a significant difference in responses from men or women, hypothesising that 'women would be less willing than men to inflict harm on a cute puppy'.

Once again, they were wrong. Levels of obedience obtained from the male volunteers were close to those obtained by Milgram in the original experiment. But, without exception, 100 per cent of the female volunteers 'complied with instructions to shock the puppy all the way to the end of the scale'.

Milgram's experiment has been repeated often, and in many countries. (Milgram himself had hoped to repeat them in Germany but his early death prevented him from doing so.) The highest rates of full obedience were found in South Africa and Austria; the lowest in Australia and Spain.[9] In particular, in one version of the experiment (Experiment 5) that featured scheduled and scripted protests from the Learner, the obedience rate went from 70 per cent to 82.5 per cent; howls of protest did not cause participants to doubt their actions.[10] And the passage of time has not produced different behaviours. In 2008, Michael Portillo repeated the experiment for a BBC television programme. He misunderstood the experiment (he was using it to make an argument about aggression) but the results were virtually identical to Milgram's. In March 2010, French television producers seemed to think that recreating Milgram's experiments would make a fine game show;[11] their motives may have been different (and Milgram would have hated the use to which his work was put) but their results were the same: most participants went all the way.

Milgram struggled long and hard to understand his own, highly disturbing, findings. And what he concluded was that when we are part of a group, or an organisation, we change our focus.

Although [he wrote] a person acting under authority performs actions that seem to violate standards of conscience, it would not be true to say that he loses his moral sense. Instead, it acquires a radically different focus. His moral concern now shifts to a consideration of how well he is living up to the expectations that the authority has of him. In wartime, a soldier does not ask whether it is good or bad to bomb a hamlet; he does not experience shame or guilt in the destruction of a village: rather he feels pride or shame depending on how well he has performed the mission assigned to him.[12]

That shift of focus is fundamental. It makes us blind both to the alternatives we have to obedience (every one of Milgram's participants was free to stop) and it blinds us to our moral responsibility for our actions. We focus so intently on the order that we are blind to everything else. When we obey orders, our concern to be a good soldier means that we no longer see that we have a choice or that we are morally responsible for it. Rear-Admiral Markham felt that he had to obey Tryon's orders and, when he did, it was the order and not Markham that was deemed responsible for the deaths that ensued.

Another way of thinking about this is that when we agree to submit to authority in order to pursue a larger good, we exchange an individual self (with responsibility for our conscience) for a social self that is responsible to the whole. The most traditional way of portraying this is that the individual self lives at home and the social self goes to work. But if you think of yourself on your own and then in a party, you recognise the same person but in different roles with different manners, styles and connections. The individual self is an actor, responsible and autonomous; the social self is an agent, working with and on behalf of others. Same people, different roles, different focus.

Milgram concluded that this shift of focus wasn't a personal failing and the problem of obedience wasn't wholly psychological. It was a necessary and inevitable aspect of belonging to a group. When the individual is working alone, conscience is brought into play. But when working within a hierarchy, author-ity replaces it. This is inevitable, because otherwise the hierarchy just doesn't work: too many consciences and the advantage of being in a group disappears. Conscience, it seems, doesn't scale.

It may even be that the more committed we are conscien-tiously to the moral purpose of an organisation, the more obedient we become. Taking this out of the laboratory into the real world, a group of Ohio psychiatrists decided to find out whether nurses would obey doctors, even when the doctors' orders clearly endangered the lives of their patients. What is so interesting about this study is that it involves a highly conscien-tious group of individuals working in a hierarchical organisation. When asked, nurses are quite clear about their primary concern for patients; that is typically what has brought them into their profession in the first place. So they bring a high degree of com-mitment and enthusiasm not just to the tasks of their work but to the purpose of their work. But this, it turns out, doesn't pro-tect them from the dilemma of obedience.

In the study, twenty-two nurses – twelve from a municipal hospital and ten from a private hospital – were instructed to administer an obviously excessive dose of medicine. The drug itself was unauthorised, which is to say it wasn't on the ward stock list and hadn't been cleared for use. The doctor ordering the drug would do so on the telephone and would be a physician whom the nurse did not know. (The drug itself, of course, was a placebo so that the patients were never in any danger.) Rather like Milgram, the Ohio team also canvassed thirty-three gradu-ate and student nurses, asking them what they would do in these circumstances. Thirty-one said that they would not give the medication.

But, in the experiment, it turned out that twenty-one of the twenty-two participating nurses were prepared to administer the drug. Moreover, they expressed no real resistance to the order and did not appear to experience any internal conflict or even any conscious awareness that there might be a problem. Only one refusenik felt any hostility to the doctor ordering the wrong drug. The rest merely felt somewhat tetchy or confused. 'Insofar as the nurse is concerned,' wrote the Ohio team, 'the psychological problems involved in a situation such as the one under discussion are operating to a considerable extent *below the threshold of consciousness* [my italics].'[13] What most surprised the team that conducted the experiment was not that the nurses obeyed but that their obedience had rendered them so entirely blind to their primary duty of care for the patient that they could see no conflict at all.

The Ohio nurses had just one test, one chance to disobey. But in Milgram's original experiment the volunteers had multiple moments when they could have refused. However, the fact that they were operating a sliding scale – from 15 volts to 450 volts – may, in fact, have helped them to obey. There was never a single moment at which the delivery of the shock suddenly seemed absolutely wrong. Instead, applying lethal shocks was something the volunteers learned to do only by making baby steps along the way.

'There was never a moment when it seemed so bad that you had to stop.' That comment comes not from one of Milgram's volunteers but from Walt Pavlo, a mid-level executive at MCI. Unlike a hospital, the long-distance phone company didn't have a high moral purpose that instilled commitment and obedience. What it did have was a highly competitive culture and big rewards for employees who played the game. But most of all, says Pavlo, it had people who wanted to be good employees.

'When I started out, I was thirty, eager and ambitious. Everything was going right. I had a new job, a great family, and MCI was a big go-ahead company, full of smart young people just like me. I was psyched.'

Now fifty, Pavlo is a likable, softly spoken but intense conversationalist. If you didn't know his background, his seriousness might worry you; it is as though he's still puzzling over a problem that just won't go away. His mind is restless and, even if he's talking about old times, he's still looking for new insights. As we sat together in a Washington DC hotel, we must have looked like just another couple of executives having a business meeting. But this conversation was different because Pavlo is a convicted white-collar criminal.

'My boss, Ralph McCumber, had been a navy commander, had served in Vietnam. He had a kind of military bearing: very neat, very methodical. And you just knew he was tough. I don't know how you knew, you just knew.'

Pavlo's job was to make sure that the outstanding amounts owed by the long-distance carriers to MCI got paid. He was really just a debt collector but excitement around the new, entrepreneurial company and around the newly deregulated industry made him feel bigger and more important than that. And highly dedicated.

'I'd get up at four thirty every morning, get to work about five thirty. I'd have a meeting with McCumber around seven thirty to go through problem accounts. It took me about three months to become McCumber's first lieutenant.'

There was much about MCI's operations that Pavlo didn't understand: how they let their customers run up such huge debts, why they took on customers delivering trashy products like sex chat and psychics and why they paid commission on sales to customers who didn't pay up. But Pavlo was the new boy and he trusted the business would eventually make sense. In the meantime, he was most concerned to make a good impression. So when McCumber came and told him about a forthcoming RIF, Pavlo felt anxious.

'What's a RIF?' he asked.

'Reduction in Force,' McCumber explained. 'We fire people in the fall to save a few months' salary, then re-hire in January. It's an annual ritual around here so MCI can make its year-end earnings numbers and clear out the dead wood.'[14]

Pavlo's assignment, three months into his job, was to fire one of the bookkeeping clerks, Eslene. She was fiftyish and suffered from vertigo but, he was told, she had to go. From Pavlo's perspective, he had to be the bad guy to a nice old lady who needed her job for the health benefits, if nothing else. And he did as he'd been ordered.

'Cheer up,' Eslene told him as she left. 'You're going to be a great manager.'

Pavlo says he felt like an executioner. But he didn't leave. He was being a good employee and a good provider to his family. A few months later, Pavlo and McCumber came up with the idea of getting delinquent customers to sign promissory notes – legally binding promises by clients to pay back what they owed. Since they represented obligations to MCI, they could be counted as assets and the company's bad debt disappeared. Pavlo knew it was a fudge but it seemed to work, so he kept doing what he was told.

'Of course there was never a direct order to cook the books,' Pavlo explained to me. 'Instead it was just a kind of wilful neglect. No one would ever ask how the debt disappeared. So since nobody told you to stop, you kept going. The only order we had was just: make the debt vanish. Don't bring me problems, bring me solutions. Nobody wanted to look into the detail.

'The other thing about it was: nobody seemed to get hurt. The company did fine. The shareholders were doing great. The customers were still running their sleazy businesses. Where was the harm? You couldn't see any. What you could see was the reward: promotions, swanky hotels, nice resorts. So you just look away. You do what you're told and you don't look too close.'

After two years, Pavlo started smoking, something he'd despised in the past. Turning a blind eye to the mess that he couldn't clear up – a mess that, in fact, he was exacerbating – was a horrific, cognitively dissonant experience. The good guy and the bad deeds just couldn't co-exist. The way he dealt with it was to anaesthetise himself.

'I hated myself. And I hated my customers. And I hated the company. Because, in my mind at the time, I thought: they're making me do this. MCI is making me smoke and drink and write these notes. It's not me, it's them. And how do you go back? I went into that company with such high ideals and after a while, I couldn't figure out how to get out.'

Twenty years later, and after serving a two-year jail sentence, Pavlo is still in pain, trying to reconcile in his own mind how he could have done things that he knows were wrong. He's devoted years of his life to teaching college and business-school students how he went wrong, hoping he can help them recognise the traps he fell into. The problem, he says, is not that you are asked to do one big, bad deed; it is that there are so many tiny steps along the way that there is never a moment when it's simple to say 'no'.

'I don't consider myself a bad person. I know right from wrong. But I could rationalise some very irrational behaviour that now appals me. Why did I think that this was right? It was doing my job. I did what I'd been told to do.'

Pavlo moved, by baby steps, from doing things that felt bad to committing acts that were illegal. His is a rare experience, though the phenomenal cost of white-collar crime – estimated at 2 per cent of all business revenues – suggests that it may be less rare than we would like to imagine. But in most cases, obedience is not about doing something knowingly illegal. It may be as simple as following orders that – like Pavlo's promissory notes – just don't make a lot of sense.

Obedience poses a troublesome problem for large corporations. In 1998, when BP bought Amoco, John Browne, CEO of the new combined company, ordered a 25 per cent cut in fixed cash costs across all refineries. The order was made regardless of the condition of each site. And so, over the next three years, the management responsible for the Texas City site reviewed everything: maintenance, service agreements, personnel, equipment testing and tools. Everything was cut, down, it was said, to the number of pencils.

The 25 per cent cut was not a target, it was a 'directive' and the cadre of managers responsible for Texas City implemented it. They did so despite their knowledge that, under Amoco's ownership, the plant had been run down and despite repeated warnings about the site's safety. An internal 2002 BP PowerPoint presentation says: 'If we do not achieve a significant improvement [in] safety performance at the Texas City refinery, one of our co-workers or a contract employee will be killed.'[15] A graph illustrating fatalities in the past twenty years powerfully illustrates the point. A further report showed the poor state of the infrastructure, citing high rates of absenteeism and a large backlog of overdue inspections. The following year, a safety report says that 'the "checkbook mentality" blame and status culture still exists throughout most of the Texas City site and this limits health, safety, environmental and general performance. Budget and HSE priorities are not aligned.'

Cost-cutting, personnel reductions and cutbacks on training put everyone at Texas City under increasing pressure. Between 1994 and 2004, the site experienced *eight* blowdown drum incidents, of which only three were investigated. In 2004 alone, three major incidents caused three fatalities.[16] Yet, that same year, prior to a meeting to discuss cuts, one manager sent the following email:

'Which bit of 25% don't you understand? We are going to be

wasting our time on Monday discussing this topic unless you come prepared to commit to a 25% cut. I have much more interesting things to do with my time than getting up at 3am to travel to Chicago for a non-productive meeting!'[17]

The order that came from London to cut costs was followed clearly and effectively – even in the face of repeated warnings that the infrastructure was not safe and that, as one report put it, 'we have cut routine budgets to the point where we are not doing the routine maintenance essential to keeping units up. We cut 10%, cut 10%, cut 10% . . . without regard for risk.'[18] When consultants working at Texas City asked executives whether they felt there were any safety problems not being addressed, those in high management positions answered 'I am not aware of any'. They had been instructed to cut costs and that's what they focused on.

Just as no one told Pavlo to cook the books at MCI, no one at BP headquarters in London said: 'Make the cuts, we don't care if people die.' Of course they didn't. But the effect of the cost-cutting directives was to block out other considerations. When employees were surveyed on corporate priorities, they cited number one as making money and number two as costs and budgets. And even though managers on site knew there were safety problems, were grief-stricken by accidents and honestly anxious about how to make the refinery safer, they turned a blind eye to the problems and obeyed.

That, of course, is the problem with targets, and managing by objectives. Implicitly they communicate the same message as Pavlo's boss: we don't care *how* the target is achieved, as long as it is achieved. Such is the power of obedience that other considerations (ethics, legality, safety) simply become invisible to social beings who want to make a contribution. When the inexperienced jailers at Abu Ghraib were told to 'soften up' prisoners, they were not told how to do so, they were not informed as to the usefulness of their work. They simply did as they were told.

That their cruelty elicited not a single valuable piece of military intelligence was not relevant: they followed orders that eliminated other concerns.[19]

Hierarchies and obedience persist even in the face of extraordinary danger. A National Transportation Safety Board review of thirty-seven aeroplane accidents concluded that up to a quarter of all plane crashes are caused by 'destructive obedience' inside the cockpit.[20] In a study eerily reminiscent of Sir George Tryon and the HMS *Victoria* disaster, many flight-crew errors were attributed to accepting the authority of the captain even when he was getting things wrong. Commercial aeroplane pilots typically enjoy tremendous authority: they have three to four times more experience than their first officers; many have come from the military and are not accustomed to being questioned. Only the pilot in command has explicit authority to deviate from rules in an emergency. As a consequence, it feels very difficult to challenge them. The NTSB study, which analysed cockpit communications captured on flight recorders prior to crashes, found that 25 per cent of all accidents could have been prevented if the pilot had been challenged when making an error.

Obedience is strong enough to blind us to our own self-interest. The classic example of that extreme is the kamikaze pilot or the suicide bomber, for whom obedience to a cause (and, in some cases, the promise of intangible future glory) is powerful enough to overrule the instinct of survival. Those cases are always cited as being culturally determined – by the Japanese love of their emperor or by religious extremism. But in far tamer, academic experiments, in which volunteers have been ordered to harm not an anonymous 'Learner' but themselves, the same results have been found.[21] Volunteers will more readily self-harm than disobey.

This is a problem the military has had generations to ponder. From a legal perspective, military law states that a soldier must obey orders unless that order is manifestly illegal. If the order is illegal, then the superior who issued it is held responsible. But any doubts that a soldier may have about the legality of the order should be resolved in favour of obedience. (Intriguingly, the same rules of conduct apply to lawyers too.[22]) We may tend to think of the military as having a culture of blind obedience, but that is far from the case. One of the few of Milgram's volunteers who did *not* obey was, he said, inspired by his military training in which he was taught that he had a right to refuse illegal orders.

The Nuremberg trials that followed the Second World War did not allow obedience as an excuse because the prisoners being tried there were the superior officers and also were high-ranking political officials. And even in more recent times the charters establishing international tribunals relating to war crimes in the former Yugoslavia and in Rwanda have not allowed obedience as an excuse. Only in the Communist bloc and some parts of the Third World does following orders provide any kind of legal protection.[23]

'When we are training young officers, we talk about duty, roles, responsibility but we never talk about obedience,' says Ian Stewart. He teaches at the Royal Military Academy at Sandhurst. Why, I wondered, didn't they talk about obedience there?

'Despite what some of our friends outside the organisation sometimes seem to think,' said Stewart, 'obedience to us sounds blind, going through the motions without thinking, without thinking yourself into the situation. That's really not a good idea, especially now. If you act like a cog in a wheel, you become very predictable – and then it is very easy to work against you.'

Instead of obedience, according to Stewart, Sandhurst tries to teach its young soldiers to belong to the organisation – but to think for themselves.

'There's a process of socialisation going on at Sandhurst, or at West Point. This is almost theatrical on a grand scale. We bring them here for a year – volunteers, who come willingly, with a spring in their step. We are inculcating values and beliefs and the way of being, in a military sense. It isn't obedience, it is about becoming one with the organisation. It's what, in business, you might call authenticity. We like to think that we are in the job of encouraging authentic leaders so that their own values and the values of organisation are aligned. Time here really is whole-person immersion; it's twenty-four seven, for three hundred and sixty-five days. Everyone is in costume, everyone is playing a role, no one ever steps out of the role.'

In an environment where peer pressure is immense, and a desire to conform inherent, how can the military teach its young officers to think for themselves, to deal with orders that may be quite uncomfortable?

'We are very good at exercises and role play,' says Stewart. 'So we intentionally put them in situations where they are supposed to feel uncomfortable. Military training is about making auto-matic a codified ethical way of behaving. Under pressure, little sleep – that's how our exercises work. Ten days with maybe three, four hours sleep a night, being assessed, people on their case, threats changing all the time. Last week – we had an exercise set around a mosque and an order to search the mosque. The men on the course decided that wasn't the right thing to do, that there was another way to deal with the situation that would not inflame it. That's the kind of thing we want them to think about. While it isn't Helmand, it is as close as dammit as we can make it. We will do exercises like that over and over again to the point where we hope that, when it is real, that second nature kicks in. That is what military training is about.

'The lesson they're supposed to learn is: if you feel too uncom-fortable, don't do what you think you are supposed to do. The more choice-making we give people, the more engagement and efficiency they show. If you just get people to press a button, we can't expect them to be thoughtful. An immoral order should never be followed; that ethical dimension must be part of who we are. But I'm not claiming we always get it right one hundred per cent of the time.'

The hard part, in all of this, is being able to recognise what constitutes an immoral or illegal order. While all soldiers are provided with legal support if they refuse to follow an order that they believe is illegal, in fact the ambiguity of most conflict means that no one can be confident their decision will be sanctioned. Most soldiers aren't trained lawyers and, despite all the exercises, confusion over responsibility persists.

In 2005, Corporal Daniel Kenyon, thirty-three, and Lance Corporals Darren Larkin, thirty, and Mark Cooley, twenty-five, faced nine charges relating to the alleged abuse of Iraqis they had taken prisoner two weeks after the conflict was declared over in May 2003. Their defence then was that they were only obeying orders. But their orders, issued by Major Dan Taylor, were to work the detainees 'hard' – and it was an illegal order. That meant it shouldn't have been issued, and it shouldn't have been followed. So who was more at fault?

'As to the officer's conduct, let's examine it,' says Stewart. 'While forcing detainees to work is an illegal order and contrary to the Geneva Convention on the treatment of prisoners, there is no evidence at all that he ordered the sort of mistreatment that they received. Given this, he cannot, in legal terms, be held responsible for their actions. There is no regulation that says an officer is responsible for every action a soldier carries out, only the ones he ordered them to. Should he have taken responsibility for their misdeeds, where soldiers have clearly gone far beyond what is acceptable conduct? It raises a lot of difficult issues, which is why it is so important to teach it and discuss it.'

At least Stewart is discussing it with his students. It's a conversation that rarely occurs within business environments, where many executives imagine that military command-and-control would make their lives easier.

'I had this conversation once at business school,' Fred Krawchuk recalled. A lieutenant-colonel in the US Army, when we spoke, he had just arrived in Kabul, in the midst of Operation Moshtarak. As you might expect of someone working in a highly volatile context, he thinks about obedience very carefully.

'I was the only one at business school who was a military offi-cer on active duty. We were discussing leadership and someone said: "For you, Fred, leadership is easy. You give orders and people follow." It is not that easy. If people don't respect you, don't trust you, there are lots of ways to get blown off without "disregarding orders". It isn't black and white. But what I think about is: we are very results-oriented. Take care of the mission, that's what we're trained to do. And there's a lot that's healthy about that. But when dealing with conflict situations, how much room is there for independent thinking?'

Before going to Afghanistan, Lieutenant-Colonel Krawchuk served as a Special Forces officer assigned to the US Pacific Command in Hawaii, where he was responsible for communi-cations, security and development strategies in Asia. This meant working with host nations, local populations, non-governmental organisations and local governments to build infrastructure – water, medical care, education – in highly volatile conditions. It doesn't, he says, lend itself to quick or simple solutions.

'Obedience is too simple. In a highly complex situation, like this one, anything too simple doesn't work. And it is a misservice to sit back and wait to be told what to do. Of course you do as you're told but there is something else about moral courage, about standing up for what is right. It might mean you assume some risk and write a position paper or schedule a briefing to help solve some of these difficult problems we're facing right now. You don't just wait to be told what to do. When do you pick the fight? How far do you take your ideas? As someone who believes we need comprehensive answers to complex situations, I think we need more than just people doing what they're told or waiting to be told. My experience is there is a lot more struggle with that than with illegal orders.'

What Krawchuk is struggling with is not obedience itself, but its side effect, which is blindness. When all you do is obey, you become blind: not seeing consequences or alternatives or better solutions. I'm haunted by that email from the harried BP executive: 'Which bit of 25% don't you understand?' It sounds so desperate, frightened of consequences if the order to make cuts isn't obeyed. Under these conditions, the independent thought Krawchuk values simply isn't possible.

What Milgram's experiments demonstrate is that, however much we think we won't obey, for the most part we do. It is a default behaviour, at least in part because its opposite – reflection, independent thinking – is so much more effortful. Obedience is another kind of shortcut, in which we trust someone else's thinking above our own. It's easy and simple, especially when we're tired, distracted and don't want a fight. And so it both amplifies and articulates all those other forces that make us blind.

The military has had to grapple with the full spectrum of obedience from Nelsonian initiative to the unquestioning following of orders. More than a few tragedies – from the sinking of HMS *Victoria* to My Lai and Abu Ghraib – have forced them to reflect on the considerable intellectual challenge that obedience presents. This has made them all wary of the power obedience confers, a wariness that it would behove corporate executives to consider. Dealing daily in life and death, the military recognises that the costs of its mistakes are high and irretrievable. But Fred Krawchuk's story about being at business school is telling: his business colleagues seemed to envy what they imagine to be the military model of obedience – just do as you're told – unaware that it's dangerous and out of date. That the military itself doesn't regard blind obedience as an admirable goal should give any executive pause. Some of the gravest mistakes in both the business and the political world have been caused by eager executives, keen to please, hungry for reward and convinced that blind obedience was their path to success. Who is more wilfully blind: the executives who believe this, or the leaders who allow them to? Military law would blame the boss.

7. THE CULT OF CULTURES

Madness is the exception in
individuals but the rule in groups.

Nietzsche

Walt Pavlo didn't stop at writing promissory notes. As bad debts
at MCI ballooned, he found himself spending more and more
time with crooks and charlatans. Some went into liquidation;
when Pavlo met with TelRoute, he caught their executives stealing crystal glasses and bottles of liquor from the office bar. This
was not, he reflected, liquidation the way he'd studied it at business school. One of his more bizarre clients made money from
porn lines and from selling pre-paid calling cards, exploiting new
immigrants eager to phone home but too poor to own a phone.
When Pavlo called into their New York offices, he felt, he said,
'like a lost kitten in a jungle full of predators'. The tables were
piled high with cash but still the company's $25 million debt
remained unpaid.

'Everywhere you looked,' Pavlo recalled, 'everybody was on the
make and on the take. At MCI, sales sneaked deadbeats on to the
network. Finance wrote worthless promissory notes. Accounting
hid MCI's past-due balances. The customers on MCI's network
were ripping off MCI and I was covering them up on behalf of
the company.'[1]

Everybody Pavlo spent time with seemed to be ripping people off. One of the most colourful, and the most dangerous, was Harold Mann, who dreamed one day of running a vast, vertically integrated porn empire. Along the way, he ran sex chat lines for his own and numerous other phone companies. He owed MCI money, of course – that's how he and Pavlo met – but he also owed about $600,000 to a smaller company called TNI. But TNI also owed MCI $2 million. Everybody was collecting from consumers, but no one was paying their bills.

One day, bubbling with enthusiasm, Mann came to Pavlo with an idea. Mann would take over collecting TNI's debt. But the money he collected wouldn't go to MCI; Pavlo and Mann would keep it for themselves – and Pavlo could cover the traces with another promissory note. After all, Mann reasoned, it's not like MCI was ever going to get the money anyway.

'Holy shit. That's what I thought. I realised that Mann knew exactly what was going on at MCI. Deadbeat balances were being shoved into every hidden corner and crevice they could find. Who'd miss a lousy $2 million?'

As Mann pointed out, Pavlo was surrounded by cheats; he was the only one who hadn't yet figured out how to make money at it. Till now. If he couldn't beat them, why not join them?

'I also thought: I've been on the road, chasing these deadbeats for years and what do I have to show for it? No time with my family. Everybody else is getting rich – and I'm taking home a lousy salary. When I could be . . .'

Four years after he'd joined MCI, Pavlo was sitting with his wife on a Cayman Island beach, smoking Cohiba cigars and thinking that life had never been sweeter. He'd finally made it.

At MCI, Pavlo had learned to obey orders, even when they were repugnant – like firing the clerk – or stupid – like issuing promissory notes. But spending most of his time with fraudsters and cheats, he learned to conform – to them. They ripped the company off; so would he. They operated without concern for anyone but themselves, and so could he. Despite a moral upbringing and a nagging sense that he was doing the wrong thing, Pavlo conformed to the crooks around him. At the time, he said, it was like he lost sight of everything he was and everything he stood for.

Stanley Milgram distinguished clearly between obedience and conformity. Whereas obedience involves complying with the orders of a formal authority, conformity is the action of someone who 'adopts the habits, routines and language of his peers, who have no special right to direct his behaviour'.[2] Milgram knew what he was talking about; he had been a student of Solomon Asch, the great American psychologist of conformity who in the 1950s had conducted a series of experiments that demonstrated just how readily individuals will conform to a group.

In his experiments,[3] Asch assembled college students for a simple test: shown a single, vertical, black line of a certain length, they needed to identify which of three separate lines matched it in length. All but one of the students had been told beforehand to choose an obviously 'wrong' line. The other, isolated, student gave his opinion last. In nearly 40 per cent of the cases, the isolated student chose the obviously wrong answer. Repeated trials of the experiment showed that only a small minority – 8 per cent – can be counted on always to conform and only about a third can be counted on never to conform but the vast majority of us – 58 per cent – will, under certain conditions, conform.[4] Under social pressure, most of us would simply rather be wrong than alone.

The distinguishing feature of conformity is that it is implicit and it feels voluntary; after all, no one is telling us to choose the wrong line and there is no legitimate or formal reason to do so. Just as we prefer to spend time with people like ourselves, so we like to fit in. When we find that we don't fit in, we can change

the people or change ourselves. Conforming is the choice –
sometimes conscious, sometimes not – to change ourselves.

Since Asch, a great deal of work has been done trying to discover whether some people are more likely to conform than
others, whether there is a 'conforming personality'. Not surprisingly, it's been found that people are more likely to conform
to those of higher status than to mere peers – we'd rather conform to models of success.[5] Minority group members are likely
to conform when they are the sole member of their minority.
Unlike in Asch's study, when the experiment was repeated at the
University of Oregon in 1979, men were found to be more likely
to conform than women. Perhaps most interestingly, those who
conformed were more likely to believe in external factors, such
as luck, chance or fate; those who believed that they alone had
control over their lives were less likely to choose the wrong line.
But, just as when Asch conducted his original experiment, when
those conforming were shown their error, they all responded
with astonishment: 'Oh, God, I must be blind! What's the matter
with me . . .'[6]

In business, companies foster competitiveness because they
think that, somehow, it will bring out the best in people. And
they put employees into teams because a diverse group of
individuals is thought to be more likely to make a better decision that one person alone.[7] But the problem with such group
collaboration is that much of its promise disappears when
individuals influence each other, which, in teams and corporate cultures, they inevitably do. Most corporate cultures enjoy
the advantages of conformity but prove alarmingly blind to its
dangers.

'When I was at Lehman, if you didn't fit it, you just weren't
there,' recalled Brad Ruderman, a veteran of the defunct firm. 'I
mean, the mentality of the business culture there – it was their
way or no way.'

Ruderman sits in a Los Angeles synagogue wearing flipflops, shorts and a t-shirt. He's forty-six, with classic American good looks and his hair is only just beginning to grey. He has beautiful manners but also, like Pavlo, an air of sadness that is strangely touching. Far from boastful, he describes his years in investment banking with a mixture of nostalgia and bafflement.

'I was a blank slate when I got in there,' he recalled. 'I had a job in investment management and one day I met a friend who worked two floors down in sales and trading. When I walked on to his floor I saw a situation I couldn't believe: energetic people just knocking the cover off the ball: energy, activity, just the most amazing scene to behold, and I said: "What's going on here?" He hooked me up with the managing director downstairs and I was able to start and work my way up. And I was one of them.'

Ruderman had grown up in California, where his father enjoyed a successful career in the securities industry. But Ruderman never thought he was quite top tier; he hadn't gone to Harvard or Wharton, he'd graduated from UCLA. So when he joined Lehman Brothers, he felt he had to prove himself.

'The people I'd work with were from Harvard, Yale, Princeton, all Ivy League people. Only two or three of us were non-Ivy League and I was gonna get them! The rewards of belonging – well, it was everything! The self-satisfaction of knowing what you had accomplished monetarily but also intellectually and that you had joined a club, a group of people seen as the best and the brightest – that was something money can't buy. When you're twenty-nine and you have a direct phone extension to the vice-chairman of the firm, it doesn't get much better. It is every cliché rolled into one. For someone with low self-esteem, this was the way to show I belonged.'

As a child, Ruderman had been a good boy, looking up to his father, working hard to get good grades and stay out of trouble. He was, he says, always looking for a pat on the back and validation, always feeling a cut below his expectation of himself.

'And then I get into Lehman and it is so competitive as to boggle the mind! We're all on commission and, every day of the week, our prior day's commission would be posted on the window of the managing director's office. So every day you walk into work your net income is posted for everyone to see. If that doesn't foster competition for someone already competitive, what would? Of course, that's what it's for. For someone like me, if you're not up there somewhere near the top, it's a disaster. You have to do something because otherwise, well, you're nothing.'

The minimum Ruderman felt he had to earn was $100,000 a month – anything less and he was a loser. But if he'd made $140,000 in July, then anything below $120,000 in August would be a flop, too. Every month, he needed a bigger and bigger hit to stay in the gang.

'I was so motivated to gain acceptance. It wasn't greed. I didn't need anything. I had a car. A house. Once I had that, I had what I needed. It wasn't about stuff. It was about my personal score-board with everyone else. Sometimes there'd be three days left in the month and I didn't hit last month's target, so I'd push the enve-lope to do some things not always in the best interest of my client. I lost all morals, all ethics, in the interest of staying in the gang.'

He got to the point, he says, where he really didn't care about his clients, only about the commissions he earned. Of course, the firm always said that client interests came first, but in the com-petitive environment in which Ruderman worked, what came first was fitting into the Lehman culture. To an outsider, one of the more bizarre features of the gang in this investment bank was the preponderance of gambling.

'You would walk into the restroom and see racing forms on the floor – because that's what everyone did in their downtime! There was nothing hidden about it. Then there were huge poker games going on after work, twice a week maybe. It would cost $50,000 to buy in. We would bet on anything that moved, like which window washer would finish first. Any time you take a chance, that is gambling.'

Getting sucked into the poker game meant that soon Ruderman was working hard to hold his own in two highly competitive environments. When he returned to California to start his own firm, he became a big fish in a small pond, taking investments from Larry Ellison, CEO of Oracle, and Michael Milken's brother, Lowell. CNNMoney even quoted him as an authority on financial bubbles:

'Everybody is in a bubble,' said Brad Ruderman, managing partner at the Beverly Hills, California-based hedge fund Ruderman Capital Partners. 'Everybody that missed the stock market bubble is intent on identifying the next one. There are people almost daily talking about a housing bubble – but every home that's getting built, people are moving into right away. Is that a bubble?'[8]

Desperate to stay and look successful in a town where he was surrounded by the rich and famous, Ruderman used his family connections to get new clients and new money to start his own fund. Most of them, he says, were just like him: professionals who'd done well, upper class, well educated.

'There's such cachet involved in being part of an exclusive group of investors. I managed a fund with limited entry and my investors walked around their country club saying, "The economy is in disarray but I have Brad Ruderman managing my money!" And I'd walk around talking about the people whose money I managed. And we all . . . there was a kind of reflected glow!'

The glow began to dim when the market went down and Ruderman couldn't maintain high rates of return. But to stay in the club, he couldn't admit that to anyone. So he misrepresented his results and hoped that something – gambling, lottery tickets – would provide enough cash to keep his place secure. But he was in over his head and in April 2009 the Securities and Exchange Commission obtained a court order halting his hedge-fund fraud.

'It wasn't that I didn't know what was going on. I have intellect. But I couldn't see any other life. I had to keep it going because . . . I mean, if I wasn't part of this, what was I? What else was there?'

In 2010, Ruderman was sentenced to 121 months in jail. Having felt that he would lose everything if he did not fit in, he discovered too late that conformity itself had cost him everything.

Competitive corporate cultures easily – sometimes deliberately – provoke conformity because, as Ruderman experienced, being left out is so painful. It's a well-recognised phenomenon of trading organisations, the butt of jokes, popular derision and political contempt. But even apparently benign organisations can provoke the same behaviours, especially when, like medicine, they're extremely hierarchical. There just aren't a lot of rewards for bucking the system.

'I had done all my anaesthetic training in London but I didn't want to bring my kids up there. So I was looking for a good hospital outside of London where I could settle down,' Steve Bolsin recalled. 'I was delighted when I got the job in Bristol, especially because Bristol had a reputation for not appointing people from outside; they tended to make appointments from within their own ranks. They seemed to have a dislike of outsiders or at least didn't take them on very well.'

Despite that reputation, Bolsin moved to Bristol in September 1988 and at first enjoyed the new city and the new job. He was particularly interested in paediatric cardiac surgery; that Bristol did quite a lot of it was one of the hospital's attractions. But quite quickly he became concerned.

'I remember from early on that operations seemed to take a

long time to complete. I'd come home late, then go back to the ICU to do a ward round on a sick child who'd spent most of the day in theatre. My wife Maggie would ask: is this what it is supposed to be like? Where I'd been working before – at the Brompton – we would finish these operations around three or four in the afternoon. But at Bristol, we'd be finishing at seven or eight.'

That the operations were taking so long meant that they were more dangerous for the children. During the procedures – usually to correct congenital heart defects – the heart has to stop beating. So you put cold solutions into the heart to stop it beating; that way they wouldn't need oxygen for about forty minutes, during which time the operation would be done.

'If you take any longer,' said Bolsin, 'the survival of the heart cells is at risk. And if it takes very much longer, heart cells would start to die and the child would not survive or else would be very sick for a very long time afterwards. So time was critical and expertise was important. And the fact that these operations were taking so long was a big worry.'

Bolsin figured out that the operations were so slow for two reasons. Some of the surgeons hadn't been trained formally in this type of surgery and each operation was a huge opportunity – but also a huge challenge – to do everything right in time. In paediatric cardiac surgery, there's no such thing as a routine case; congenital abnormalities are all slightly different and surgeons without tremendous experience might not have the understanding to deal with subtle changes. That was one reason that might apply to any hospital. But the second reason was unique.

'As far as the surgeon, Mr Wisheart, was concerned, there was a real issue of technical competence.'

Bolsin tried to figure out how to tackle the problem without a full-frontal attack on Wisheart, who was, at the time, both Medical Director and chair of the hospital Medical Committee.

This meant that he was, for a number of years, one (if not two) of the 'Three Wise Men', a system designed to respond to concerns about fellow doctors in the NHS.

'In 1991 we had some mixed audit meetings – meaning there were cardiologists, surgeons and anaesthetists there – where we discussed the hole-in-the-heart operation. The surgeons recognised that our mortality rate was higher than for the rest of the country. And they thought the thing to do was to improve the case management – improve the way we prepped the kids for operation, improve the ICU. They were looking everywhere except where they needed to!'

Bolsin collected data on the operations, showing that Bristol's mortality rate was 27 per cent – compared to 5–8 per cent for the rest of the country. So Bolsin called more meetings, trying to get to the bottom of the problem. But when he circulated the meeting minutes, in which he described paediatric cardiac surgery 'reaching crisis proportions', he was told: 'these minutes will not be circulated, this is not how we do things, I do not want you keeping minutes again'.[9] Part of the problem, he discovered, was the ancient tribalism of doctors.

'There were a lot of structural changes going on within the NHS at the time and a big debate within Bristol about whether anaesthesiology be part of surgery or should become part of support services. Of course we didn't want either! And it was certainly well known that surgeons don't like being told what to do by anaesthetists. On several occasions, it was mentioned to me that anaesthesia doesn't want to raise its profile too much because we were already under fire, with people trying to pick it off. So there was a lot of jockeying for position. That warfare and tribalism was a feature of what was happening.'

From 1989 to 1992, Bolsin collected data – not itself an easy task as cross-disciplinary audits weren't customary and incurred a fair degree of defensiveness. As the Kennedy Report said, 'they [the hospital] were actively collecting and discussing data. They were quick, however, to deny any adverse inferences drawn from the data, by resort to plausible justifications such as case mix. To some, this could be seen as wilful blindness; to others, a justifiable reaction in the context of difficult procedures with low numbers performed under less than ideal circumstances.'[10] Bolsin also continued to ask everyone he could think of to help him tackle the problem. Many of his senior colleagues assured him that the matter would be raised with Mr Wisheart or with the trust's CEO, Mr Rylance, but none of those attempts succeeded in achieving any open discussion. Most of Bolsin's senior colleagues felt that they should just be trusted to get on with things.

Bolsin became so frustrated that he suggested to his fellow anaesthetists that they simply stop giving anaesthetics. After all, he reasoned, no anaesthetics would mean no operations. But his colleagues wouldn't hear of it; the department was getting too much flak. If it caused more trouble, it might just get lumped in under surgery – and no one wanted that.

Bolsin continued to search for allies anywhere he could. By 1991, mortality rates at Bristol were twice the national average. In 1992, Bolsin discussed some of his data with Phil Hammond, who (unbeknownst to Bolsin) wrote for *Private Eye*. The appearance of Hammond's articles in the *Eye* led to a flurry of questions and meetings but no action. By 1994, a new paediatric cardiac surgeon had been appointed and on 6 January 1995, he approached Wisheart, asking that he not carry out an operation on an eighteen-month-old boy, Joshua Loveday. Claiming that this was the first he had heard about any concerns over these operations, Wisheart persevered and the child died.

'Wisheart was the most stubborn man you can imagine,' says Bolsin. 'He never accepted that he should stop doing paediatric cardiac surgery. He was incredibly stubborn, more stubborn than you can ever imagine.'

Everyone in the hospital knew. When Bolsin, frustrated and demoralised, tried to find work elsewhere, he soon realised that everyone in the NHS knew what was going on in Bristol. One reason Cardiff medics wanted their own paediatric cardiac unit was because Welsh doctors felt it wasn't safe to send their patients to Bristol for operations. Everyone knew what Bolsin both knew and documented: Wisheart was an unsafe surgeon.

'My wife Maggie was working as a nurse in the hospital,' Bolsin recalled. 'She worked in the emergency room and she was often seeing surgeons. One day, she saw the cardiothoracic registrar come down and, after he'd seen the patient and admitted him, she covered her name badge and went over to chat to him. And she asked him, "What's going on in the cardiac unit? What's all the fuss about paediatric cardiac surgery?" And he said, "Everyone knows Wisheart can't operate but all the trouble is just being stirred up by someone who has it in for him." She said, "But you said he can't operate!" And the registrar looked at her and said: "I know that. But I'll tell you what: you don't shop your colleagues." Then Maggie uncovered her badge and he looked really embarrassed – but he'd given the game away. You can kill children in large numbers but don't shop your colleagues.' This was conformity beyond Asch's wildest nightmares.

Frustrated, ostracised and convinced his reputation as a troublemaker would prevent him getting any other appointment within the NHS, Bolsin emigrated to Australia. A new cardiac surgeon was appointed to Bristol and the problem might have remained invisible but for Bolsin's decision first to contribute to a Channel 4 documentary, *Broken Hearts*, about the hospital and, finally, to report Wisheart to the General Medical Council.

'The GMC rather half-heartedly said to me, "We will have to tell the people you're complaining about." I said I could deal with that. They really didn't want to investigate, but they had to. I remember being told by their investigator, an old Met Police investigator who came out here to interview me: "You realise you are the only doctor who ever complained?" I had no idea! I would have thought there would have been other complaints. There had been complaints by parents but the GMC had managed to ignore them. But they had to do something when a doctor complained. The GMC only acted when it had to. They really hoped it would go away. I think that is still true today. The profession in the UK has never come to terms with Bristol, they have never acknowledged my role in improving the standards of health care in the NHS. It's worth noting that even after the TV programme and even after he was being investigated for serious professional misconduct, the hospital Medical Committee – that's all the hospital's doctors – still passed a vote of confidence in him. It's absolutely incredible and tells you everything about hierarchies in medicine. They just didn't want to see what might be true.'

The subsequent Kennedy Report referred to a 'cardiac club' but in fact the club at Bristol extended well beyond the cardiologists and cardiac surgeons. Many doctors, managers, clinicians and nurses had known what was going on for years. And while the exact number of children who would not otherwise have died can never be known for sure, the report puts that number at thirty to thirty-five infants. The cost of conforming to this club was very high.

It's easy, and perhaps comforting, to look at people like Pavlo or the Bristol doctors, to condemn them and imagine that they're utterly different from us. But the powerful urge to belong, to which they succumbed, isn't a criminal urge but a human one. It runs very deep because our self-esteem is delicately dependent on what society thinks of us. In a 2007 study, psychologists at Tufts and Princeton experimented with just how subtly that self-esteem can be influenced. They invited forty-six female college students to take an Implicit Association Test that measures self-esteem. Some of the students were overweight and, of these, some were supervised by an experimenter wearing a t-shirt that read 'everyBODY is beautiful' while the others were supervised by an experimenter wearing a plain t-shirt. Would the self-esteem of the overweight students be influenced by the mere sight of a supportive t-shirt?

Of course it was. The one-time expression of an egalitarian attitude about weight on the t-shirt of an experimenter was enough to improve the self-esteem of the overweight women. While Walt Pavlo was receiving hundreds of thousands of dollars as signals that told him he was part of the in crowd, even as trivial an expression of support as a t-shirt slogan might have made him feel better about himself.

There is a physical reality to the pain that we feel when we are excluded. Uncomfortable feelings of social exclusion and phys-ical pain arise, in part, from the same regions of the brain; and the same neurochemicals that regulate physical pain control the psy-chological pain of social loss, too. When we form and validate our social relationships, this stimulates the production of opioids that make us feel great. (When relationships dissolve, likewise, opioids aren't produced and we feel awful.) As the pioneering psychopharmacologist Jaak Panksepp put it: 'social affect and social bonding are in some fundamental neurochemical sense opioid addictions'.[11] In other words, our desire to seek social connections with others comes from chemical rewards as well as social ones.[12]

We can all remember how this feels from schooldays: the fun of being part of a clique, or the misery of being left out. The silent treatment, being 'sent to Coventry' or, within the penal system, being sent to solitary, these are all forms of punishment because they make us feel cut off from sources of power and self-esteem. However independent we may be (or want to be) we know that we can achieve little alone; to be excluded is both to be lonely and to be impotent. But when we gang together in like-minded groups, we become more effective, learn shortcuts and feel ourselves validated.

Conformity is compelling because much of our sense of life's meaning depends on other people. Pavlo felt foolish because he didn't have any of the measures of success valued by the people he spent most of his time with. He conformed because, by doing so, he could join a group that appeared to give his life meaning and respect. Even though he was fully aware that what he was doing was wrong, his need to belong blinded him to alternatives and consequences. And just as our sense of well-being may be sufficiently fragile to be influenced by t-shirt slogans, so our sense of leading a meaningful life hinges crucially on being included.

Cyberball is mostly known as a 1980s arcade game, first released by Atari and maintained, to this day, for lovers of retro video games. Multiple players, each on a separate computer console, can throw a ball back and forth. But there's another version, refined by psychologists, with the aim of simulating social exclusion. Using this software, you can pit volunteers against each other or against pre-programmed players who will behave as you need them to. So you can play this cyberball with lots of players or, as in one experiment, with just one real participant who, after a brief period of inclusion, is slowly but surely ostracised. This experiment wasn't designed to prepare students for college life or investment banking; it was designed to measure how 121 individuals respond when they're not part of the game.[13]

In the experiment, after the experience of ostracism, the volunteers took a test, the Kunzendorf No Meaning Scale, which assesses the extent to which life is viewed as meaningless (e.g. 'Life is a cruel joke' or 'I don't care if I live or die'). As you might expect, the excluded players were more likely to feel their lives to be meaningless. A similar experiment, but with real people delivering positive or negative feedback, showed similar results: those who were rejected not only found less value in life; they also felt no desire even to search for new meaning. The experience of exclusion left them feeling hopeless and demotivated.

The Florida State University team that conducted these studies devised several more, but they all led to the same conclusion: ostracism makes individuals feel they lack purpose, have less control over their lives, are less good moral beings and lack self-worth. Those secondary-school cliques aren't uniquely adolescent experiences: human beings hate being left out. We conform because to do so seems to give our life value.

This is so fundamental a part of our evolutionary make-up that it is strong enough to make us give the wrong answers to questions, as in Asch's line experiments, and strong enough to make us disregard the moral lessons we've absorbed since childhood. The carrot of belonging and the stick of exclusion are powerful enough to blind us to the consequences of our actions.

Once we conform, there are many rewards. Not just Cayman Island bank accounts and media coverage, but tiny, daily reinforcements that come from being with the in crowd. Of these, perhaps the most profound is jargon, the secret language that identifies those in the know, reinforcing the bonds of conformity. All groups use acronyms, nicknames and abbreviated technical language to communicate quickly but also, subliminally, to reinforce belonging: we know what we're talking about but no one else does.

In the thousands of hours of recorded phone conversations by Enron power traders, what's most striking (after the criminality of the deals they're discussing) is their language: not just the code names of illegal power contracts (Get Shorty, Death Star and Fat Boy) nor the saturation of language in expletives, but the pervasive derogation of anyone or anything that is *not* Enron: from 'little old grandmothers' to dumb consultants to the whole state of California: 'Best thing that can happen, fucking earthquake, let that thing float out to the Pacific . . . they're so fucked.' There's even tacit recognition that the company operated as a quasi-cult, in repeated references to 'drinking the Kool-Aid'. The sense of belonging to a superior team was so strong that no one seems to have remembered that the real people who conformed by drinking the Kool-Aid (in the Jonestown massacre) all died.

Nicknames operate in the same way as jargon: denominating the in crowd from the outsiders. If you don't have a nickname, you clearly aren't an important member of the group. If you do have one, then that provides some status and, of course, if you are the person doling out nicknames then you're the most powerful of all. The contemporary accounts of Bush's White House all illustrated this dynamic in action, where a nickname bestowed by the President was a sign of favour even if some of them (Turd Blossom – Karl Rove, Big Time – Dick Cheney and Fredo – Attorney General Gonzales) didn't seem especially complimentary.

Aggressive, cultish language is characteristic of highly competitive, deeply conformist organisations, as Frank Partnoy recalled when writing about his time as a derivatives trader at Morgan Stanley.[14] Partnoy arrived shortly after an internal coup had placed John Mack – 'Mack the Knife' – at the top of the firm. He had displaced Robert Greenhill, whose supporters were known as the 'Branch Dividians', named after the religious cult best known for the siege at Waco, Texas. 'This kind of aggressive fervour was new to me. I had never belonged to a militia before. The salesmen at First Boston might have played practical jokes on their clients, but they certainly hadn't discussed firing shotguns at them or blowing them up or ripping their faces off. In contrast, Morgan Stanley was a savage cult.'

Partnoy found the pull of the cult irresistible. Before long, he was as eager to rip someone's face off or blow someone up as any of his peers. He honed his killer instincts at the Fixed Income Annual Sporting Clays Outing (FIASCO for short) but he was dimly aware that he had started to become just like his boss (nickname: Scarecrow).

'I wondered how much I had changed in the past months. Scarecrow's influence was pervasive and I suspected we were becoming more and more like him. Why were two intelligent young men awake before dawn on a dreary April day, excited about sloshing through the mud in the pouring rain so that we could, if we were lucky, pump a few pounds of birdshot into little pieces of clay? What was happening to us?'[15]

Assimilation into the cultural norms of an organisation is a profound experience. It isn't always as colourful as Partnoy's or Ruderman's but it always leaves a deep imprint. Of course, the first step of conformity is taken by the choice to enter a particular profession or organisation: those that are chosen are already selected and, importantly, self-selected to fit in. In medicine, academics studying new students found that young medical students were unlikely, if they saw something unethical, to blow the whistle. But what was more striking was that, after three years of medical training and ethics classes, they were even *less* likely to rock the boat. In other words, these students came in as conformists – and ended even more so.[16]

'By the time you are at med school you are pre-selected as someone likely to be intimidated by hierarchy,' says Steve Bolsin, the anaesthetist at Bristol Royal Infirmary. 'By end of training – in four years – ninety-seven per cent will not rock the boat. It's recognised in research from the US, Germany, UK, all over the world. It is called the hidden curriculum of medicine. We know that mistakes are a huge problem in medicine – in the US, they're estimated to cost between seventeen and twenty-nine billion dollars a year – but the profession doesn't seem to have any real urgency around the issue. "I want to be in the right group" is a very important part of it. I don't want to be seen not supporting my peer group. Everybody wants to be part of the in group.'

What was happening to Partnoy and what happens to trainee doctors turns out to be physiologically interesting. Asch's conformity experiments have puzzled psychologists and neuroscientists for years, but now the development of fMRI technology allows them to study the brain at the point that it conforms.

In 2005, neuroscientist Gregory Berns and a team of researchers at Emory University placed thirty-two 'normal, right-handed volunteers' into an fMRI brain scanner and asked them to compare not lines, but three-dimensional objects.[17] In one version of the experiment, they had to decide by themselves which two objects were the same. In another, they decided after knowing what their fellow participants had decided. And in a third version, they cast their vote after knowing what a computer had decided. What the scientists sought to discover wasn't whether the volunteers would conform; they knew by now how likely it was that they would. Instead, they wanted to know what kind of brain activity was involved. If, in the act of conforming, activity in the prefrontal cortex was dominant, this would indicate that conformity was the result of conscious decision-making. But if activity centred in the occipital and parietal regions of the brain, then that would suggest that conformity was an act of perception – that social influence had altered what the volunteer *saw*.

The three-dimensional test was harder than Asch's and so the participants made more mistakes, even without any external input. But they conformed at the same rates. And when they did so, there was *no* activity in the prefrontal cortex – that is, a conscious decision was not being made. The brain's activity centred on those areas of the brain responsible for perception. In other words, knowing what the group saw *changed* what the participants saw; they became blind to the differences.

The scientists concluded that the areas of the brain responsible for perception are altered by social influences. What we see depends on what others see. That was a remarkable enough finding. But several other insights emerged from this experiment. Knowledge of the group's decision seemed to reduce the mental load on the volunteers; less thinking took place when they knew what the others thought. A good match could stop thinking because it felt right. So instead of the group benefiting from the collective wisdom of many, in fact what it got was reduced thoughtfulness from each one.

When asked in a debriefing questionnaire how they explained their conforming errors, the participants had no sense of having conformed; they believed that they had all reached the same decision purely serendipitously. They may have thought that they'd made a free choice where in fact they had not. Just as Asch and Milgram had surmised, the conforming decision was not experienced, not felt at all but was entirely implicit.

Furthermore, in the rarer examples of a participant taking an independent stand against the crowd, something else happened: the amygdala, the area of the brain that governs emotions, became highly active. Something tantamount to distress seemed to take place. Independence, it seems, comes at a high cost.[18]

Berns's findings have all kinds of interesting applications, from the profound to the trivial. Studying teenage taste in popular music, the same researchers found that a big determinant is anxiety about not matching the taste of the in crowd. The same may be applied to all kinds of fads and tastes: do you read the new Dan Brown because you want to – or because you worry about being left out of the discussion? Does the little black dress make you feel good because it suits you, or because it reduces your anxiety in a crowd? How far did clients who invested with Brad Ruderman or Bernard Madoff do so because they carefully considered their options or because they wanted to belong to the same club? How far are we capable of even scrutinising our choices, never mind summoning the emotional energy to make them? How often in life are we really just going along for the ride?

Of course, we all assimilate to a degree – society would cease to function if we did not. But one of the biggest risks of conformity, according to the psychologist Irving Janis, is that our sense of belonging (which makes us feel safe) blinds us to dangers and encourages greater risk-taking. He cited the example of Picher, a mining town in Oklahoma, which was, at one time, the largest producer of lead and zinc in the world. Residents were proud of the fact that bullets for two world wars were made from lead in their mines. But the mines were so extensive that some of them ran underneath the town. In February 1950, some 200 residents were told to evacuate because of the imminent danger of a cave-in. But the city fathers just laughed; one attended a Lions Club meeting wearing a parachute, just to show how silly the rumours were. Unfortunately the other inhabitants in Picher followed their lead, costing some of the men and their families their lives when the town collapsed days later.

Janis was working in the 1970s, well before the advent of fMRI scanners. But he hypothesised that lack of vigilance and excessive risk-taking are a form of 'group derangement' and he argued that this kind of behaviour could be found in any kind of group. Most famously, he outlined his hypothesis in detailed studies of military disasters: the Bay of Pigs, the Korean War, Pearl Harbor and the escalation of the Vietnam War. Well before the neuroscience was available to support his theory, Janis believed that, in a group, the pressures to maintain a consensus results in less thinking. Members don't look for information to confirm or disconfirm. 'Selective bias is shown in the way the group reacts to factual information, mass media, experts and outside critics. They spend little time deliberating the obstacles to the plan and therefore fail to work out contingency plans.' And he concluded by summarising a groupthink 'law' which is the central irony that lies at the heart of all corporate cultures: 'The more amiability and esprit de corps among the members of a policy-making in-group, the greater is the danger that independent critical thinking will be replaced by groupthink, which is likely to result in irrational and dehumanising actions directed against out-groups.'[19] The downside of the cosy feeling of togetherness is that everyone is less vigilant and more vulnerable to bad and dangerous decisions.

Groups subject to groupthink typically imagine themselves invulnerable, like the Picher city fathers. They rationalise warnings out of existence and believe passionately in the moral superiority of their group. Enemies and outsiders tend to be demonised and dissenters are subjected to immense pressure to conform. Dissent is rare and difficult because self-censorship mostly expunges it and because consensus and unity are deemed the ultimate good. In most organisations, the good team player is implicitly defined as the person who goes along with the team, not the one who asks hard questions. I've even heard boards discuss how, and why, they are invulnerable to groupthink, oblivious to the irony inherent in their confidence. In fact, of course, being a truly good team player involves having the confidence to dissent – but this is rarely what's implied in this trite accolade.

Serving on the Bear Stearns board of directors, Henry Bienen, the president of Northwestern University, learned just how prized board unanimity can be. Completing an annual questionnaire about the board's effectiveness, he opined that some meetings seemed somewhat perfunctory, short on discussion and debate. He was subsequently subjected to what he called a 'woodshed' discussion when he was roundly chastised by Jimmy Cayne, the same CEO who had rejected Pat Lewis's risk-assessment model. Bienen quickly saw that criticism was not welcome and he was not invited to stand for re-election when his term expired.[20]

Just before the UK bank HBOS was taken over, I chaired a panel in the City of London about board governance. Taking part was Dennis Stevenson, then chairman of HBOS. We were all pretty amazed when he turned up at all – everyone knew the bank teetered on the edge of collapse. But he did more than turn up; he eulogised the outstanding board he chaired, citing as evidence the fact that, even in this crisis, 'we are as one'. He seemed oblivious to the notion that the unity of his board may have been a contributory factor to the bank's mess in the first place.

Since Janis first published his hypothesis in 1972, scholars have applied it to a wide range of decisions, from the fiasco of Classic Coke to the Iraq War. The emphasis within the Bush White House on loyalty and consensus meant that dissent, dissonant data or disconfirming information could not be entered into discussions. The desire to be part of the in crowd, at the centre of power, played heavily against discursive, exploratory debate.[21] As Scott McClellan, a Bush spokesperson and fan, wrote, '[Bush] failed to spend enough time seeking independent input from a broad range of outside experts, those beyond the White House bubble who had firsthand experience on the ground in Iraq, and – perhaps most important – those with different points of view, including those who disagreed with his policies. The failure to open up the Bush White House to fresh perspectives in the second term was already beginning to exact a price.'[22] Otherwise intelligent human beings steadily blinded themselves to alternatives and to the consequences of their choices. Thinking themselves masters of the universe, they became slaves to their group.

But the concentric circles of conformity and groupthink may ripple wider still. Individuals influence each other, reducing thought. Groups influence other groups, pushing each other into positions of greater extremism. But in a competitive marketplace, the moral dislocation that Pavlo and Ruderman experienced can spread, like a contagion, to entire institutions and industrial sectors. That's certainly what it looks like when you examine the chain reaction that led to the implosion of the mortgage industry in the United States in 2008. What you see is the contagion of conformity spreading from one institution to another.

In California, Florida and most of the Northeastern states, house prices appreciated at an average rate of 10 per cent in the years 2001–6. Because, during that same time, Alan Greenspan at the Federal Reserve was bringing interest rates down to record lows (reaching 1 per cent by 2003) you didn't need to be a great mathematician to understand that you would get a higher rate of return on your house than on your savings account. So home ownership ballooned, reaching an all-time high of 69.2 per cent in 2006. But many of these new purchases weren't really homes; they were investments.

'I started buying houses because, well, that's what everyone was doing!' Looking somewhat abashed, Deborah Laird still struggles in her effort to capture how she felt just a few years earlier. A high-school science teacher with a pension, she'd never been a very active investor. Left a small sum of money by her mother, she had put it into mutual funds that, after the tech bust of 2000, had delivered disappointing returns. Deborah wasn't greedy; she had always lived modestly and remains rather proud of her thrifty lifestyle. But, in 2003, that started to change.

'All you ever heard was how much money people were making, selling houses, buying houses. I'd lived in the same house for fifteen years; I started to feel stupid! I reasoned with myself that it wasn't like I was actively helping anybody by staying out of the market. So I decided to trade up.'

Laird sold her Boston apartment and bought herself a house. She was surprised by how much money she'd made. And it had been so easy.

'The mortgage was simple. Finding properties wasn't hard.

And after teaching physics all day, it was fun to have something else to talk about in the staff room. I realised that everyone was doing it and it was, well, it was kinda fun!'

By 2006, Laird wasn't just a science teacher any more; now she was a landlord, with three apartments and two houses. But whereas being a schoolteacher and a property investor might have made Laird peculiar years ago, now it made her part of the club.

'And then I had a cancer scare. It wasn't a big deal – I mean, now I can see it wasn't a big deal. But at the time, my God, I was scared. And I just stopped everything. I mean – it's not like I needed another house! And between appointments and scans and teaching and looking after all the properties, I was just burned out. And the money seemed so stupid – if I was going to die next year, what would it bring me? So I just stopped.'

Her home today is comfortable but not ostentatious. It's decorated mostly with pictures of nephews and nieces; the sofas are dotted with cushions she embroidered herself. It's not the headquarters of a property tycoon. But Laird feels she had a lucky escape.

'Looking back, I feel like I went kind of mad. It was like: property was the hot thing and I was doing the hot thing and everyone was doing the hot thing and we were all in it together. And I have *never* been someone who ever cared about that stuff before! Now I think my cancer was a kind of warning, or a blessing. Because if it hadn't come along – I might never have stopped. And where would I be now?'

Halfway across the country, in Plano, Texas, Laird's conformity to her peers was amplified at the corporate headquarters of Countrywide, the company that had supplied mortgages for Deborah Laird's tiny property empire. There, Catherine Clark was aggressively recruited to help build the business even faster. With deep experience at a senior level in large corporations, Clark had an exemplary résumé and high moral standards. What enticed her to Countrywide was its entrepreneurial energy and ostensible appetite for change.

'They told me they wanted my experience of different corporate cultures in other places I'd worked. But once I got there – they just wanted me to conform. Working at Countrywide, there wasn't a lot of change and no desire for change. There was no real liking for new people. Everyone talked about the "Countrywide way" and that's what you were supposed to stick to. It meant that newcomers were all frustrated – they wanted to change, and had often been recruited for change – but we were just shut down.'

The company needed her to bring in more senior executives, to deepen the talent pool and diversity of the team. But, once again, she was frustrated.

'I found an African American from Bank of America – perfect for the position. And my boss says, "Why would we consider him? He would be hard to understand." (In other words: he's not like us.) There was another potential candidate from WaMu. He was very well qualified but he was gay.'

What shocked Clark most was the lack of dissent within the organisation. 'Where I'd worked before, my most trusted advisers would argue with me. No one was afraid of conflict. People would scream at each other – and then, the next day, they'd be playing golf together. It wasn't that it was a culture of screamers either; it's just that dissenting voices were OK.

'At Countrywide, in meetings, there was no dissent. There were lots of whispers afterwards, but no argument in the meetings. In the Consumer Markets Division, Joe was known for his tirades. You would be called to his office, he'd scream and yell at you with his door open so everyone could see. So everyone got the message: toe the line or else.'

Clark started as an outsider and left because she felt she couldn't accomplish anything. The overwhelming conformity of the aggressive sales culture, however, was part of the appeal to many who stayed.

'I love this business!' says Pamela Vincent, who stayed with Countrywide until it merged with Bank of America. 'Housing is an important American value. There is something worthwhile in what we do, helping someone buy their first home. And I love the sales culture; there's a lot of celebration, a lot of deadlines, a lot of ups and downs and it's exciting because this is where the money is made. Each month you start from zero and you can see the money made producing loans.'

Vincent isn't persuaded that anyone did anything wrong. She defends NINA loans (available to those with no income and no assets) as 'great for the self-employed'. All she will concede is that the company shouldn't have let sub-prime lending extend quite so far or expected appreciation to continue indefinitely.

'At Countrywide, we weren't the first to do sub-prime mortgages but we did start applying sub-prime practices because we continued to see housing appreciation. The bedroom ATM! The house goes up – why not take a new mortgage? These kinds of loans can be very valuable in the hands of a very astute homeowner who is economically savvy. My former brother-in-law put four girls through college, just refinancing his house. Lots of people did that. Appreciation was thought to cover all ills.'

But didn't she think that, some day, market appreciation of properties would have to stop – or at least slow down?

'Well, no one else thought they would. And it's like Chuck Prince at Citigroup said: you had to keep dancing. Why wouldn't you? It was fine as long as everyone else kept doing it, too!'

That infamous quote from the CEO of Citigroup perfectly describes how conformity works in the marketplace: everything's fine as long as no one dissents, bucks the trend, or fails.

Vincent worked in retail mortgages. In Florida, Jim Kennedy saw what was happening at the wholesale end of the market.

'With wholesale mortgages, you are the middleman. The retailers originate the deals and we fund them. That meant we saw what happened when you put a lot of loans together. And what we saw was a lot of fraud – like multiple homes all being bought by one guy on the same day as an owner occupier! I'd report it back to the broker and he'd just say, "Jim, we are just focused on getting the sale." So I'd report it to headquarters and all they ever did was turn a blind eye. We took it to upper management because it left a sour taste in the mouth. We knew what was going on. And what did management say? If we didn't do it, someone else would. All they cared about was market share. It was just like a game of chicken, waiting to see who'd bail out first. No one was gonna go first.'

'There was endless wilful blindness,' says Michael Sarnoff, Chief Credit Officer at a large Midwest bank. 'The entire food chain from borrower to lender to securitiser to auditor to rating agency to end investor. They all went along for years, they all got sucked in and conformed to perpetuate the madness.'

Sarnoff worked in the mortgage industry for twenty years. His vantage point allowed him to see how, at every step of the way, all the participants conformed to the same errors.

'In 2003, I think we hit an all-time high in terms of volume. The sub-prime lenders were multiplying and everyone knew the loans were just stupid: loaning to people with terrible credit, no income, occupancy fraud, income fraud – but nobody cared because appreciation was taking place. Then they all started throwing wood on the fire in the form of additional lending so you could lend to anybody, to a dead person! The amount of crime in the mortgage industry was just incredible but even if you segment that out, you still, today, have incredible greed and stupidity among consumers who are buying property they can't afford.'

Theoretically, the market was hugely diversified: a plethora of borrowers, lenders, securitisers, auditors and rating agencies competing with each other was supposed to spread risk and generate a wide diversity of products and business models. But competition between the participants was so fierce that instead they all copied each other. The drive to compete just created more and more uniformity. It wasn't just that everyone was working from the same assumptions; they all used the same software.

'Desktop Underwriter is software that has about one hundred fields and you put the data in and it produces either an approval or a caution,' says Sarnoff. 'You can't close a loan with a caution. So it's really the industry standard – everybody uses it – so everybody was judging the same people the same way. The software was written by employees at Freddie Mac and Fannie Mae; they were right there at the table and, because they're such a force in creating standards in the marketplace, they just perpetuated it.'

That so much of the market was fraudulent perturbed Sarnoff and he'd complain to anyone who would listen. But even so, and despite his seniority and proven competence, he couldn't change the game. In order to compete, he needed to be able to attract and retain a sales force. And no salesperson would stay working for him if they didn't have the same chance to earn the huge commissions their peers were making. So even at his own bank, Sarnoff sometimes had to turn a blind eye to the absurdity of NINA loans and the proliferation of fraud.

Nevertheless, he remains especially critical of the ratings agencies that were asked to grade the debt that was packaged up into mortgage-backed securities.

'Moody's, Standard and Poor's, were manipulating the data to keep securities going through, making them appear larger or more secure than they were. I knew people who'd rate a security and, by the time the paperwork got through, all the data had been changed and falsified. The real problem was that since the seller paid for the rating, they didn't mind incompetent audit teams or falsified results, as long as they got their AAA ratings. I have friends on audit teams who'd see their final results changed. I wouldn't do it, but many did. Everyone was in on it. But it really was: if you can't beat 'em, join 'em.'

And of course by the time the packaged securities reached Wall Street, there were plenty of traders to sell them and rip someone's face off.

Sarnoff says the last few years have been like watching a plague sweep through a town as, slowly but surely, each part of the industry succumbed to the same disease. This was conformity on an epic scale, as institution after institution caved in to the same thinking: if you can't beat 'em, join 'em; if we don't do it, some-one else will; toe the line or else; you have to keep dancing.

What he was seeing was wilful blindness amplified: we may all know it's wrong, but if I won't see it, then you won't see it and they won't see it. We may not have seen collaborative, collusive conformity on such a scale since the totalitarian regimes of the 1930s. This time, however, there were no dictators; there was only the market. And the central challenge of the episode is the revelation that the more competitive the market became, the more it also became uniform. What Pavlo and Ruderman and Partnoy saw on a personal level turned out to be true on a global scale: the more competitive a society becomes, the greater is the compulsion to conform.

With so many involved, did Sarnoff think that any one person could be said to be responsible? Who was blind?

'Insane consumers, greedy lenders, loan officers who'd do any-thing to get information through the system, poor underwriters who were no more than box checkers, a cheap labour force, Fannie Mae and Freddie Mac and a President who pressured them to increase home ownership, biased rating agencies, secu-ritisers, and all the stupid investors who bought CDOs and CDOs squared,' says Michael Sarnoff. 'All equally blind. All greedy. There was just a horrible deterioration in the moral fabric of people. And a lot of wishful thinking. But the structure of the industry means no one feels responsible.'

In their mutually reinforcing conformity, each of these businesses perpetuated and exacerbated each other's errors and flaws until they comprised a system that could not change without collapse. Though many claimed merely to be 'obeying the market' no one told them what to do; they merely copied one another. As fragile as Brad Ruderman, as anxious as Walt Pavlo, thousands of organisations chose not to think but to conform. What none of the experiments or the neuroscience or the biochemistry can tell us about conformity is how bad it feels when it goes wrong. Because in choosing to stick with the crowd, we steadily blind ourselves – to alternatives, to bad news, to doubt, to the individual values that we think are steady but turn out to be susceptible too – until we find ourselves dazed and confused in the dark.

8. BYSTANDERS

'As I was leaving the tier that night, I was told that I didn't see shit. And me being the person that I am – I try to be friends with everybody – I said, "See what? I didn't see nothing."'

US Army Specialist Jeremy Sivits on Abu Ghraib[1]

In January 2001, Walt Pavlo pleaded guilty to wire fraud and money-laundering and was sentenced to two years in prison. It might as well have been twenty, for he had lost everything: his job, his wife, his family, most of all his sense of himself. The little boy who'd been brought up to know the difference between right and wrong now had to wrestle with the incontrovertible fact that good Walt had done bad things. Who was he now? A bad-guy fraudster who'd burned through shareholder cash partying like a rock star on the Cayman Islands? Or a fundamentally good guy who had, somehow, lost himself?

Pavlo doesn't think many people with a conscience get away with white-collar crime because, he says, you can't bear the reality of what you've done. To this day, you can read the anguish on his face as he struggles to reclaim the good man he always thought he was. He's working again, for a small recycling firm that's glad to have someone more qualified than they might be able to afford. But the battle still goes on inside Pavlo's head. He's neat, well dressed, attentive, punctual and these things matter to him, disproportionately: every detail signals whether he's still on track. He has to convince a tough jury: himself. But he still isn't sure of the verdict.

When he got out of prison, Pavlo contacted Frank Abagnale, the famous fraudster whose life story was the subject of Spielberg's film, *Catch Me If You Can*. Abagnale advised him to start talking to people about his experience. If you stick at it, Abagnale advised, you can be successful, but you have to have the right message. You have to bear the consequences of what you've done, and you have to go it alone. Pavlo took this advice and started teaching business-school students how easy it is to go wrong. He would give up to eight talks a day for a single fee. Punctilious about not making too much money, he didn't want to profit from his crime.

One day, he was giving a talk in South Dakota.

'It was very cold outside. I was talking to a bunch of sopho-mores and I smelled smoke. But I kept on with my talk. Ten minutes later, smoke started rolling in through the air vents. We evacuated the building. About ten minutes later, it turned out it was no big deal – just someone burning pizza boxes. But when we all came back in, I asked, "How many of you smelled smoke and said nothing?" Everyone giggled and raised their hand. "How come no one said anything?" Some said they didn't want to look stupid; others said they weren't sure it was smoke. But that is how it is in business. You smell the smoke. You know there's something wrong and you think: maybe it's just me, maybe I'm wrong – and you don't do anything. By the time there's a fire in the building, it's too late.'

Although he didn't know it, Pavlo had witnessed an accidental re-enactment of a famous experiment conducted in 1968 by two young psychologists, Bibb Latane and John Darley, in which they placed one, two or three volunteers in a room and asked them to fill in a questionnaire. As they did so, the room slowly began to fill with smoke. The two psychologists wanted to know under which conditions the volunteers would be most likely to do something about the smoke: were you more likely to respond to an emergency when alone or with confederates?

Their results were shocking. One person alone would, within two minutes, do something about the smoke: look for its source, check its temperature, go and get help. But when there were two people in the room, only one out of ten reported the smoke. The rest stayed there, doggedly filling out their questionnaires while coughing and rubbing their eyes. And when there were three people in the room – which the psychologists theorised should produce three times the response rate of one person – only one in twenty-four people reported the smoke within the first four minutes, even though, by then, they could scarcely see.[2]

Darley and Latane coined the phrase 'bystander effect' to describe what they'd discovered. Their interest in the phenomenon had been sparked by the murder of a young New Yorker, Kitty Genovese, who was stabbed to death in the middle of a street in New York City. At the time, it was thought that up to thirty-eight people had witnessed the attack, which lasted more than half an hour, yet not one had so much as phoned the police. Preachers, news commentators and politicians instantly pontificated about callous New Yorkers and inner-city anomie, but Darley and Latane were sceptical – and they were living in New York themselves at the time. Was it just New Yorkers who were especially venal – or would anyone respond passively to an emergency? Which, if any, of us was so superior?

Their very first experiment isolated volunteers in booths and led them to believe that they overheard someone having an epileptic seizure. In cases in which the volunteers thought that they alone knew what was happening, 85 per cent reported the incident. But where the volunteers believed that others elsewhere would also know about the seizure, only a third did anything about it. What the experiment indicated was that the more people witness an emergency, the fewer will intervene.[3] Collectively, we become to blind to events that, alone, we see readily.

In that first experiment, the witnesses knew others shared their knowledge, but they were isolated from one another because Latane and Darley wanted to rule out conformity as one of the explanations for the behaviour. Just knowing that other people were aware of the problem – even without knowing whether anyone had actually taken steps to address it – was enough to prevent any form of intervention. Once you put people together in a group, as in the smoke-filled room, bystander behaviour might be exacerbated by conformity but it clearly was not determined by it.

Their results provoked a flurry of variations, in which men and women, black and white, young and old, were witness to all kinds of emergencies: robberies, faints, asthma attacks, screams, falls, crashes and electric shocks.[4] They all confirmed the original thesis: the more people that witness an event, the less likely it is that any will respond to it. Even just thinking about other people reduces levels of altruism.

Unlike in the US, English law recognises the importance of bystanders and attempts to formulate a response to them. The legal doctrine known as 'joint enterprise' says that even bystanders can find themselves convicted of murder, even where there is no evidence as to who inflicted the fatal blow. It was most famously used in 1952 to convict Derek Bentley, whose words 'let him have it' led to the death of a police officer. More recently, four men were convicted of murder in the case of sixteen-year-old Tyrone Clarke, who was stabbed to death by a gang of up to thirty youths. Even though it wasn't clear who had struck the fatal blow, the four that could be identified were all regarded as guilty.[5]

But the law doesn't change behaviour and new headlines keep confirming Darley and Latane's findings. The advent of mobile phones should have made reporting incidents faster and easier, but they haven't changed our willingness to do so. In 2001, a thirty-year-old security manager named Kenneth was attacked by five youths on a London bus when he asked them to stop throwing biscuits around. One of the gang gouged out Kenneth's right eye, as at least fifty people sat by and no one did a thing. These stories are legion and repetitive: unmotivated attacks on innocent victims, witnessed by dozens of people who, for the most part, merely stand by and look away.

In the spate of tragic deaths of young children, like Tiffany Wright and Khyra Ishaq, both of whom starved to death, the press has been quick to blame social services. But what is so striking in these cases is that the children were seen by neighbours and bystanders who did nothing. In the case of Khyra Ishaq, a neighbour witnessed the little girl eating bread off a bird table because she was so underfed. Screams and cries of 'let me out' had reportedly been heard coming from Khyra's house, where a neighbour said she once saw Khyra whimpering in the back garden before her death, dressed just in her underwear. But cultural norms – don't be a Nosy Parker sticking your nose in where it isn't wanted – meant that Khyra died seen, but not seen. When Tiffany Wright died, Alan Jones of the Safeguarding Children Board pointed out that family friends and neighbours were more aware of what was going on than the authorities were, but this provided the starving child with no help or protection whatsoever. And when David Askew, a 64-year-old man with learning difficulties, was bullied to death after years of abuse, blame fell on the local council for failing to rehouse him – even though his neighbours, who had witnessed his torment for years, had done nothing to prevent such cruelty. These crimes needed no CCTV cameras to be seen; they were seen by a broad community of bystanders.

There is no reason to conclude that these witnesses were exceptionally bad people. That's what Latane and Darley's work had proved. We are all likely to behave this way. When we are in groups, we see bad things happening but act as though we are blind to them. Just as we all think we won't obey Milgram's instructor, so we do not believe that we would be passive bystanders. But the evidence is against us.

Internet chat rooms have, in recent years, shown just how far bystander behaviour can scale. In 1998, Larry Froistad, a 29-year-old computer programmer, confessed to 200 people in a chat room for recovering alcoholics that he had set his house on fire to murder his five-year-old daughter.[6]

'When she was asleep, I got wickedly drunk, set the house on fire, went to bed, listened to her scream twice, climbed out the window and set about putting on a show of shock and surprise.'[7]

Only three of the 200 members of the chat room reported him and Froistad was subsequently tried, convicted and sentenced to forty years in prison. Subsequent studies of over 400 different chat groups' behaviour just reinforced the bystander thesis: more people, less response. But one salient detail did emerge: you were more likely to get help if you could ask for your helper by name.

What the bystander effect demonstrates is the tremendous tension between our social selves and our individual selves. Left on our own, we mostly do the right thing. But in a group, our moral selves and our social selves come into conflict, which is painful. The non-intervening subjects of Darley and Latane's experiments had not, they said, *decided* not to intervene. Rather they were frozen in a state of indecision and conflict about whether and how to intervene. Looking for a way out of that discomfort, they choose the easier path, a kind of moral shortcut.

One of the initial explanations for bystander behaviour was ambiguity: it can be hard to know quite what's happening or what response is most appropriate. But perhaps too we are ambiguous about our own role within the event. We hope that the situation isn't so dire that it needs our intervention. Perhaps it will pass or we've just misinterpreted it. Responding could provoke conflict and we don't like conflict. Conformity comes into this, too: I sure would look like an idiot if I rushed to help and it turned out to be nothing. Our fear of embarrassment is the tip of that iceberg that is the ancient fear of exclusion and it turns out to be astonishingly potent. We are more likely to intervene where we are the sole witness; once there are other witnesses, we become anxious about being judged by the group.

The most common experiences of bystander behaviour are trivial, or at least feel that way. You may hear a young employee being mocked by her peers for her dress sense. You don't intervene because the gossip doesn't matter to you. But harm is being done because being mocked at work is professionally damaging. So we may think of intervening, but most of us talk ourselves out it. Likewise, most of us will never witness a crime. But we are all bystanders to something: homelessness, poverty, cruelty, sadness. Our most frequent exposure to bystander apathy occurs at work, where we see (or think we see) colleagues indulging in abusive, unsafe or illegal activity. We don't want to be the ones to complain and, anyway, we might be wrong. Where this concerns clothing, it might not matter. But where it involves vulnerable people, it can be highly dangerous. This emerges powerfully in a study of nurses. (I'm not quite sure why nurses get studied so much – perhaps they make striking examples because we expect such high standards of empathy and altruism from them, and so it is so much more meaningful when disappointed.) They regularly observed a colleague, Annie, cruelly abusing patients.

'She had a really negative effect on patients, especially the elderly ones or those who were long-stay,' one of the nurses, Sean, recalled. 'Making a big deal about getting them a bed pan or helping them to the bathroom during the night meant a lot of them would stop taking anything to drink from late afternoon to ensure they didn't need the bathroom during the night . . . and yet dehydration is a big problem with elderly patients. And we had a number of patients who suffered a long, painful night because she had been really abrupt with them when they'd first asked for something for the pain, and they were too scared to ask again.'[8]

Annie was the talk of the hospital; everyone – even those on other wards – knew she was a terrible nurse. But no one did anything. Some said she was intimidating: 'When drunks were admitted to the ward, she never had any trouble from them. If even a big, drunk aggressive guy gets the vibe that he should behave himself or else, you can imagine how easily the rest of us were intimidated by her.' They were afraid that if they did say anything, and nothing happened, working with her would only get worse. Others blamed themselves, hoping they could figure out how better to work with Annie.

'At first, I thought of this as my problem,' Sean admitted. 'I was pretty new and I'm not the most assertive of people.'

Some nurses made excuses for her, explaining what a hard life she had had, while others tried to focus on her redeeming qualities: she was good in a crisis (when caring takes a back seat). All the nurses tried to avoid working with her and they all talked about her. Like all workplace gossip, the fact that everyone knows what is going on turns out to be part of the problem. Talking about the problem feels like action – but it isn't.

'Knowing that colleagues were concerned and keeping an eye

on her made me feel a bit better about it for quite a while,'
recalled another nurse, Mandy. 'It was only gradually that it
dawned on me that nothing had actually changed: she was no
better, in fact she was probably getting worse.'

Responsibility for Annie was being diffused: since everyone
knew about it, in theory everyone was responsible for it – which
means that they all wanted someone else to act. But by remaining passive, the nurses actually *reduced* the likelihood that anybody
would bring about a positive resolution. Diffusion of responsibility – the rule of nobody – is a common feature of many large
organisations, where almost nothing is done alone. Even one of
the most famous whistleblowers of all time – Daniel Ellsberg –
succumbed to it for a while.

Ellsberg started working in 1964 for Assistant Secretary of
Defense for International Security Affairs John T. McNaughton
'on secret plans to escalate the war in Vietnam', although both of
them personally regarded these as wrongheaded and dangerous.
Unfortunately, by decisions of President Johnson and Secretary
McNamara, these plans were carried out in the spring of 1965.[9]

Despite his belief that the war was wrong, Ellsberg continued
to work for the government. In 1967, he was assigned to work
on the top-secret McNamara study of US decision-making in
Vietnam – what came to be known as the Pentagon Papers, a
7,000-page analysis of twenty-three years of American policy in
the region. Ellsberg kept hoping – quite reasonably – that those
with access to the papers would read them; he personally urged
Henry Kissinger to do so. He also kept hoping that someone
else – any of the 'scores of officials, perhaps a hundred' that had
access to the papers – would give them to the Senate. Still no one
did. It was not until 1971 that Ellsberg finally took action himself, risking life imprisonment by leaking them to the press.

That Ellsberg waited in no way undermines his courage; rather
it illustrates how even a tremendously brave man could think, and

hope, that someone else – with more authority, more power, more protection – would act. In Ellsberg's case, as in the more mundane case of the nurses, there were so many people who could act that no one felt uniquely responsible for doing so.

Sometimes diffusion of responsibility can be no more than a fancy phrase for passing the buck. We take our cues from those above us – especially in hierarchical organisations – and if they do nothing, what are we supposed to do? We can always use our salary, our career, to justify turning a blind eye to what we know is wrong.

When she was a contract specialist at Enron, Lynn Brewer completed a legal brief concerning a large gas contract that she knew to be 'a quarter-billion-dollar scam'. Enron simply did not own the gas it had used as collateral; the company was in default of the agreement the day it entered into the deal. But no one else seemed worried by it. Brewer had the nerve to track down the detail – something no one expected her to do – but she had absorbed enough of the company's competitive ethos to know not to include details of the fraud in her brief. She agonised at length, knowing that ignoring the scam and helping to cover it up was wrong, but she was loath to jeopardise salary, career and the excitement of a new job. So she drafted the brief as though there were nothing wrong with it, and then conveniently diffused responsibility for the fraud on to others.

'Bound by attorney–client privilege and a legal code of ethics, going outside the company and blowing the whistle was not an option. It would cost us not only our jobs but our careers . . . Why hadn't the banks caught the minor missing detail? Or had they too been wooed by the promises of Enron's Yellow Brick Road the same way I had?'[10]

The Yellow Brick Road reference is germane. In 1997, Enron's mining and metals team had staged a holiday skit of *The Wizard of Oz*. Sherron Watkins played the Wicked Witch and

the Wizard was played by Jere Overdyke in a scarlet satin pimp
suit, pretending to be the CFO, Andy Fastow.[11] Everyone could
read the subtext: just as the wizard is a fraud, so the company's
financial wizardry was nothing more than smoke and mirrors.
In the audience, everyone laughed knowingly – every one of
them a bystander. They may have felt themselves merely passive
witnesses to a crime too big for them to stop – but the reality
was that, with every crooked contract, the Enron employees
were validating their crooked corporation. The crucial point
about bystanders is that they have potential influence, and their
choice not to use it means that they aren't neutral but run the
risk of morphing into perpetrators. A neutral stance isn't
possible. The collapse of the sixth-largest corporation in America wasn't achieved by a few bad guys but by thousands of
bystanders.

That everyone was well paid, that they all liked each other and
had so much in common, that many were exhausted by long
hours and global travel, all helped to secure their collusion. But
what moral clarity they might have had was also severely
confused by the intense ambiguity of their environment.
Orientation videos and TV ads for Enron specifically celebrated
the 'defiant and the visionary'. CEO Skilling and Chairman Lay
deliberately set out to build a vast company that operated with
the freedom and latitude of entrepreneurial start-ups. They
actively poured scorn on rules and regulations and encouraged
competitive risk-taking. At the same time, they were spending a
fortune lobbying Washington to get any inconvenient regulation
abolished. It could be very hard, at any given time, to know
whether a law was to be taken seriously, or merely an obstacle to
be circumvented. The cliché – don't ask for permission, ask for
forgiveness – was understood as licence to do anything that generated revenue.

Such shifting sands make it intensely difficult to keep hold of any clear sense of moral norms. If everyone is doing crooked deals, and being rewarded for it, then what is normal? If everyone is taking moral shortcuts, where can you see signs for the main road? How can you maintain a sense of yourself as a good person if the definition of 'good' keeps changing?

'As a child,' says Walt Pavlo, 'when you did things wrong, your parents said so. I know right from wrong. But as an adult when I was hiding money, I knew I was doing wrong but I was being rewarded and promoted! It's extremely confusing. You rationalise: it can't be that wrong if nobody's stopping me. So I'm going to call it OK because it fits my life model that good things happen to good people. Good things are happening and therefore I must be good.'

Of course, Pavlo had a boss. Didn't the boss start to wonder how such huge debts managed to disappear? No. In a classic example of 'don't ask, don't tell' his boss – who was, anyway, under a lot of pressure and exhausted – never asked: what are you doing and how are you doing it?

'If he had asked, that would have relieved me of so much pressure. It would have been a *relief* if he'd said anything!'

But instead the boss chose to be a bystander, too.

Bystander behaviour need not always involve a crime. In companies, it is more often implicated in the failure to respond to strategic business threats. Classically, this is taught as the blindness of buggy-whip manufacturers to the all too obvious rise of the automobile, or the myopia of American car manufacturers to the emerging excellence of Japanese automobiles. The cases are legion but teaching the stories of these industrial train crashes never seems to reduce their number.

In 1999, the advent of the Internet and the rise of digital music had all of the record labels dazed and confused. Why were kids stealing their music? How could they be stopped? Although the music business is the closest thing to organised crime I've ever witnessed, you could feel their pain. The business that had done so well from kids for decades suddenly seemed to be in melt-down. Years before the iPod had launched, kids were ripping CDs and sharing them – via email, Napster, Kazaa or any number of file sharing sites. Nobody wanted to pay for music any more – anything you wanted could be found for free online some-where. Of course, the record companies didn't do nothing. They dabbled in a few Internet initiatives but were too venal to make good partners for anyone. And they invested heavily in lobbying, hoping that they could buy enough friends to stop the future happening. As profits melted before their eyes, torn between denial and aggression, they presented a disunited, incoherent front to a consumer base years ahead of them. Whatever they tried to do, it was always too late.

If you weren't in the music business, this was easy to see. And it didn't take a gigantic leap of the imagination to see that what was happening in music was just a glimpse of the future for the movie industry. But it hadn't happened to them yet. Broadband penetration in the late 1990s was still under 50 per cent in the US. Even though, theoretically, you could download a movie, in practice nobody had the patience to do it down phone lines. But the music business presaged the looming disaster lying in wait for the film business.

At any rate, that's what it looked like to me when I approached the studios with a proposal that was, in essence, a precursor of iTunes. Wouldn't it make sense to seize the initiative and learn about online distribution and consumption now, rather than wait to have it owned by someone else? At the time, I ran an online media business called iCAST. Well connected and extravagantly well funded, we had a lot of meetings in Hollywood; even if people didn't like or understand all of our ideas, they wanted our money. I remember in particular one meeting with an army of executives from Disney, many of whom are still in place to this

day. We laid out the threat, as we saw it, and proposed a number
of ways we could work together to seize the initiative. I didn't
recognise it at the time, but in this meeting we witnessed the full
panoply of bystander behaviour. They all saw what was happening in the music business. They understood that the same crisis
awaited their business. But no one was willing to take the risk of
intervening. The market, they said, was ambiguous; no one knew
for certain how digital entertainment would develop. And whose
responsibility was it to take the first step? Corporate politics
meant that doing nothing would always be safer than recom-
mending a bold course of action. Besides, the executives asked,
if the strategic risk were real, wouldn't some of the other studios
be doing something about it? If they weren't, why should
Disney? Nobody in the room – though they were all proudly
very senior – felt quite senior enough to take a decision. I
remember sitting there thinking: in the 1980s, the TV companies
were dubbed the 'three blind mice' because of their failure to take
the advent of cable seriously. Now the film studios were producing the remake.

You only have to mention the words 'wilful blindness' to hear
the same story about any industry: how beverage companies
ignored vitamin drinks, packaged-goods businesses didn't think
it mattered whether products were environmentally sound; pharmaceutical companies don't pay attention to off-label prescribing
and gun manufacturers pretend a secondary market (selling to
kids and criminals) has nothing to do with them. The knowledge
is there, spoken or unspoken, but the executives do nothing. In
these cases, it is their livelihoods, not their lives, that are threatened – but their pattern of behaviour is just the same as Kitty
Genovese's bystanders.

These are classic business stories, because it is so human and so
common for innovation to fail not through the lack of ideas but
through lack of courage. Business leaders always claim that

innovation is what they want but they're often paralysed into inaction by hoping and assuming that someone else, somewhere, will take the risk. They may see a looming crisis but, like the experiment participants, would rather continue earnestly to complete their questionnaires than get up and acknowledge that the room is full of smoke and they can no longer see. Just like the witnesses to a crime, once someone does seize the initiative, bystanders are left feeling anxious and uncomfortable, dimly aware that they missed their moment.

Nobody really knows if bystander behaviours are innate or learned, but they certainly start very young. Most children witness bullying at school, by teachers or peers or both, and feel uncomfortably grateful not to be the victim. They may even learn, as my son did, the invaluable life lesson of how to stay off a bully's radar screen. But a salient characteristic of all bullying is that it craves an audience that most kids, acting as bystanders, provide.

In recent years, America's Department of Justice and the police have become very interested in bullying, calling it the most under-reported safety problem on American school campuses.[12] Two-thirds of school-shooting perpetrators (for which the shooters were still alive to report) had previously been bullied; that they occur at all may, in some part, be attributed to the rage and frustration felt by the victim, for whom all bystanders are colluders. Similarly, teenage suicides often uncover a history of bullying, usually at school where it is visible and known about but never acted on.

Bystanders play a big part in bullying. Despite many campaigns, and the requirement that all UK schools have an anti-bullying policy, a national survey into bullying in 2006 showed that 69 per cent of schoolchildren said that they had been bullied, 87 per cent of parents said that their children had been bullied but 83 per cent of teachers said that they had not seen bullying at their school.[13] In many instances, student bystanders act as 'reinforcers', providing an encouraging audience, while others merely protect the bully by their failure to intervene. Both validate the bully by their very presence. Only 10–20 per cent of witnesses ever provide any real help. Perhaps most disappointing of all is the police observation that bullying is little reported because children follow adult examples.

'It is at school that children learn to be bystanders,' says Ervin Staub.

Staub has devoted his life to the study of good and evil. He is a Holocaust survivor and his work on genocide and mass violence has led him to work in Rwanda, Burundi and the Congo, as well as New Orleans and Los Angeles. His interest in bullying derives from his observation that all mass violence requires, and is also inflamed by, bystanders. It's for that reason that he conducted a lengthy study of bullying in schools, which is where, he believes, the behaviour starts.

'Sadly, teachers don't intervene often. It turns out that some teachers think kids should take care of their own business. So they don't do anything. But this is problematic because, as adults, we should provide kids with guidance. When we are passive, that sends a message that there's no need to act.'

Teachers and parents often won't intervene because they think the children need to learn to deal with the problem themselves. But the kids take the wrong message, learning instead to do what the adults do: nothing. And then that message gets amplified.

'I very much believe that bystanders give perpetrators and bullies a message that what they are doing is accepted. It tends to make them believe that they are supported.'

In Western Massachusetts, Staub has begun to develop a curriculum to teach kids how better to respond when they see bullying. Its goal, he says, is to create a sympathetic but unaccepting attitude to bullies.

'We try to help the students understand the impact on kids who are bullied; kids don't process that necessarily. And we train them to engage. They don't have to do it alone, just turn to a friend and say: "Hey, we need to do something here, we have to stop this." We also try to get them to turn towards and support the victim because the passivity of bystanders makes victims feel there is no sympathy for them. You know, it often takes very, very little to stop a bully; people just don't realise the power that they have.'

So far, Staub has run his programme only once, but early indications are that students emerge more confident of ways in which they can and will intervene. He'll be running it again because he wants those kids to understand the power they have. Staub is dedicated to understanding the processes of mass violence in order to prevent it.

'I have done work in Rwanda for many years now and one of the things we do there is try to help people understand the influences that lead to violence, what are the social conditions and psychological changes that people undergo. By providing this kind of information, I believe it is less likely that people close their eyes. They know what to look for. Things that normally go under your radar, when you know what you are looking for, those things are likely to connect, to click in. You think: I have to pay attention to this, this matters.

'One of my strong positions is that in the case of mass violence, we must act early. It is easier to act earlier – before ideologies and positions have developed and intensified. It's just the same in individual situations, even if you're not thinking about ideology, just thinking of a bully. Once they're a little way down the road, they're in a position where if they stop in response to someone, they lose face. So it's easier to intervene before they have too much to lose.

'The same is true in other group situations. We tend to think:

this is a small thing, it's not big enough to worry about it. But by the time it is big enough to worry about, it is too late. Mass violence evolves progressively, always with small steps like excluding people, creating offices that serve discrimination. When no one does anything about those changes, that sends a sign: a sign that they can go further. I'll give you an example: Goebbels. After the Evian Conference in 1938, when the community of nations gathered in Switzerland to talk about taking in Jewish refugees from Germany, no one wanted to take them in. Goebbels wrote in his diary: "They would like to do what we are doing but they don't have the courage." He took the message that if, at the first step, no one would stop him, then he could keep going.'

Today, over forty years since he collaborated on the bystander experiments, John Darley works within the leafy enclave of Princeton. He's since moved on to do important work that explores how large organisations, and the people in them, become corrupt. In many ways, he has not strayed so very far from his original, groundbreaking work. The greatest evil, he argues, always requires large numbers of participants who contribute by their failure to intervene.

Darley was born into psychology; as a teenager, he remembers his father helping Leon Festinger with logistics when he infiltrated the cognitive dissonance of Marian Keech and her flying-saucer devotees. For someone who has spent his life delving into such dark aspects of human behaviour, Darley is a delightfully affable and mellow character, open, accessible and still eager to explore human behaviour and the social and corporate structures that reinforce it. He's particularly intrigued by the way that morality impinges on thinking only intermittently.

'The moral mind is not our default mind,' he says. 'In very competitive environments, where you're under a lot of stress, a lot of cognitive load, you won't necessarily even see that there is a moral consideration at all. Most corruption, I think, starts with an intuitive act, not a deliberate one. Is this a System 1/System 2 error? I wonder.'

Darley is referring to a body of work by the psychologist and Nobel laureate Daniel Kahneman, who argues that we operate two modes of thinking: System 1, which is intuitive, associative, very fast, and born of habit. It is, in essence, shortcut thinking – and much of the time, it is good enough. System 2 is more deliberative, analytical, slow and requires much more effort; it's what we use if we want to solve a maths problem correctly but one of its other purposes is to monitor System 1 for errors.[14]

'Many decisions made intuitively are reasonable,' Darley continues. 'But the problem is that sometimes they are not. And the reasoning system monitoring – System 2 – is intermittent and lax. That's the problem: no alarm goes off. So you sell mortgages to people who can't afford them but you're in a competitive environment, under a lot of pressure to perform, so you don't monitor the morality of your actions. And of course, as soon as that mortgage is securitised, you're not responsible for it, so you don't care if the owner defaults. Responsibility has been diffused. From your perspective, System 1 has worked just fine. And of course the most bonused are the most blind because for them to look carefully is, quite literally, too costly. I think when you look at how all of that plays out, you see that conditions of high stress – from competitive environments, compensation structures or just company politics – the high stress tends to distance moral reflection.'

Darley has written extensively about the degree to which corruption on a wide scale, and evil on a wide scale, require large numbers of participants and bystanders. Corporate meltdowns like Enron, MCI, or the banks require the work of thousands of people, all failing to see the moral implications of their work.

And you can't have historic catastrophes, like the Holocaust, unless millions of individuals have taken, in effect, the same moral shortcut.

'Under conditions of high stress,' Darley continues to gnaw on the problem, 'you may still have inklings, suspicions. But you may inhabit an environment that valorises blindness, so you don't look. Who or what is it you are blind to? In the end, I think it's you. You become blind to yourself. To your better self.'

In 1938, the residents of Mauthausen were feeling optimistic. Their quarry was once again being used, as massive rebuilding in Germany and Austria brought new business to the town. In nearby Linz, Hitler had great plans for his home town: a new bridge, town hall, art museum, party headquarters and two monuments, one commemorating the *Anschluss* and one commemorating the composer, Anton Bruckner. The town's economy was looking up too because the building of a new concentration camp created jobs and new business for suppliers and craftsmen.

When prisoners began to arrive in August, the SS tried hard to keep the population at a distance. But the camp was in full view, and ordinary life had to continue. Inevitably that meant that the brutal treatment of prisoners was witnessed by many bystanders. One was a farmer, Eleanore Gusenbauer, who didn't like what she saw. So she wrote to complain:

In the Concentration Camp Mauthausen at the work site in Vienna Ditch inmates are being shot repeatedly; those badly struck live for yet some time, and so remain lying next to the dead for hours and even half a day long.

My property lies upon an elevation next to the Vienna Ditch and one is often an unwilling witness to such outrages.

I am anyway sickly and such a sight makes such a demand on my nerves that in the long run I cannot bear this.

I request that it be arranged that such inhuman deeds be discontinued, or else be done where one does not have to see it.[15]

9. OUT OF SIGHT, OUT OF MIND

St James's Square is one of London's most elegant addresses. A short stroll from Buckingham Palace, it is lined with fine, tall Georgian buildings embracing a quiet, shady park square. Prohibitive parking charges prevent it from being too crammed with cars, while the refined inconvenience of its layout stops taxis using it as a rat run. Just off Pall Mall, it's in the heart of gentlemen's clubland. The fine sweeping staircases and high marble halls of the Naval and Military Club suppress the acoustic, while deep armchairs envelop hushed conversations. The Dukes of Norfolk and of Cleveland have kept family houses in the square since the eighteenth century, just two of the seven dukes and seven earls in residence. A few doors down is Chatham House, home of the Royal Institute of International Affairs, and scene of many a high-level confidential briefing on world politics. The 'Chatham House Rule' is a byword for frank but confidential conversations that don't leave the building. At one time, the elegant terraced house was home to the Earl of Lovelace and his wife, Ada, daughter of Lord Byron and an early computing pioneer. For the young couple, the square was the perfect London residence: exclusive, close to the heart of power. Next door is the London Library, the world's largest private lending library, founded by Thomas Carlyle. Thackeray was its first auditor, Dickens, George Eliot, Kipling, Shaw, Henry James and T.S. Eliot among its members.

Its Piranesi staircases bind together a maze of buildings packed
with over a million volumes. St James's Square is picturebook
London: intimidating as an oyster on the outside, seething and
expensive within.

It's a long way from the sulphur-scented streets of Texas City.
But St James's Square is also the headquarters of BP. It's here
that Lord Browne of Madingley issued his order for cost-cutting and here too that the Group Chief Executive of Refining
and Marketing, John Manzoni, ensured that it was implemented. If you look at an organisation chart for BP, you'll see
Browne at the top and Manzoni immediately underneath. From
there, it's about seven layers of management down to the guys
operating the Texas City refinery. Seven layers, 4,800 miles, a
six-hour time difference and a cultural chasm between the two
locations.

Like many multinational corporations, it's impossible to put the
whole org chart on a page because nothing is simple. The Business
Unit Leader (BUL) is responsible for the refinery but alongside
him works an HSSE (health, safety, security, environment)
manager and a process-safety manager; they're responsible for
numerous sites, so, on any given day, they could be in Texas City –
or somewhere else. Towards the bottom of the pyramid, it gets
particularly hairy, with Tier 1, Tier 2, Tier 3 and Tier 4 managers,
each with accountability of various kinds. It got complicated, not
just because there were so many titles, acronyms and responsibil-
ities, but because the people kept changing: five plant managers
alone, between the years 2001 and 2003.[1]

Additional organisational change occurred in 2003 and 2004,
when BP issued its 'Management Framework'. The BP South
Houston complex was dissolved, the director became the refinery Business Unit Leader, and the process-safety department
became part of the new HSSE department with a new manager.

The impact of these organisational changes on process safety was summed up by consultants studying the refinery just weeks before the explosion. 'We have never seen an organisation with such a history of leadership changes over such a short period of time. Even if the rapid turnover of senior leadership were the norm elsewhere in the BP system, it seems to have a particularly strong effect at Texas City. Between the BP/Amoco mergers, then the BP turnover coupled with the difficulties of governance of an integrated site . . . there has been little organisational stability.'[2]

Instability, of course, is just a word that means a lot of people moving up – and out. No aspiring manager wanted to stay in Texas City. Why, the site wasn't even in Houston, America's oil capital, but a half-hour congested drive on the Galveston freeway. High flyers might do a stint but they'd soon be on their way – wasn't that the fun of working for a global business? The managers could move, and did – frequently. Everyone else, the guys 'closest to the valve', stayed put; where else were they going to go?

The men running the isomerisation unit reported to bosses on site who reported to a Regional Vice President, Pat Gower in Illinois, who reported to a Group Vice President, Mike Hoffman, who reported back to Manzoni in leafy St James's Square. And Manzoni's job wasn't simple either.

'I have ultimate accountability for several of the businesses inside BP,' Manzoni explained in his deposition, taken after the explosion at Texas City. 'It's the refining business. There is a retail business. There is a lubricants business. There is a marketing business. There is [a] chemicals business. If I were to give you a sense of that, these are very diverse businesses. In language and in companies that you may be more familiar with, it's a bit like putting Coors, Whirlpool, GAP, General Motors all together and running those businesses all together.'

With so much on his plate, detail was never going to be at the heart of his working day. Asked about the Texas City 'assets', Manzoni was unapologetic. 'It would be very unusual,' he said, 'for me to look at individual assets.' The year that Manzoni became Group CEO, Texas City had been described as 'in complete decline'. In 2003, an audit claimed that the 'condition of the infrastructure and assets is poor at the Texas City refinery'. In July 2004, Manzoni finally actually paid a visit to this, the largest refinery in his portfolio. But, according to his deposition, he still had no inkling that anything was wrong.

Q. And you are telling me no one told you about the problems that existed at the plant during that visit?

A. Actually, I left the plant with a sense that programs were being put in place and that – and there was something called the 1000-day program.

Q. Have you ever talked to any superintendents?

A. I have done it in the past. I can't remember whether I did on that visit in Texas City.

Q. Did you ever talk to a guy named Ray Hawkins?

A. No.

Q. If he – if you had spoken to him and he told you, 'Do you know what? My day-to-day activity is nothing more than crisis management, eventually something is going to fall off the plate,' what would that tell you?

A. There is a problem.

But of course, no one told Manzoni – they knew about him, but they rarely saw him. No one at the refinery had the kind of relationship that would make them seek him out to tell him the truth. Just that year, the site had already seen $30 million of damage due to a ruptured furnace pipe, and two months after Manzoni's visit, two workers died opening a pipe flange. But apparently Manzoni didn't notice this either.

I am not sure I was made aware of compliance issues or gaps in operations. You know, we obviously focus on continuous improvement in all aspects of our business but I am not sure that I was specifically made aware of any gap. I believe nobody knew the level of risk at Texas City because, if they had known, I have absolutely no doubt we would have taken different and substantively different actions.

Manzoni's argument is intriguing because he's using a logical shortcut: assuming that there could not have been a problem because, if there had been, someone somewhere would have taken action. Since no one took action, the problem could not have existed. But the deposition reveals all the details Manzoni never saw: the impact of budget cuts, the absence of updated fire equipment, deferred maintenance, cut safety training. It rehearses the sequence of reports, audits, consultants reports, surveys and warnings that all drew attention to safety issues at the plant. But all of it, it seems, passed Manzoni by.

Q. Tell me why the plant wasn't shut down to fix these problems before this explosion occurred.
A. I can't tell you actually because I wasn't aware of the problems before the explosion occurred.[3]

Throughout his deposition, what is so surprising is the frankness with which Manzoni demonstrates his own blindness. Not only did he not know what was going on, he doesn't appear to think that there was anything to know. He is so vague in his deposition that his critics might just conclude he's lying, but I don't think he is: the very fact that he is so brazenly unconcerned by his own ignorance makes him weirdly credible. Although he acknowledges the gravity of fifteen deaths, he seems at a loss to understand why he should be involved. He has no real understanding of Texas

City, is unprepared but also strangely unworried, annoyed only that everyone insists on digging up history when what he really wants is to fix the problem now he finally sees it.

What comes out loud and clear in his testimony is the unbridgeable gulf between Manzoni, the élite, educated British executive, and the men close to the valve whose issues can neither be heard nor seen. Watching Manzoni, it's tempting to ask the question: where was he? And the answer would be: a very, very long way away. Separated by miles, by background, by culture, by status. Even the deposition was conducted in Chicago, a long way from everything, and everyone, that mattered in the case.

In 2007, Lord Browne resigned from BP, for a host of reasons not least of which was the damage done to BP's reputation and stock price by the Texas City accident. Between 2005 and 2008, as other oil companies saw their stock prices rise by 30–40 per cent, BP went through prolonged losses and only modest gains. This provoked a great deal of soul-searching within BP as it struggled, under new CEO Tony Hayward, to reorganise the business. The company chastised itself for 'poor listening' and for its celebration of complexity as a virtue rather than a problem. Attempts were made to reduce the organisational chaos of the company, by keeping executives in their jobs for longer, rewarding crisis prevention over heroic crisis management and by ostensibly simplifying corporate structures. By the end of 2009, the company leadership was feeling confident again, its share price rising and it was nearly ready to start talking publicly about how profoundly it had changed. But executives were cautious. After all, it wasn't as though Texas City was over. At the end of the many lawsuits that had followed that explosion, BP had reached a plea bargain with the US Justice Department, in which the corporation paid a $50 million fine to avoid criminal charges for violations of the Clean Air Act related to the fatal explosions. But that deal was contingent on BP fulfilling its settlement agreement with the Occupational Safety and Health Administration (OSHA), something it hadn't done. Instead, in every year that followed the refinery explosion, another worker died on the job at Texas City and by October 2009, the corporation still faced 439 outstanding safety violations at Texas City alone. Less than six months later, the Deepwater Horizon oil rig exploded and then sank, leaving the largest offshore oil spill in US history. When, after weeks of trying and failing to contain the disaster, CEO Hayward complained that he wanted his life back, the distance between St James's Square and the Gulf of Mexico yawned wider than ever.

One of the arguments put forward to support globalisation is that, because we have the technology to connect everyone, business can and must expand across the globe. We don't need to be in the same room together any more. Between the Internet, video conferencing, email, mobile phones and social networks, distance doesn't matter. What's so painfully obvious in BP's case is that none of this technology bridges the gulf. The distance does matter. Manzoni couldn't see the people who work for him, he had no relationship with most of them. Much more likely is that he truly did not know most of the 80,000 people working for him, he didn't ever see their working conditions and, perhaps worst of all, he didn't see that not seeing might pose a problem. When Tony Hayward said he wanted his life back, he seemed utterly impervious to the oil-rig workers who would never get their lives back or the fisheries workers who had lost their livelihoods for ever.

Technology can maintain relationships but it won't build them. Conference calls, with teams of executives huddled around speakerphones, fail to convey personality, mood and nuance. You may start to develop rapport with the person who speaks most – or take an instant dislike to them. But you'll never know why. Nor will you perceive the silent critic scowling a thousand miles away. Video conferencing distracts all its participants, who spend too much time worrying about their hair and whether they're looking fat, uncomfortable at seeing themselves on screen. The nervous small talk about weather – it's snowing there? It's hot and sunny here – betrays anxiety about the vast differences that the technology attempts to mask.

Physical distance isn't easily bridged, no matter how refined the technology. Instead, we delude ourselves that, because so many words are exchanged – email, notes and reports – somehow a great deal of communication must have taken place. But that requires, in the first instance, that the words be read, that they are understood and that the recipient knows enough to read with discernment and empathy. What's tragically obvious in Manzoni's deposition is that he has no idea who is working for him or what they are worried about. It's extremely hard to communicate well with people you don't really know, whose concerns you cannot see.

Communication technologies have developed exponentially since Milgram did his obedience experiments, but there's one version of those experiments that has become more relevant than ever. In the original experiment, the victim could not be seen or heard and 65 per cent of obedient subjects delivered shocks to the maximum limit. In that version, one of the subjects commented, 'It's funny how you really begin to forget that there's a guy out there. For a long time, I just concentrated on pressing the switches and reading the words.'[4] But in a second version, the victim was in the same room as the subject, sitting just a few feet away. That proximity reduced the number of fully compliant subjects to 40 per cent. And when the subjects were made to touch their victims' hands, placing them on a shock plate, human contact meant that only 30 per cent finished the course. With the victim sitting in the same room, establishing eye contact, and eventually physical contact, everything changes. It is so much easier to be blind to the consequences of your actions when you do not have to see them play out.

Similarly, John Darley conducted a variation on his bystander-effect experiments, when he placed some pairs of participants in a room face to face, and others sitting back to back. They were left to draw. After four minutes, they heard the sounds of an accident: a workman apparently fell to the floor, groaned and exclaimed, 'Oh my leg!' Eighty per cent of those working face to face responded to the accident; only 20 per cent of those sitting back to back did so. Relationships – real, face-to-face relationships – change our behaviour.[5]

This is, of course, why some leaders like distance; they feel that they could not do their jobs if they were immersed in the messy, human detail of the mission. Britain's General Haig, who presided over the slaughter of a whole generation of young men in the First World War, could not bear to visit a military hospital. One of his subordinates, on first visiting the battlefront, is reported to have burst into tears, crying, 'Good God, did we really send men to fight in that?'[6] Albert Speer was always very careful not to visit the labour camps he oversaw – or, on the one occasion he visited Mauthausen, to stick firmly to the guided tour that shielded him from reality. Even Eichmann and Himmler became physically ill when confronted with the consequences of their decisions.[7] In Iraq, Brigadier-General Janis Karpinski was responsible for sixteen prisons – 17,950 inmates – spread across a country slightly smaller than France. Although Abu Ghraib, with 6,000 prisoners, was the largest, she didn't spend a lot of time there. And the only interrogation she witnessed was one that she was invited to see. Like all the other senior officers, she never visited at night when the abuses occurred. The argument for distance is that eliminating proximity clarifies the mind and facilitates more objective decision-making. But it can also blind you to the details that you'd prefer not to see.

Structural blindness was built into the way that BP did business, not because its leaders wanted to be blind but because, to be competitive, Browne believed the business had to be big, it had to be a 'super major'. Built through aggressive mergers and acquisitions around the world, it was inevitably spread across continents, time zones and cultures. The company was well aware of the problem; it's why so many surveys and processes were put in place to attempt to hold everything together. But structure alone, when presented with such a challenge, won't fix the problem. Manzoni and his boss, Lord Browne, were both blind to the routine risks being run at Texas City in part because they weren't familiar enough with the site or the people to care about them. They were abstractions, numbers, profit generators and cost centres. But it wasn't just geography that left them so dangerously out of the loop. It was also power.

Power imposes distance between those that have it and those that do not. The powerful are quite often unaware of this, the best struggle against it, but the distance is always there. Power circumscribes whether you're spending most of your time in elegant London clubs or at the Grand Prize Barbeque on Texas City's Palmer Highway. Power determines whether you are talking to chief executives or superintendents. Power decides whether you fly in the splendid isolation of a private jet or first class instead of in economy, next to the young mother who needs help with her restless child. Limousines and catered lunches, personal assistants and flattering friends teach new habits of privilege and entitlement. But while these may seem attractive luxuries, they come at a cost: isolation. The bubble of power seals off bad news, inconvenient details, hostile opinions and messy realities, leaving you free to inhale the rarefied air of pure abstraction. Like the cave dwellers of Plato's parable, the powerful see only shadows of reality flickering on their walls, grateful to be so comfortably protected from external realities. The rough gives way to the smooth in a frictionless ascent.

Moreover, recent research into power shows that the powerful appraise information differently. A team of American and French academics got together to try to figure out whether power alters judgement. In one experiment, they recruited teams of students and divided them into two groups: one group had the power to choose applicants for an internship, the other group could advise but not select. The powerful participants paid more attention to information that conformed to stereotypes. In other words, having power seemed to make them less inclined to challenge received wisdom.

In a further experiment, the participants were subjected to personality appraisals that evaluated the need for dominance. Those who scored higher were put into a separate group from those who scored lower and both groups were then asked to evaluate students for internships. While the powerful did not completely ignore information that challenged stereotypes, they still gave it less attention. Dominant people, it appears, use snap judgements and conform to received wisdom more than do the less dominant. Those who need power, and those who have it, think differently. The stereotypes they fall back on can be counteracted – but doing so requires a great deal of motivation and cognitive effort.[8] Power does corrupt, but more insidiously than even the powerful appreciate.

Frances Milliken, one of the academics responsible for work on organisational silence, did a marvellous study comparing how those in power communicate differently from those who lack power. She found that, like the rich, the powerful are different from other people. Confronted by risky situations, they are more likely to expect positive outcomes. They're so optimistic at least in part because they have – or think they have – the power needed to overcome most adversity. That psychological distance between themselves and others means that they can't think as concretely as other people; inevitably they have to think in far more abstract terms. But what is frightening about Milliken's study is that the combination of power, optimism and abstract thinking makes powerful people more certain. The more cut-off they are from others, the more confident they are that they are right.

Just to add a little spice to what might otherwise have seemed a rather dry linguistic inventory, Milliken chose to focus it on the response of officials during Hurricane Katrina. Milliken and her team collected a vast array of public statements by officials during the disaster and analysed the language of each piece according to the amount of power held by its speaker. It must have been a lugubrious process but the conclusions feel real. Sure enough, she found that federal officials – those with the most power and who didn't live in New Orleans – were very much less troubled by events, more optimistic that the crisis would be effectively dealt with, and far less prone to doubt. Psychologically this becomes self-reinforcing: the less they knew, the less curious and concerned they became.

The poster child for this conclusion, of course, must be Michael Brown, the director of the Federal Emergency Management Agency (FEMA). Although Milliken is wonderfully discreet and doesn't shape her argument around his pronouncements, he was a walking demonstration of her argument. On the day that the hurricane first hit landfall in Louisiana, Brown seemed relaxed, reminding emergency-services personnel 'not to respond to hurricane impact areas unless dispatched by state, local authorities'.

Two days later, he received an email from a FEMA colleague: 'Hotels are kicking people out, thousands gathering in the streets with no food or water. Hundreds are still being rescued from homes. We are out of food and running out of water at the dome.'[9] But Brown, despite the detail he received, didn't seem worried as he responded: 'Thanks for update. Anything specific I need to do or tweak?'

Four days later, he told ABC's Ted Koppel that he had been unaware that 20–25,000 refugees were stranded at the city's convention centre without food or water.

BROWN: We first learned of the convention center – we being the federal government – today.

KOPPEL: Don't you guys watch television? Don't you guys listen to the radio? Our reporters have been reporting about it for more than just today.

BROWN: We learned about it factually today that that was what existed. When we first learned about it, my first instinction [sic] instinct was: Get somebody in there, give me truth on the ground, let me know because if it is true, we've got to help those people.

KOPPEL: But here we are five days after the storm hit and you are talking about what is going to happen in the next couple of days.

BROWN: I just want to say to the American public that they do need to understand exactly how catastrophic this disaster is. And they do need to know that we are going to have every available resource to do everything that we can. We're going to take care of these victims. We are going to make it right. We are going to make certain that the devastation that has been reaped [sic] upon these people is taken care of and that we get their lives back in order.[10]

What's so striking about all of Brown's responses is that they are so remote, so confident and so extraordinarily abstract. There are no individuals, there is no fear or hunger in his response. There are only abstract 'victims' whose lives someone somewhere is going to get back in order. Koppel's responses, while polite, finally exploded with disbelief – and real detail.

> KOPPEL: Mr Brown, some of these people are dead. They are beyond your help. Some of these people have died because they needed insulin and they couldn't get it . . . You say you were surprised so many people didn't make it out. It's no surprise to anyone that you had at least 100,000 people in the city of New Orleans who are dirt poor, who don't have cars, who don't have access to public transportation, who don't have any way of getting out of the city simply because somebody says, 'You know there's a force-five storm coming? You ought to get out.' If you didn't have the buses there to get them out, why should it be a surprise to you that they stayed?

Brown wasn't as far away as it might seem – he was in Baton Rouge, Louisiana. But psychologically he was miles away, not just because he was part of the Washington élite but also because he had been hoping for some time to retire from FEMA. He didn't want to be in his job and, mentally, he was already gone, which is why, three days after the levees broke, he wrote his infamous email: 'Last hurrah was supposed to be Labor Day. I'm trapped now, please rescue me.'[11] That Brown can make a joke, comparing his professional bondage with the physical and tragic trap the citizens of New Orleans found themselves unable to escape, illustrates how unbridgeable the gulf between them was.

In a far less tragic context, Geoff Hoon, former UK Secretary of State for Defence, appeared entirely out of touch when he apologised for having been caught, in secret recordings, cosying up to American lobbyists. At a time when over 2.31 million people were unemployed, Hoon seemed to see his own predicament, as an MP confronting future unemployment, as so uniquely painful that it would justify his actions.

> My pension is not payable in many years in my case . . . I don't think I was in any different position from anyone else who leaves a job or loses a job or is thinking of moving on to another. I'm not quite sure what the average length of time that people serve as MPs is these days – it used to be around seven years. I think it's about two terms, so ten years. In that period of time there will be MPs who lose their seat who will find it very difficult in mid-life to find alternative employment. I was aware – you mentioned that I was Chief Whip – I was aware that several colleagues who lost their seat in 2005 spent actually years trying to find something else. Because the skills and experience of a former MP are not readily translatable to other walks of life.

But nowhere does Hoon betray any awareness that long-term unemployment is not an MP's special problem but a national and economic tragedy, with over 687,000 adults unemployed for longer than a year.

The distance imposed by geography and implicit in power is reinforced by the structures within which work gets done. It's been that way ever since 1776, the year Adam Smith published *The Wealth of Nations* and extolled the glories of the division of labour. While it might take one man a day to make a single pin (or ten pins if he were skilled), he explained, ten men could produce 48,000 by each taking on a separate part of the work. (Today, Smith's observation is commemorated on the twenty-pound note.) As most manufacture became a good deal more complex, and more lucrative, than pins, the idea became embedded in industry. In Europe, Toyota makes its cars' engines, carpets, and instrument panels in the US, headlights and brakes in France, steering wheels in Turkey, airbags in the Czech Republic, wheels in Germany, suspension parts in Spain and windscreen wipers in Italy. The modern American automobile can contain components designed in the US, manufactured in Asia, and assembled on Native American reservations in Canada before returning to the US to be completed.[12] Such attenuated processes have multiple aims: to reduce costs, to use the most specialised labour, to provide employment and take advantage of tax breaks. Division of labour has become central to our concept of work: governments, for-profit, non-profit, service and commodity businesses all seek to use specialised talent to deliver faster, better, cheaper results. As Adam Smith argued, with greater specialisation comes greater efficiency and productivity.

But in an established corporation like BP, that meant that the cost-cutters didn't know much about safety. Why should they? It wasn't their department. They had – or claimed to have – very little insight into the consequences of mandated savings; that wasn't their job. Manzoni lacked refining experience and, according to his executive assistant, Lord Browne showed 'no passion, no curiosity, no interest' in safety.[13] In theory, there were plenty of other people to look after those details, but the company's internal inquiry shows a concatenation of poor communication between them all.

The division of labour isn't designed to keep corporations blind but that is often its effect. The people who manufacture cars aren't the people who repair them or service them. That means they don't see the problems inherent in their design unless a special effort is made to show it to them. Software engineers who write code aren't the same as the ones who fix bugs who also aren't the customer-service representatives you call when the program crashes your machine. Companies are now organised in ways that can facilitate departments becoming structurally blind to one another.

This was perfectly illustrated by America's Food and Drug Administration, where (before 2007) one vast bureaucracy was responsible for approving drugs – the Office of New Drugs – but an entirely different set of individuals – the Office of Drug Safety – was responsible for the safety of drugs once they were on the market. On one level, the separation seems to make sense; after all, if the approvals process worked, the Office of Drug Safety shouldn't have anything to do. That is why their funding was so different, with new drug approvals taking nearly 80 per cent of the budget.

But there were inherent problems in the structure. The smaller team, responsible for ongoing safety, had less money but was responsible for policing the entire market of drugs being consumed by millions of consumers. Moreover, its funding could be taken as a reasonable indicator of its organisational clout. To overturn an approved drug would always require a great deal of research and data, both of which took money. To cap it all, the safety team didn't even have final authority to withdraw a drug. All they could do was recommend withdrawal – to the very people who had approved the drug in the first place. Without money or clout, they needed to ask colleagues publicly to change their minds. No wonder they met denial and resistance. In effect, therefore, the monitoring of drugs that were approved in small-scale trials was abandoned once they were being taken by millions of patients, leaving the FDA effectively blind to the outcome of its own decisions.

In 2004, when the arthritis drug, Vioxx, was eventually shown to cause heart attacks and strokes, all of these structural issues came into sharp focus. Of course it didn't help that the pharmaceutical company responsible for the drug, Merck, struggled mightily to conceal concerns that the drug could cause heart attacks and strokes. But in this it seemed like the approvals team within the FDA were their allies, not their watchdog. The only reason the scale of the problem came to light was because Dr David Graham, associate director in the Office of Drug Safety, was able to collaborate with health company Kaiser Permanente on a three-year study of the arthritis drug. What he found suggested that many patients were at risk. When he later testified to Congress about how things had gone so wrong, he was at pains to describe the scale of the problem.

> Imagine that instead of a serious side-effect of a widely used prescription drug, we were talking about jetliners. (Please ignore the obvious difference in fatality rates between a heart attack and a plane crash, and focus on the larger analogy I'm trying to draw.) If there were an average of 150 to 200 people on an aircraft, this range of 88,000 to 138,000 would be the rough equivalent of 500 to 900 aircraft dropping from the sky. This translates to 2–4 aircraft every week, week in and week out, for the past 5 years.[14]

Of course, Graham was counting only American deaths. But the FDA carries such influence that American approval had spearheaded global acceptance, meaning Vioxx became one of the most prescribed drugs in history. Eighty million people around the world used the drug regularly, 400,000 of them in the UK, of which it is estimated that at least 2,000 died from taking the drug.[15]

But, despite evidence that Vioxx might be very unsafe for a very large number of patients, Graham's concerns found no support within the FDA.

> An email from the Director for the entire Office of New Drugs was revealing [he later testified]. He suggested that since FDA was 'not contemplating' a warning against the use of high-dose Vioxx, my conclusions should be changed.

Even more revealing, a mere 6 weeks before Merck pulled Vioxx from the market, CDER, OND and ODS management did not believe there was an outstanding safety concern with Vioxx. At the same time, 2–4 jumbo jetliners were dropping from the sky every week and no one else at FDA was concerned.

The same month that Dr Graham was encouraged to change his conclusions, the FDA approved Vioxx for children with rheumatoid arthritis. The following month, they called Dr Graham's study 'a scientific rumour'. But eight days later, Merck pulled the drug off the market.

In his testimony, Graham went to great lengths to explain that Vioxx was not unique. The problem wasn't just the drug – it was the FDA's structure, which seemed designed to ensure that problems could not, or would not, be seen. The vast power and funding of one division effectively masked the insights and recommendations of its lesser partner. It took an Act of Congress – the Food and Drug Administration Amendments Act (2007) – to change things.

Where you put information makes a difference to how visible it is. When, as in the case with Vioxx, important information resides in an under-funded department that doesn't have much power, the organisation becomes structurally blind. Similarly, if large amounts of money are parked in off–balance-sheet vehicles, special-purposes entities and offshore subsidiaries, getting a comprehensive overview of a business becomes impossible. When the banks began to teeter in 2008, one of the biggest problems they faced was that they simply did not know how much money – or debt – they had. The monolithic insurance giant, AIG, could not answer the simplest questions about their assets because so many of them had been buried in accounting complexity. At the time that Enron went bust, it later turned out that the company had far more money than they imagined – they just couldn't see it because it sat off the balance sheet. Goldman Sachs invented creative derivatives deals in order to help their client, the Greek Government, mask the true extent of their deficit – as though merely stashing the debt where it could not be seen would solve the problem. Ernst & Young, together with the solicitors Linklaters, were accused in 2010 of having figured out a way – known inside the bank as Repo 150 – to camouflage as much as $50 billion dollars of Lehman Brothers debt, thus rendering their client effectively blind to its own danger.[16] In the desire to boost their balance sheet, such manoeuvres wilfully blinded their organisations to their own vulnerabilities.

Structural blindness assumes a physical reality with the development of outsourcing. Corporations, eager to reduce fixed costs and overheads, suddenly realised that they didn't have to employ all the talent they needed. If they could buy it in, then they could eliminate swathes of management while retaining, or even increasing, negotiating power. The markets loved the idea because it looked as though huge areas of expense and exposure were eliminated from balance sheets permanently. Entrepreneurs leapt at the idea because it meant that, instead of working for dreary monolithic organisations, they could set up their own businesses and be masters of their own destiny in a competitive marketplace. At least that was the idea.

In reality, the disaggregation of work has made it harder than ever to connect all of the pieces; you need huge swathes of management to oversee outsourcing, competitive bidding, partnerships and contractors. What used to be departments are now outside firms but someone still needs to get them all to work well together. At least at the FDA the fight between the approvals people and the safety people was clearly, if painfully, visible. But, once you outsource or subcontract work, it loses its visibility.

When he came to investigate the *Challenger* space shuttle disaster, this is exactly what the great physicist and iconoclast Richard Feynman discovered. As an outsider, he had little concern for the hierarchies within NASA; in telling the story, he revels in his contempt for rank and deference. Focused as a cat on a rat as he chases down every conceivable source of information, truthfulness and insight, he delights in crashing through barriers and filling in gaps. He eventually, and triumphantly, figures out that a major cause of the disaster was the O-rings, which, in the extremely low temperatures to which they were subjected, must have cracked. But the O-rings, of course, weren't made by NASA. They were made by Morton Thiokol, an aerospace company that used plastic specially made by the Parker Seal Company. NASA was based at the Kennedy Space Center in Georgia but also at the Marshall Space Flight Center in Huntsville, Alabama, Morton Thiokol was based in Brigham, Utah, and Parker Seal in Lexington, Kentucky.

When the Morton Thiokol team became concerned about the low temperatures forecast for launch, they did their best to relay their concerns. But the engineers couldn't raise a red flag until they got support from their management. As subcontractors, they had little leverage; after all, NASA was their customer. Nevertheless, two meetings were called to address concerns. Given the geography, of course, these had to be conference calls and, given the number of people involved, not everyone could attend, or attend both calls. NASA was under political pressure to launch, Morton Thiokol was under commercial pressure and could never have had the power to stop the launch. In the inquiries which followed the disaster, the sheer difficulty in understanding what had happened aptly reflected the endemic nature of the problem: a director from Morton Thiokol had to turn up – uninvited – at one of Feynman's meetings in order to be able to share what he knew.[17]

More recently, SIGG, the Swiss makers of trendy aluminium

water bottles, discovered that outsourcing their manufacture didn't give them the control their high-end brand needed. SIGG's chic products had developed a substantial following from conscientious consumers worried about the bisphenol-A found in many hard plastics. BPA has been linked to diabetes, heart disease, premature puberty in girls and lower sperm counts in men. The claim that the SIGG bottles didn't pose this hazard was important to their consumers, who wanted a permanent water bottle to reduce waste (good for the environment) and one that was free of BPA (good for the drinker). But, in fact, SIGG did not manufacture the lining of their bottles; a third party did. And that third party did not tell SIGG what materials they were using.[18] When it transpired that there was, after all, some small amount of BPA in the liner, the company was publicly trashed by its customers and the CEO lost his job. The company had been manufacturing blind.

SIGG was making a simple product in Switzerland. There wasn't anything especially stressful, dangerous or complex about their business. In conditions of great ambiguity and danger, however, the difficulties inherent in the division of labour become pronounced and even fatal. In Iraq, the US military works with some 180,000 private military contractors – some building Pizza Huts, some bringing commercial supply-line expertise to the delivery of gas and ammunitions. With so many moving parts, each under separate management and under commercial pressures, dumb but tragic things happen. When Staff Sergeant Ryan Maseth, a decorated Green Beret, was electrocuted taking a shower, a subsequent investigation showed that the contractors concerned had been instructed to fix anything that was broken; nothing in their contract required that they uncover or fix potential hazards. The army wasn't sufficiently aware of its own electrical problems and the contractor never had its work inspected. They were both blind to each other.[19]

The same attenuated supply chain underlies Primark's business model. First lauded for its combination of high fashion and low cost – 'Primani' – most consumers turned a blind eye to how this financial miracle was achieved. But by subcontracting its clothing manufacture, the company could keep itself blind – with the result that it could then also deny all knowledge when children as young as nine were found sewing sequins on to clothes destined for Britain's high streets. Who was most blind – the consumers buying implausibly cheap clothes, the company selling them, or the Tirupur Exporters' Association, whose Executive Secretary Mr A. Sakhtivel claimed that the children were 'just helping their parents after school'? The sheer complexity of trading relationships obscured who did what for whom.[20]

That same confusion was reflected in the chaos, scapegoating and finger-pointing that immediately followed the explosion on BP's Deepwater Horizon oil rig. BP, of course, didn't make the rig; the Deepwater Horizon was built by Hyundai in Korea to a design from a Texas firm, R&B Falcon, which was bought by the Swiss operators, Transocean, who leased the rig to BP. Most of those killed weren't BP employees and therefore were not the responsibility of the British company. Once you outsource critical functions, you may be blind to how the work gets done. The cynical will conclude that that is precisely what outsourcing is for.

It's challenging to recognise that outsourcing has become so embedded in Western economies, that there are no areas in which it is not considered. We outsource our wars now, through private security firms, and much of our policing: in the US and the UK, the number of private guards is now more than twice the number of public police officers.[21] Current debates, over the outsourcing of clinical trials for new drugs to India, China and other cheap labour markets, focus entirely on whether or not ethnic differences will generate different data. But those debates overlook the far bigger issue, which is about the imbalance of power, between rich Western pharmaceutical companies, and poorly paid, unprotected volunteers half a world away. When a very rich Western firm employs a far less wealthy foreign firm to do clinical trials, what are the pressures upon that dependent business to deliver good results? And how convenient is it to the larger company to take those 'good' results at face value? Disregarding these inequalities of power is a form of blindness in itself.

Everyone who's ever worked in an organisation knows how intensely difficult it can be to prevent silos, to find people who are intellectually able and politically prepared to connect the dots. It takes effort, commitment and mistakes to overcome the sheer difficulty people have working with each other, negotiating the complex interface between their personal ambitions and organisational goals. But the silos, which should be a metaphor for disconnection, take on a substantial reality when we are talking about separate institutions – be they companies or organisations – with different mandates, goals, power bases and agendas. When John Snow, former US Secretary of State of the Treasury between 2003 and 2006, testified before Congress on the role of financial regulators in the 2008 financial crisis, he explained how part of the problem was that he couldn't even see the problem.

> Nowhere in our financial regulatory system is there anyone with full accountability and full 360-degree view on risk and leverage. I remember in 2005, sensing that there were developments in the debt markets, the sub-prime and the mortgage markets that needed to be better understood. I took what was deemed to be a fairly extraordinary step and called in all of the substantive regulators of the mortgage market. I asked them to give their considered views on

whether or not undue risk was being created. We didn't yet have a housing crisis. We didn't yet have a sub-prime crisis. But I wanted to get their view. But no one of them had that view. They had pieces of the puzzle. It's like the blind man and the elephant. They are all touching a piece of it, but they don't know what the big picture is.[22]

Nor was financial regulation within the City of London any better. With the FSA responsible for banks, the Bank of England responsible for monetary policy and the government responsible for economic policy, and all of them warring with each other for power and influence, any one of them could take the part of the blind man in Snow's elegant metaphor.

If he had difficulty peering through a structural morass of regulation, how much more difficult was the challenge of gaining a holistic view of the market itself? The division of labour, institutionalised into different organisations, had taken the once simplistic task of buying a home and blown it into so many different transactions that, apparently, no one could put the pieces together any more. That was the conclusion the London School of Economics drew when asked by the Queen why no one saw the banking crisis coming. 'The difficulty was seeing the risk to the system as a whole rather than to any specific financial instrument or loan. Risk calculations were most often confined to slices of financial activity, using some of the best mathematical minds in our country and abroad. But they frequently lost sight of the bigger picture.'

The mortgage market, comprised of buyers, brokers, primary and secondary funders and securitising banks, had spectacularly become the ultimate expression of Smith's division of labour: each institution doing what it was best at, generating products at a faster rate than any individual was capable of, but with a level of complexity no one could understand any more. Most pernicious of all, financiers came to see banking as its own universe, separate and distinct from the rest of society, so siloed by its wealth, power and intellectual abstractions that they could not even perceive public outrage when the banking failure destroyed jobs, businesses, and funding for all those activities – education, health, the arts – that knit society together. Boasting, or joking, as Goldman Sachs chairman Lloyd Blankfein did, that his bank was doing 'God's work' just articulated his blindness.

We don't see things that are too far away, that are too distant from our own experience, too separate from our own concerns, or simply too complicated to assemble. But we also don't see things that are too far away in time. The past recedes from view unless we find ways to memorialise it and keep it within our lines of sight. In Libby, Montana, Gayla Benefield and Gary Svenson used to make wooden crosses every year, each one painted with the name of a victim of asbestosis. Some in the town complained; they didn't want their loved ones' names used in a campaign. So Gary has built a pergola down by the river and intends to raise money by selling small medallions, each engraved with the name of one of those lost to the dust of the vermiculite plant. That way, he says, people can choose to have their kin memorialised or not. He wants the town to remember, and visitors to the town to learn, what happened there. But already another, bigger, pergola has been set up next to his, as though to make sure his doesn't get all the attention.

In Texas City, one man carries with him a searing memory of the explosion. Dave Senko supervised the contractors who were killed but he was at another site on the day of the accident. Today, his hands shake as he talks about the friends he lost. Many of them had wanted to quit the project, he says, because they didn't feel safe working at the site. But Senko had persuaded them to stay. He misses these men and carries them on his conscience. BP, he told me, wouldn't allow a memorial to them on the site; they weren't BP employees. So he waged a one-man campaign to get a memorial at the contracting firm's offices. They eventually gave in.

'What is on the memorial?' I asked him.

He was too upset to speak. I waited. Silence. Then he handed me his phone; on it was a picture of a small stone slab. All it says is: 'March 23, 2005'. No names. No description. After he'd pestered his company a little more, Dave was able to add a light and a small pear tree. He still goes there some evenings to check it's still there and that the light still works. One time, the security guard came over and asked him to move. He was outraged and said they could call the police if they wanted to. He wasn't moving.

'Remembering is important,' he said. 'It matters. If you can't see these things, they'll just keep happening.'

Why do we build institutions and corporations so large and so complex that we can't see how they work? In part, it's because we can. Human hubris makes us believe that if we can imagine something, we can build it; and if we can build it, we can understand it. We are so delighted with our own ingenuity and intelligence and it gives us a sense of mastery and power. But the power is problematic as it takes us further and further from the reality of what we have built. Like Daedalus, we build labyrinths of such cunning complexity that we cannot find our own way out. And we are blind to the blindness these complex structures necessarily confer. So we forget all about it.

10. DE-MORALISING WORK

History and ideas enjoy a strange relationship. Sometimes they seem to develop in lockstep, like Rousseau and the coming of the French Revolution. At other times, ideas emerge as a critique of prevailing social moods, as when the Romantic idealisation of sentiment grew out of the Industrial Revolution. That contentious relationship is analogous to what happened at the turn of the last century when so much public energy suddenly centred on money. As the Western world experienced a financial bonanza, with global markets reaching new highs daily and consumers avid for each new avenue of expenditure, along came a bunch of psychologists and economists with a challenging message: money doesn't make people happy.

What? In the middle of a consumer explosion, when £5,000 handbags flew out of stores and people bought homes whose garages were larger than their former houses had been, how could it be that money didn't make us happy? But that's what positive psychologists like Martin Seligman and economists like Richard Layard were saying. And to prove it, they could show that, despite increases in GDP, overall life satisfaction hadn't gone up. And the richest countries weren't the happiest.

The data, and its corollaries, caused a big stir, as they should have. After all, if GDP growth didn't make people happy, why were all Western economies pursuing it so ferociously? Wasn't happiness itself a more meaningful goal? If it was, then how would it be measured – and, if money couldn't increase it, what would? At that point, a lot of thinking stalled. Hmmm. If money wasn't going to make people happier, how could a government, or political movement, measure success?

In companies, the money/happiness debate was a bit of a poser, too. Some CEOs thought they saw a light at the end of the tunnel: did this mean they didn't have to pay their employees so much? Not surprisingly, nobody was volunteering to take pay cuts on the grounds that they thought it would make them feel better. Did it mean that sharcholders wouldn't be so insistent on growth or dividends? If there were any shareholders who thought they would be happier with less, they were a consistently silent minority – with plenty of stocks to choose from.

The reason the argument started to peter out was simple. Just because money can't make people happy doesn't mean that we aren't motivated by it. We are. In a 1953 experiment, patients were asked to hang on horizontal bars for as long as they could; most could take it for about 45 seconds. When subjected to the power of suggestion and even, in some cases, hypnosis, they could stretch to about 75 seconds. But when offered a five-dollar bill (which today would be worth about £20) the patients managed to hang from the bars for 110 seconds. Anything that allows you to increase your performance by 150 per cent is pretty motivating.[1]

Nor was that some weird anomaly of 1950s America. More recent studies have shown that the mere idea of money can make people persevere more and work longer.[2] Another study showed that money changes what we remember. In that experiment, volunteers were show a selection of images, each accompanied by a price. Remembering one picture was worth five dollars; remembering another was worth merely ten cents. Testing their subjects the next day, they found that their participants were far more

likely to remember the high-price scenes.[3] Much of this motivation may not even be conscious; humans tend to adapt the
degree of effort they expend according to the magnitude of
reward they expect.[4]

Serious students of motivation like Daniel Pink argue that
money may make us work harder but it doesn't make us work
smarter. Citing experiments conducted by Dan Ariely, he argues
that money inhibits creativity and problem-solving, the kind of
higher-order thinking on which developed economies depend.[5]
The problem is that knowing money doesn't make us smarter may
not stop us wanting it.

We want money for a very good reason: it makes us feel better.
A fascinating series of experiments by a team of Chinese and
American researchers put volunteers through their paces in a
Cyberball game in which they were slowly but surely socially
excluded, with the result that they registered distress. But then,
in their distressed condition, they were made to count money
and their mood lifted. As a control, some were asked to count
paper, just to ensure that it wasn't the repetitive task of counting
that had the ameliorative effect. Paper, it turned out, wasn't an
analgesic, but money was. Simply counting the money made
people feel stronger.

What held true for psychic pain turned out to be true for
physical pain also. Students submerged their hands in very hot
water: 43°C (109.4°F) for ninety seconds, 50°C (122°F) for
thirty seconds and then again 43°C for a minute. The pain they
experienced was lower after counting money than after counting paper. And while it might be tempting to dismiss the results
as indicative of loan-depleted American students obsessed with
cash, the students who volunteered for the experiment were
Chinese, rewarded by nothing more than course credits for their
participation.[6]

Money does influence us and it does make us feel better. That's why companies pay overtime and bonuses. It may not, in and of itself, make us absolutely happy – but, just like cigarettes and chocolate, our wants are not confined to what's good for us. The pleasure of money is often short-lived of course. Because there are always newer, bigger, flashier, sweeter products to consume, the things we buy with money never satisfy as fully as they promise. Psychologists call this the hedonic treadmill: the more we consume, the more we want. But we stay on the treadmill, hooked on the pleasures that, at least initially, make us feel so good.

What all this has shown is that money may be the richest area ever discovered for the study of unintended consequences. From which it should follow, but rarely does, that managers and compensation committees need to be tremendously thoughtful when deciding how to apply such a powerful, even irrational, motivator. Because money has a more complex influence on people than just making them work longer.

'Money certainly changes the way you think,' says David Ring. He's an internationally renowned orthopaedic surgeon at one of the top hospitals in the United States. Ring's tall, handsome and, for the most part, silent – except when he starts talking about his work, which is when he really comes alive. He loves what he does, but doesn't love the role that money plays in medicine.

'Doctors who own stakes in testing labs order more tests; I've experienced that, first hand. Colleagues working in surgical centres that they own – they take the money, the government pays the facility fee and they get some of that money. Now if you're doing that kind of case, the way to make money out of that is to spend less. So if you're working at your own surgical centre, you will treat a fracture with pins. Then the same doctors will go to treat the same kind of case but this time they're in a hospital, so they'll use an expensive plate. They will tell you that with a straight face. They bypass questionable ethics. Some of it is conscious and some of it I'm sure they just don't see.'

Could that mean, I asked him, that money might influence a diagnosis?

'Change diagnosis? I think so. The minute you see dollar signs in your patient's eyes, it changes how you think. You have to learn not to look at their insurance – get as far down the diagnostic path as you can before you know their income. It's impossible not to be swayed by the profit motive. I'm an academician and devoted to things that don't earn money but I watch people come in on my path and gradually get off of it. First, they just want to do well in their practice, just to be good surgeons. After a few years, they start to realise that what they do determines how much money they make and they start to learn a new game. The old game was: diagnose well, communicate well, do the surgery well. The new game becomes: make money. They don't really see the game change, they're blind to it. But it changes.

'Arthroscopy for arthritis, that's a classic example. You definitely don't cure osteoarthritis with arthroscopy. There was one brave guy in a Veterans Administration hospital in Texas who did a pilot study comparing knee arthroscopy with washing the knee and with cleaning the knee out. All three treatments were equally effective! But there's a lot of money in arthroscopy. So the response of American orthopaedic surgeons was very defensive. It is a wilful blindness – you bypass curiosity and scientific knowledge and concern for your patient and go straight for profit motive and preserve your position.'

Ring is a vocal critic of the role that money plays in medicine. But that doesn't mean that he feels himself to be immune to its influence.

'You could say that I'm really high-minded because I'll fly to Sheffield to teach or do research in my free time – but I still get caught up. You can see the temptation, especially in Massa-chusetts where there is only one good payer – workers' comp. It is devilishly good. You can make so much out of one case. So I can make a lot of money – ten times what I can make from Medicare or an HMO [health maintenance organisation]. It is so tempting; with just a few workers' comp patients, you've made your year's income in a month. If this is the going rate, why should I be the sucker?'[7]

It would be easy enough to dismiss Ring's insights as merely indicative of the American medical system which, notwith-standing Obama's reforms, signally lacks the sense of social purpose and service that characterise the NHS at its best. But you don't have to spend very long talking to British doctors before one theme becomes very clear: one reason the NHS hierarchy is so powerful is because consultants have the power (or influence) to allocate private work, and time for private practice. Aspiring doctors don't want to rock the boat because that's one way to ensure such lucrative work never comes your way. The transfor-mation of GPs' surgeries into small (or not so small) businesses has, similarly, threatened to drain some of the social impulse out of the service. At the same time, cosmetic surgeons, weight-loss nutritionists, homeopaths and teeth-whitening dentists have embraced a market outlook with a fervour Ring might find daunting.

What is striking about Ring's perspective is not just that he's so forthright but that, unlike most of us, he is highly conscious of the influence that money has on him, as well as on his col-leagues. Money is not making these doctors less motivated; they're as motivated as ever – maybe even more so. What money changes is their behaviour.

In a series of experiments carried out in 2007, participants got to play Monopoly (or were forced to, depending on your view of the game). Some came away with £3,000 of play money, some with £125 and some with none. They were then taken across the lab, ostensibly to another room for another experiment. But on their way, they encountered a woman who spilled a box of pencils. The volunteers who had made the most money from the Monopoly game turned out to be the least helpful, picking up the fewest number of pencils. In another version of the experiment, volunteers encountered a colleague who seemed to be highly confused about a task. The participants who were not thinking about money spent 120 per cent more time helping their colleague than those who had money on their minds.[8]

Then the researchers wondered whether they were just asking for a form of social interaction of a kind that the money-primed participants weren't very good at. So they designed an opportunity to do something that was easy and money-related: donate to the University Student Fund. But the participants who had been reminded of money donated only 39 per cent of their payment (on average) to the Student Fund. Their peers, who were not so conscious of money, donated 67 per cent.

The volunteers who had money uppermost in their minds weren't entirely without values however. When they were given difficult or impossible tasks to perform, they worked 48 per cent longer before asking for any help. They persevered – but they persevered alone. What the researchers concluded was that, while money was great at motivating individual effort, it carried with it significant negative social side-effects. In the conflict that we all experience – between our interest in ourselves and our concern for others – money appears to motivate only our interest in ourselves, making us selfish and self-centred.

A further set of experiments confirmed this insight. When reminded of money – by screensavers, posters or watercolours – participants put greater physical distance between themselves and others. Given the choice, they were also more likely to want to work alone and to prefer solo leisure activities. Small reminders of money produced large changes in behaviour, making people less social, less connected to others. They were more motivated than ever, but more isolated, less helpful and less concerned for their fellow man.[9] They became socially disengaged. Over time, the researchers concluded, the mere presence of money elicits a market-pricing orientation toward the world. Money makes people feel self-sufficient, which also means they don't need or care about others; it's each man for himself.

The most striking live demonstration of this phenomenon in recent years has been Guy Hands, a former executive at Goldman Sachs. Today, he heads up his private-equity firm Terra Firma, best known for its acquisition of the music business EMI. Hands is demonstrably successful and has made enough money to be very comfortable. Nevertheless, in his desire to preserve his assets and avoid paying tax, Hands has left the UK, which means that he never visits his school-age children, who remain in England with their mother. Neither has he visited his mother and father there. 'I do not visit my parents in the United Kingdom and would not do so except in an emergency,' he said.[10]

Few of us are likely to worry about tax to the degree that Guy Hands does, but that doesn't mean we are immune to the impact of money on our motivation. Performance-related pay, performance bonuses and all kinds of incentive plans are designed to elicit harder work and perseverance from the workforce. But the unintended social consequences of such plans are far from straightforward.

'Every branch office had its own incentive scheme,' Paul Moore told me. Between 2002 and 2005, Moore was head of Group Regulatory Risk at HBOS, the largest mortgage lender in the UK. 'I remember one in particular: every Saturday, once the office closed for the day, the sales staff would all get together. And the sales advisers who'd beaten their targets, they got cash. But if you'd failed to beat your target, you were given a cabbage. Cash or cabbage, in public, every Saturday.'

The ritual humiliation of employees was just one aspect of the company culture that alarmed Moore. To him, it signified that money had obliterated all other motives within HBOS, even concern for employees' respect for each other, and for their customers.

'When we were doing a review,' Moore said, 'one woman in Scunthorpe told me: "We hit our targets but we have never hit our sales targets ethically." What she meant by that was that the pressure to hit targets was so great that they were all anybody thought about. So there was a culture of bullying in HBOS, focused on sales numbers. I don't think people had started that way; it's what working for the company turned them into. The management just didn't think carefully enough: if you demand a sales increase of ten per cent, and then only allow a cost increase of three per cent, then you are going to get some highly improper sales and some very anti-social behaviour. And that's what happened.'

Moore's job was to look for all aspects within a company's processes and procedures, as well as within its balance sheet, that exposed it to risks. That meant, inevitably, spending a great deal of time poring over balance sheets. But, for Moore, the greatest exposure didn't lie in the numbers. It lay in the people, the culture and their incentives. What he came to see within the firm was that the management – the CEO and his executive teams – were so driven by earnings (and their own compensation, which derived from earnings) that they couldn't, and wouldn't, see the impact that the company's culture had on individual morality or the wider society that the company served.

When he shared his insights with the CEO, Moore was fired. He was later vindicated when, in September 2008, the bank collapsed. Testifying to the parliamentary select committee six months later, his rage was still palpable.

Anyone whose eyes were not blinded by money, power and pride, who really looked carefully, knew there was something wrong: that economic growth based almost solely on excessive consumer spending, which was based on excessive consumer credit, which was based on massively increasing property prices which were caused by the very same excessively easy credit could only ultimately lead to disaster. But sadly, no-one wanted or felt able to speak up for fear of stepping out of line with the rest of the lemmings who were busy organizing themselves to run over the edge of the cliff behind the pied piper CEOs and executive teams that were all being paid so much to play that tune and take them in that direction.[11]

A subsequent survey of 563 risk managers undertaken by Moore, in conjunction with Cranfield School of Management, cited culture and remuneration practices as two of the chief causes of the banking failure. These most hard-nosed and numerate of analysts didn't think regulation or economic models were chiefly at fault, and they were entirely dismissive of the idea that banks had failed due to 'global circumstances beyond anyone's control'.[12] What went wrong, they thought, was the culture: people's attitudes to money. Pursuit of profits had effectively displaced concern for people. 'A constitution for knaves may produce knaves' is how one economist described what happens when money becomes the chief motivator.[13]

Of course we all want to earn a living but the moral fading that accompanies financial incentives may be more profound than anyone is quite willing to acknowledge. When companies overpay, as firms like Enron and many banks routinely did, in effect they are saying: Look at the money, don't look at anything else. And employees often absorb exactly that message. 'I reckon that for the first ten years, all I'll focus on is the money,' one trainee

banker told me. 'Then I'll start to think about my family.' Even
before he had joined his firm, he expected to have to leave all
other considerations behind – and was prepared to do so. And I
have met many men and women just like him.

The trade-off between social and financial motivations and
the sense that one works against the other is intuitively understood even if it isn't scientifically demonstrable. Surely this is
what lies behind the public outrage surrounding bankers'
bonuses. It is not just envy, or fury at the increasing gap
between rich and poor, but an implicit understanding that the
more money an individual earns, the less engaged he, or she,
becomes in the general welfare of the nation. If I earn ten million pounds a year, I need not concern myself with the
condition of NHS hospitals or my local school, the mental-
health issues confronted by young isolated mothers or the lack
of employment available to young people in rural communities
because I can buy my way out of any of these predicaments.
Given enough money, I can be an island. I might even come to
believe that there is no such thing as society because I don't feel
dependent on society to get what I want. The overpaid may not
feel it but one consequence of their compensation is that they
become disengaged from the rest of us. It's an interesting
thought that high rates of pay might become indicators of low
levels of social engagement.

One of the first people to identify the strange and often unintended consequences of money was the social scientist, Richard
Titmuss. Born in 1907 to a Bedfordshire farmer, his family
moved to London where, at the age of fourteen, Titmuss went
to work in his father's transport business. When his father died a
few years later, he moved to an insurance firm; now the family's
major breadwinner, a serious salary and a permanent position
were crucial. Working in insurance taught Titmuss a great deal,
about how people lived, moved, worked or lost their jobs. He

had boundless energy and deep curiosity about how the world worked. Why did people behave as they did? Why was there so much inequality?

Self-taught and highly motivated, Titmuss eventually left the dusty world of insurance to work on social policy; by the time the Second World War was over, he was well known and highly regarded. Despite never having attended a university, Titmuss became Professor in Social Administration at the London School of Economics. He was, demonstrably, a man who knew a lot about motivation.

Much of Titmuss's academic work informed the post-war development of the welfare state and the creation of the National Health Service. To all intents and purposes, he was a good, old-fashioned policy wonk: embroiled in the minutiae of social legislation and politics, a man who never really lost his passion for statistics. And then, three years before he died, he published a book that blew up the world of economics. *The Gift Relationship* argued that money didn't always motivate people; in fact, paying people could undermine their moral motivation. Using the example of blood donation, Titmuss showed that paying donors made them less willing, not more willing, to donate blood and it increased chances that the blood supply would be contaminated when donors were paid. The book caused a sensation worldwide because it dared to challenge the two fundamental tenets of modern economics: first, that individuals make rational economic decisions; and second, that individuals are motivated only by self-interest. If people did less when offered more – what could that mean for economics?

Titmuss died before he could follow up his argument, but his book, and the questions he posed, continued to infiltrate and disrupt economic thinking. The idea that we make economic decisions rationally came under a lot of fire, with an army of behavioural economists demonstrating that biases and cognitive shortcuts interfere with our reasoned decision-making. And evidence mounted that money and behaviour might have a more complicated relationship than was allowed for in the popular economic models of the time.

One of the most interesting studies came out of Switzerland, where two economists wanted to test their theory (derived from Titmuss's work) that, far from enhancing our motivation, money might destroy it.[14] In 1993, they visited two communities in central Switzerland designated as potential sites for nuclear waste storage, and asked 305 residents whether they would be willing for the storage facility to be located in their neighbourhood. More than half of their respondents (50.8 per cent) said that, if asked, they would vote in favour of having the facility in their community. This wasn't because they were enthusiastic about nuclear waste: nearly 40 per cent believed there was a chance of a serious accident and nearly 80 per cent believed that many local residents would suffer long-term effects from it. But they thought, if the storage facility was necessary, it might as well be in their area. In other words, their sense of a common, social good overcame their individual reservations.

What was most interesting, however, was what happened when the two economists offered to pay residents to house the nuclear waste store. The amount offered wasn't trivial: between $2,175 and $6,525 per individual per year – near or above the community's median monthly income. But now the level of acceptance *halved*. The two economists tried raising the amount of compensation offered to see if that could influence their respondents. Only *one* person who declined the first offer was prepared to accept anything higher and only 4.9 per cent said that the amount of the compensation mattered. You might have thought that, with two reasons to support the project, commitment would be higher. After all, now the Swiss residents could do good *and* make money. But that isn't the way it worked. Just as in the lab experiments, the mere prospect of money reduced people's sense of connectedness to the community.

Nor was this some weird Swiss peculiarity: an experiment in Nevada reported similar findings: pay diminished the respondents' sense of commitment to one another. Subsequent studies reinforced these findings.[15] When there was no penalty for lateness when collecting their children from a childcare centre, parents were rarely late. But once they were fined for being late, the possibility of losing money didn't make them more punctual – it made them less so. Nor could their previous punctuality be revived; when penalties were abandoned, parents still didn't care as much about being on time. What had started as a social relationship had been reduced irrevocably once money was introduced.

What these group studies showed was just what the lab experiments with individuals had gleaned: money blinds us to our social relationships, creating a sense of self-sufficiency that discourages co-operation and mutual support.

Nobody yet quite understands why money works the way that it does. Economists have speculated that motivation may work in ways similar to cognitive load.[16] Just as there is a hard limit to how much we can focus on at one moment, perhaps we can be motivated by only one perspective at a time. When we care about people, we care less about money, and when we care about money, we care less about people. Our moral capacity may be limited in just the same way that our cognitive capacity is.

We're at the raw edge of brain science here. A number of fMRI experiments have attempted to understand what happens when the brain makes a moral choice. Some have looked at the brain as it decides between two conflicting options; others have tried to see the difference between a utilitarian decision (do I take the bus or the train?) and a moral decision (should I lie?).[17] The findings are unclear. Certainly moral choices occupy a great deal of brain capacity, and they seem to employ autobiographical memories (which implies empathy) and social awareness. But no one knows how to trace motivation, at least not yet. It seems to sit on the cusp between brain and mind in a relationship that is endlessly fascinating but still obscure.

Empirically, however, we do know that one incentive – money – seems to crowd out our more social motivations. Since the mere presence of money evokes a market-pricing orientation, people become commodities and every commodity has a price. That is one reason why the use of money to enforce social behaviours is, and feels, so inappropriate and doomed. The idea that you can keep couples together by offering them tax incentives is, in effect, to use an anti-social tool to enforce pro-social behaviour. Proposals to engage parents in their children's school conduct by issuing fines for non-attendance of parent–teacher meetings follow the same pattern. You can't commoditise relationships and then expect people to care more; it's like trying to accelerate by pumping the brakes.

Knowing that economic incentives diminish our concern for others, we ought to deploy them with tremendous delicacy. But most firms don't. Instead, they're used like sledgehammers in the delicate china shop of human motivations. When economic incentives are over-weighted, they send a signal that it is money, and money alone, that matters. Financial incentives that appeal to self-interest may fail in ways companies don't expect because they undermine the moral values that you need people to bring with them to work. As David Ring said, money changes the way you think – and it changes the way you think about everything. But most companies remain blind to how profoundly, and pervasively, this impacts the way that people do their jobs.

The social disengagement induced by money would explain why, when senior managers at Countrywide would gather to look at the company three years out, they could have such extraordinary discussions.

'A lot of us on the operations side and risk-management side would have meetings which led to a discussion of sub-prime mortgages,' Catherine Clark recalled. 'The sales people got such high commissions, they wouldn't stop. We kept asking: what happens in three years' time? And the only answer we ever got came from the guy in charge of all the back-office servicing: he said the technology infrastructure would not keep up with all the foreclosures.'

What is so memorable about the scene Clark paints is that there aren't any real people in it. There are just sales – and a looming IT problem. Nobody can see that the IT problem represents thousands of families losing their homes. By the same token, when we learn how many investors identified the looming failure of the banking industry, what's remarkable is not that these bright individuals had such foresight – but that their only thought was to cash in on it.[18]

At a time when BP was so focused on cost-cutting, mergers and acquisitions, it's perhaps not surprising that market thinking predominated. In 2002, the company was on a very aggressive growth path, about to deliver one of the strongest financial performances in its history. That's when members of the Health and Safety Team got together to run a course. Part of the training involved an analysis of the decision whether to place contractors at Texas City in temporary trailers, permanent trailers or permanent buildings. But that isn't how they chose to think about the cost-benefit analysis. Instead, a PowerPoint presentation shows an analogy with the Three Little Pigs. Each trailer option is designated a straw house, stick house or brick house – with, for good measure, a fourth option which is a blast-resistant house. This is BP's cost-benefit analysis of the three little pigs:

Frequency: the big bad wolf blows with a frequency of once per piggy lifetime.

Consequence: if the wolf blows down the house, the piggy is gobbled.

Maximum justifiable spend (MJS): a piggy considers it's worth $1,000 to save its bacon.

1.0 piggy lifetime × $1,000/piggy life = $1,000

Which type house should the piggy build?[19]

In making their decision about what kind of trailer to build, the BP executives had to calculate the value of a life ($1,000), the number of people in a trailer, the cost of a trailer and the likelihood of a fatal accident in which a 'piggy' might be killed, or 'gobbled'. You have to ask how this analogy helped them towards a moral decision. I often ask how BP employees responded to this presentation. I hope somebody was appalled but I can imagine a fair amount of laughter as the metaphor was teased out. It isn't clear from the presentation whether this was a training exercise, a decision process or both. What is clear is that human beings weren't under consideration. The Texas City contractors were animals, with a market value. And they were, ultimately, allowed to work and die in houses of straw.

It would be wrong to say that BP is the only company in the world that thinks this way. Many have been shown to: Ford, when it calculated the costs of reinforcing the Pinto's rear end, as compared to the cost of lost lives; A.H. Robins when it chose not to recall the contraceptive Dalkon Shield; W.R. Grace when it chose bankruptcy as a means of shaking off the dust of Libby, Montana. And when the Archbishop of Dublin, Kevin McNamara, took out insurance against claims resulting from priests abusing children, what was he doing but placing market concerns over social ones? He could have removed accused priests from their ministries and tried to get them help, he might have launched a thorough investigation, imposed a child-protection policy or alerted other bishops – but he turned a blind eye to people and focused instead on protecting the Church's assets. In treating people as less important than things, work becomes both demoralised and demoralising and we become blind to the moral content of our decisions.

Money and wilful blindness make us act in ways incompatible with what we believe our ethics to be, and often even with our own self-interest. Driven by our desire to see ourselves as good, we value money because it appears to be the external proof that we are good – and much of society reads it just the same way. So the problem with money isn't fundamentally about greed, although it can be comforting to think so. The problem with money is that we live in societies in which mutual support and co-operation is essential, but money erodes the relationships we need to lead productive, fulfilling and genuinely happy lives. When money becomes the dominant motivator, it doesn't co-operate with, or amplify, our relationships; it disengages us from them. The further removed we become from our neighbours, the more siloed in our self-sufficiency, the easier it is to treat people as things, to turn a blind eye to the human costs of toxic cultures and to make immoral decisions.

This isn't caused by money alone. All the other organisational forces of wilful blindness – obedience, conformity, bystander effects, distance and division of labour – combine to obscure the moral, human face of work. Money keeps us very busy, often too busy, to see clearly and work thoughtfully. It keeps us silent too, fearful lest debate or criticism jeopardise salaries. Money re-inforces and often appears to reward those core, self-identifying beliefs that blind us to alternatives and to argument. You could say that if we are just obeying orders, fitting in, diffusing responsibility for people who are a long way away and, anyway, maybe not our concern at all – then money is the final incentive to keep looking away. The fact that money tends to be addictive – the more we have, the more we feel we need – merely ensures that the cycle is rewarded and perpetuated. To paraphrase Burke, all that evil needs to flourish is for good people to see nothing – and get paid for it.

No one visiting Stanford University could fail to be impressed by its sheer scale or its wealth. Over twelve square miles, it's ten times larger than Vatican City and the vast avenues of palms leading to fountains and Spanish courtyards are reminiscent more of Renaissance papal power play than 21st-century cutting-edge research. Such lavish public buildings feel brash in their confidence, but their rooms harbour perpetrators of doubt and scepticism. At the heart of the campus, ensconced in an unremarkable lino-floored, booklined room, sits Albert 'Al' Bandura. In many respects, Bandura is the grand old man of psychology: its most cited living author, the father of social-learning theory and one of the first people to argue that children's behaviour derived not just from reward and punishment but from what they observed around them. That this seems such an obvious thought to us nowadays is testimony to how profound Bandura's impact has been on our thinking. The very phrase 'role model' would scarcely exist without him.

Much of Bandura's work has so seeped into public consciousness that we are barely aware that it is there, and his work has attracted scores of awards, honours and distinctions. But today, at the age of eighty-five, this hasn't stopped him working, nor has it rendered him complacent. For all his eminence, he's an engaging and accessible man whose mild manner belies a tenacious mind. And one of the issues he has wrestled with for years is the process by which individuals lose sight of morality in their need to preserve their sense of self-worth.

'People are highly driven to do things that build self-worth; you can't transgress and think of yourself as bad. You need to protect your sense of yourself as good. And so people transform harmful practices into worthy ones, by coming up with social justification, by distancing themselves with euphemisms, by ignoring the long-term consequences of their actions.'[20]

One of the most prominent ways in which people justify their harmful practices is by using arguments about money to obscure moral and social issues. Because we can't and won't acknowledge that some of our choices are socially and morally harmful, we distance ourselves from them by claiming they're necessary for wealth creation. Nowhere is this more dangerous, he argues, than in our attitudes to the environment and population growth. The easiest way for those who resist calls to curb population growth, and who oppose environmental controls, is to represent themselves as the good guys because they just want to make everyone better-off.

'To defend their positions, they can't say "Sure, we're the bad guys and we want to rape and pillage the planet",' Bandura told me. 'They have to vindicate harmful practices that take such a heavy toll on the environment and the quality of human life – they have to make out that what's harmful is, in fact, good. And one way they do that is to use the notion of nature as, in fact, an economic commodity. So they see nature in terms of its market value rather than its inherent value.'

That's why, Bandura argues, those who claim to love nature can also support, for example, drilling for oil in Alaska. They can't see themselves as destroyers, so they position themselves as the rational liberators of natural wealth. In this vein, Bandura quotes Newt Gingrich: 'To get the best ecosystem for our buck, we should use decentralised and entrepreneurial strategies.'[21] Similarly, when China signed a multi-billion-dollar deal with the Indonesian Government to clearcut four million acres of forest, in order to replace it with palm-oil plantations, a clan elder could not conceive of himself as doing the wrong thing. As he put it succinctly, 'Wood is gold.' It is, says Bandura, the economic justification that makes the environmentally damaging decision possible. Seeing nature as just a source of money blinds such decision-makers to the moral consequences of their decisions.

Bandura has spent a lifetime dissecting the moral disengagement required for the perpetration of criminal and inhuman acts, a journey that has taken him from the tobacco industry, the gun lobby, the television business to the multiple industries implicated in environmental degradation. He has a deep understanding of the forces at work which encourage employees to be blind to their collusion in these processes. But nothing enrages him more than the economic justifications used to defend continued population growth.

'I went to a conference in Germany,' Bandura recalled, 'where a young African woman spoke about the tremendous difference that birth control and health education had had on her community. The fact that she and her peers now had control over the number of children that they conceived and raised had transformed their lives. And she spoke of this very eloquently. And there, in that audience of well-heeled Europeans, rich Westerners, *she was booed!*'

When he recovered from his shock, Bandura analysed what was going on in the minds of the audience. What drove them, he reasoned, was their recognition that Western birth rates won't pay for the pension requirements of the elderly; if the West doesn't produce more children, it can't produce the wealth needed to look after parents when they retire. Therefore, even though consumption and environmental degradation are clearly linked, the needs of the market trump the needs of the planet.

Nor was this a purely Western phenomenon. The need for money effectively positions infants as money-making machines.

In some countries [Bandura writes], the pressure on women to boost their childbearing includes punitive threats as well. The former prime minister of Japan, Yoshiro Mori, suggested that women who bore no children should be barred from receiving pensions, saying 'It is truly strange to say we have to use tax money to take care of women who don't even give birth once, who grow old living their lives selfishly and singing the praises of freedom.' In this campaign for more babies, childbearing is reduced to a means for economic growth.[22]

In this mindset, children are nothing more than money–makers in the eyes of politicians merely crunching the numbers, blind to the moral, environmental or humanitarian consequences of their policies. Market thinking has obliterated moral thinking on a grand scale.

So persuasive (and pervasive) has the economic argument in favour of population growth become, says Bandura, that all of the major NGOs have had to stand aside from it. Fear of alienating donors, criticism from the progressive left and disparagement by conservative vested interests claiming that overpopulation is a 'myth' served as further incentives to cast off the rising global population as a factor in environmental degradation. Population growth vanished from the agendas of mainstream environmental organisations that previously regarded escalating numbers as a major environmental threat. Greenpeace announced that population 'is not an issue for us'. Friends of the Earth declared that 'it is unhelpful to enter into a debate about numbers'. The fear of losing money disabled those very organisations best placed to understand the ultimate consequences of thinking only about money.

What money does, Bandura argues, is allow us to disengage from the moral and social effects of our decisions. As long as we can frame everything as an economic argument, we don't have to confront the social or moral consequences of our decisions. That economics has become such a dominant, if not the prevalent, mindset for evaluating social and political choices has been one of the defining characteristics of our age. As long as the numbers work, we feel absolved of the harder, more inchoate ethical choices that face us none the less. We appear to have gone from having a market economy to being a market society (if that isn't an oxymoron) and it's an interesting thought that our obsession with economics has just been one long sustained phase of displacement activity.

Money is just one of the forces that blind us to information and issues which we could pay attention to – but don't. It exacerbates and often rewards all the other drivers of wilful blindness: our preference for the familiar, our love for individuals and for big ideas, a love of busyness and our dislike of conflict and change, the human instinct to obey and conform and our skill at displacing and diffusing responsibility. All of these operate and collaborate with varying intensities at different moments in our lives. The common denominator is that they all make us protect our sense of self-worth, reducing dissonance and conferring a sense of security, however illusory. In some ways, they all act like money: making us feel good at first, with consequences we don't see. We wouldn't be so blind if our blindness didn't deliver rewards: the benefit of comfort and ease.

But in failing to confront the greatest challenge of our age – climate change – all the forces of wilful blindness come together, like synchronised swimmers in a spectacular water ballet. We live with people like ourselves, and sharing consumption habits blinds us to their cost. Like the unwitting spouse of an alcoholic, we know there's something amiss but we don't want to acknowledge that the lifestyles we love may be killing us. The dissonance produced by reading about our environmental impact on the one hand, and living as we do, is resolved by minor alterations in what we buy or eat, but very few significant social shifts. Sometimes we get so anxious we consume more. We keep too busy to confront our worries, a kind of wild displacement activity with schedules that don't allow us to be as green as we'd like. The gravitational pull of the status quo exerts its influence and global conferences end when no one has the stomach for the levels of conflict they engender. In our own countries, no politician shows the nerve for the political battles real change would require.

We're obedient consumers and we might change if we were told to, but we're not. We conform to the consumption patterns we see around us as we all become bystanders, hoping someone else somewhere will intervene. Our governments and corporations grow too complex to communicate or to change and we are left just where we do not want to be, where our only consolation is cash.

This is wilful blindness on a spectacular scale and it would leave us abject with despair, were it not that, all around us, are individuals who aren't blind. That they can and do see more, and act on what they see, offers a possibility that we can be wilfully sighted too.

11. CASSANDRA

I cannot leave the truth unknown

Sophocles, Oedipus

'I wasn't surprised. I'd been saying for months that something like this was bound to happen. It was so obvious. You push these boys too far, what's in their heads is so awful and so violent. Of course you're going to have problems with violence.'

On 5 November 2009, Nidal Malik Hasan shot and killed fourteen people on Fort Hood military base. Cynthia Thomas was deeply upset but she was not surprised by what had happened. Earlier that year, she had started the Under the Hood coffee house to offer soldiers a refuge from the base, a place to hang out where they could find comfort and, if they wanted it, psychological, psychiatric and legal help.

'This stuff happens, on a smaller scale, all the time: soldiers killing someone or stabbings, shootings. All the time. People don't understand. We can have two weeks and there will be three, four, five violent incidents. And people don't see them. The violence. Everything is just all the time. A soldier snapping and doing this is not surprising. People don't want to see it, they don't want to hear about it. But it's here. It will go on happening.'

Cynthia Thomas is a Cassandra. In ancient Greek mythology, Cassandra was royalty: the daughter of King Priam and Queen

Hecuba. Besotted by her beauty, Apollo fell in love with her and gave her the gift of prophecy. But when she spurned him, he retaliated by adding to her gift the fate that no one would believe her. So the Trojans ignored her when she warned them not to bring in the great wooden horse left by the Greeks. And it was Cassandra who warned Agamemnon of Clytemnestra's murderous rage on his return from the war. She must have known she was doomed to die then too, because that was her unique talent: to see what others did not.

The savage irony of Cassandra is that, as we read her prophecies, we know that they are true, but no one else does. As such, she is one of the first characters in literature to offer readers that invaluable plot device: superior knowledge. Believing Cassandra, when everyone else derides her, we see simultaneously two contradictory points of view. We learn that any situation can contain truths that we may not be able to see but that are, none the less, visible. And she teaches us that often it is the despised who know most.

But Cassandra captivates our imagination also because she embodies that baffled rage that we all feel when no one else can see what we see. The epitome of frustration, because Cassandra is doomed always to be right, she shows us that the truth is knowable but won't necessarily set us free.

The world is full of Cassandras, individuals whose fate it is to see what others can't see, who are not blind but feel compelled to shout their awkward, provocative truths. That's why, after any industrial or organisational failure, individuals inevitably surface who saw the crisis coming, warned about it and were mocked or ignored. In Libby, Montana, Gayla Benefield was a classic Cassandra when she insisted that there was something wrong with her town. But when you meet Gayla, she has none of the wild eyes or inspired fury of the classic portrayals of Cassandra; there is nothing physically that marks her out as a rebel or nonconformist, but she seems, from an early age, to have seen things that others did not.

'In high school, I remember our teacher wanted us to have silhouettes, taken behind a sheet. And there was just something about it that made me uneasy. I didn't know why it wasn't right but I knew it wasn't.' Gayla paused for a moment, reaching for the facts, trying to make sure she captures an accurate memory. Then she laughed. 'Maybe it was just that I wasn't going to take off my false boobs! Whatever it was, I led the walkout.'

Taking a stand seems to have become something Gayla did easily. She felt comfortable being different, even when it meant being pilloried or left out.

'I took mechanical drawing in high school – no girl ever had done that at our school, but I didn't know why. I remember: I was sat in a far corner away from the boys! My grandfather was a Russian immigrant who ended up in eastern Montana. He taught me not to fight the system – but always to question it. He was the best American you could ever find. He was always trying to find a better way to do things. I never danced to a different drummer but I questioned. I've never been a blind follower. I've always questioned.'

Cassandras are often also whistleblowers, determined not just to see what others see, but to act upon it, trying to alter fate. Both see things that others don't see because they are questioners, driven to ask: What is really happening? Does it have to be that way? Am I missing something? Is there some other explanation or solution? They're driven, dedicated, often quite obsessive truth seekers – even (or sometimes especially) when no one agrees with them. But that is almost the only generalisation you can make about these extremely and wilfully sighted people.

The world contains millions of Cassandras, in all walks of life and all different. Academics have struggled to find identifying qualities they all have in common, but to no avail. It used to be thought that whistleblowers were more likely to be women because, as newcomers to most institutions, they didn't have the same stake in the status quo. It was a nice theory but turned out not to be true.[1] There doesn't seem to be any correlation between age or years or service and neither pay nor education level turn out to be good predictors either. Religion doesn't seem to play a definitive role; while all Cassandras have a pronounced sense of right and wrong, as many derive their morality from history or personal experience as from any formal faith. And, despite the fact that these troublesome truth-tellers are sometimes thrown into jail or sent for psychiatric assessments, there seems to be no evidence that, as a group, they are crazy.

What we do know is that society needs people like Cynthia Thomas and Gayla Benefield: individuals willing to ask awkward questions, trace tricky connections and challenge embedded assumptions. Because although it's fiendishly difficult to size the level of threat, corruption and crime within organisations, no attempt to do so has ever emerged with good news. It's difficult to come up with reliable numbers in the UK because tax and benefit fraud are treated separately from price-fixing, insider trading and corruption, such as in the BAE case. But in the United States, in 2000, the Ethics Resource Center found that a third of public and private employees had personally observed misconduct. A far higher percentage – 80 per cent – of directors of internal auditing said they had observed wrongdoing by their organisations. And when Harry Markopolos testified before Congress about the Madoff fraud, he argued that 'white collar criminals cause far more economic harm to this nation than armed robbers, drug dealers, car thieves and other assorted miscreants put together. These fraudsters steal approximately five per cent of business revenues annually, dwarfing the economic losses due to violent crime, yet not nearly enough federal law enforcement resources are devoted to catching them'.[2]

In the United States, vast amounts of federal legislation have been introduced to try to protect whistleblowers. The first of these, in 1912, protected federal employees who wished to offer information to Congress, and much subsequent legislation has been focused on ensuring that government employees in particular are protected. The No Fear Act (2002) and the Whistleblower Protection Act (1989) seek to protect federal employees from retaliation and the loss of their jobs, while the False Claims Act sought to elicit help from ordinary citizens against contracting fraud. That law offers a percentage of the settlement to the whistleblower and, since Congress reinforced the Act in 1986, the Justice Department has recovered more than $20 billion. The Office of Special Counsel was also created to investigate complaints by federal whistleblowers.

By contrast, the UK legislative response has been strikingly muted. Only the Public Interest Disclosure Act of 1998 provides a legal framework to protect individuals who report malpractice, and it covers all employees, not just those employed by the government. The number of cases brought has risen steeply, from 157 in the year the Act became law to 1,761 in 2009. Employees have logged 9,000 claims alleging victimisation but, of these, 70 per cent were withdrawn without a public hearing, and of the remainder only 22 per cent were won. The organisation Public Concern at Work runs a helpline for whistleblowers. It was founded in 1993 in the aftermath of the sinking of the *Herald of Free Enterprise*, the Clapham rail crash, and the collapse of BCCI. Every one of these events had revealed that staff had been aware of dangers but had not felt able to raise the matter internally or to pursue it if their concern was not taken seriously. Since the introduction of the Act, PCaW has been the first port of call for whistleblowers who, in the majority of cases, have attempted to raise their concerns but found that they were either ignored or victimised. The organisation has an excellent track record of advising callers; what's worrying is that, in their own survey, only 23 per cent of UK citizens knew there was any law at all to protect whistleblowers.

Although the 1911 Official Secrets Act had contained a provision for a public-interest defence, the Official Secrets Act of 1989 removed it after Clive Ponting, a civil servant, leaked documents showing that the navy had attacked the *Belgrano* when it was sailing away from the battle zone during the Falklands War. In 2004, the law might have been tested when Katharine Gun leaked GCHQ documents concerning a request by the US National Security Agency to help bug UN delegations. But the outcome was something of a fudge, with the Crown Prosecution Service failing to submit evidence. Whether a public-interest defence could have held up in this case therefore remained moot.

What whistleblowers demonstrate, time and again, is that, as obsessed as so many are by surveillance, secrecy and conspiracy, the greatest harms are perpetrated not in private but public, and not alone but by large numbers of people with many witnesses and bystanders. Cassandras and whistleblowers stand in that crowd, see what is happening, but somehow find within themselves the courage or the need to speak out.

They are not cynics, but almost always start as optimists, not nonconformists but true believers. They are not, typically, disgruntled or disappointed; they're not innately rebels but are compelled to speak out when they see organisations or people that they love taking the wrong course. When Stephen Bolsin started investigating the poor success rate in paediatric cardiac surgery, his aim was simply to improve it.

'I was new to Bristol. I expected to raise my family there. And I thought: let's make this a centre of excellence. If there's something we can improve, let's do it. If there's something we're doing wrong, we can fix it!'

Similarly, when Pat Lewis designed his risk model for Bear

Stearns, or Paul Moore drew the board's attention to risks within HBOS, they did so as committed employees trying to contribute to stronger businesses. They might have expected to be treated as heroes, certainly not as pariahs.

'I thought I was there to do some good,' Moore told me. 'It was a bit of a mission – integrity and financial services meant a lot to me. I think that came from a mixture of what my parents taught me and what you might call what you're given from Him upstairs. I always believed that I was a representative of the customer and the shareholder and those who could not see and understand all the detail that I could see. I was supposed to be the honest broker.'

When Sherron Watkins wrote to Enron CEO Ken Lay, she thought he would welcome her questions and appreciate that, far from trying to wreck the company, she was trying to save it.

'I'd been so loyal!' Watkins recalled. 'I thought his first response would just be to want to get to the truth, to know what was going on in his company! It was the sense that, if you tell the captain the ship is sinking, he is going to man the lifeboats.'

The letter that Watkins wrote, detailing accounting problems she could not resolve, and risks she believed Lay did not know about, did not go to the press; she wrote to Lay as the person she believed was most likely to fix the problems she'd identified. And Watkins never went public. Only after the company had collapsed did investigators find her letter.

'I thought good would prevail, that we'd unwind some deals, restate earnings, that they'd be grateful to me for identifying the problems. I only found out later that Lay almost instantly took legal advice about whether he could fire me!'[3]

When Harry Markopolos first started examining Bernard Madoff's investment strategies, it wasn't with a view to discovering criminality. The last thing on his mind was identifying systemic failures in the Securities Exchange Commission. Markopolos explored Madoff because he wanted to see if he could copy him, not bring him down.

In many instances like this, what enables Cassandras to see what others don't is a tremendous eye for detail. Markopolos says that thousands of hours of doing maths by hand is what prepared him for the moment that he saw Madoff's numbers.

'I knew immediately that the numbers made no sense. I just knew it. Numbers exist in relationship, and after you've studied as many of them as I had it was clear something was out of whack. As I continued examining the numbers, the problems with them began popping out as clearly as a red wagon in a field of snow. Anyone who understood the match of the market would have seen these problems immediately.'[4]

Like many Cassandras, Markopolos didn't allow distance or theory to obscure the nitty-gritty of what he saw. But when he provided the SEC with all of that detail, no one there had the skill, training, patience or experience to understand what they were looking at. 'The magnitude of this Ponzi scheme,' Markopolos wrote, 'is matched only by the wilful blindness of the SEC to investigate Madoff.'

For many Cassandras, God is indeed in the detail. They don't wrap themselves up in dogma, but relish facts and arguments. In just the same way that Alice Stewart immersed herself in all the domestic detail that might explain childhood cancers, Cassandras typically like getting down to the bare bones of otherwise abstract problems.

That's what James Hansen did, in the late 1970s. Having completed his Ph.D., writing on the atmosphere of Venus, he was a geek, not a dissident, buried in his data and oblivious to the student riots that surrounded him. Soon Earth's atmosphere became more captivating than Venus's, as he grappled with the detail of chlorofluorocarbons and the ozone layer. One of his key interests, he wrote, was 'radiative transfer in planetary atmospheres, especially interpreting remote sounding of the earth's atmosphere and surface from satellites'. In 1981, he published a paper predicting that the following decade would be unusually warm, and the decade after that warmer still. He was right, and he kept being right, but his work was full of detail and caveats, identifying areas of ignorance and uncertainty that would constitute a lifetime's work.[5] He had not set out to prove or disprove theories of climate change; his work didn't begin with ideology. He started with detail and merely kept following where the data led him.

It's also what Daniel Ellsberg did. He was perhaps predisposed to be sceptical of authority; at the age of fifteen, Ellsberg lost his mother and sister when his father fell asleep while driving. 'I think it did probably leave an impression on me: that someone you loved and respected could fall asleep at the wheel and they needed to be watched.'

But it was detail not dogma that turned him finally against the Vietnam War. Ellsberg had been in favour of the war – even to the degree that he had broken up with his girlfriend who opposed it. After working for McNamara at the Defense Department, Ellsberg insisted on going to Vietnam and seeing for himself, first hand, what the reality of government policy was. On his return, he read the 7,000 pages of the Pentagon Papers and learned in immense detail of the many times the public had been misled by administrations that said one thing while doing another. It was the detail of those documents, coupled with first-hand experience, that made him risk 115 years in jail for sharing what he'd found out.

Detail, evidence, research drove Sheila Bair too when, in 2006, she was appointed to head the Federal Deposit Insurance Corporation – the government insurance company that guarantees some 800,000 American banks. Bair had been worried for some time about the amount of debt that banks were carrying.

She had watched the growth of sub-prime mortgages with alarm and now she wanted to find out what was really going on. What she did was simple: she bought a database of sub-prime loans and studied it, something any federal regulator could have done.

'We just couldn't believe what we were seeing. Really steep payment shock loans and sub-primes . . . Very little income documentation, really high prepayment penalties.'[6]

Without the beguiling fog of ideology, and with the gruesome details right in front of her – data about real people buying real loans for real houses – she was in no doubt about what was going on around her. In March 2007, she issued a cease and desist notice to shut down one of the sub-prime offenders, Fremont Investment and Loan.

From an entirely different vantage point, Aaron Krowne gained the same insight. Krowne wasn't a financier, far from it. He was a computer-science and maths graduate working as a software developer. Fascinated by economics since the dotcom bubble, he was just a keen, smart observer who liked asking himself questions about what he saw around him.

'I have a strong moral sense from my father and I learned you collect the data, form a hypothesis and try to confirm or disprove the hypothesis. You don't impose your views on *a priori* findings; you present what you find even if it isn't what you want. Because it is important for all our lives and the wellbeing of society. I just felt a need to say something and speak up.'

What gave Krowne something to speak up about was his experience in 2005 when he tried to buy a home.

'I was in a situation where I had to leave the apartment I was in or buy it. The owner wanted to sell, so I looked at the buy-versus-rent fundamentals and made a chart of the price for that kind of unit over ten to twenty years. And it spiked up just like a bubble! Everyone was saying – you have to buy! But I said: Look at the fundamentals. I'd have had to get an exotic loan to come out ahead monthly and I just didn't feel comfortable after such a rapid run-up. So I declined and had to move.'

Towards the end of 2006, Krowne noticed a lot of sub-prime lenders going under. He thought that the bubble he'd spotted was about to pop so he launched a little website to ask hard questions about what was going on, why, and who was responsible.

'It started as just a single page, with seven or eight lenders on it. I called it Implode-O-Meter for a little humour, the whole thing was so ridiculous. I posted it on some economic blogs I frequented and it caught on. Traffic steadily increased and it got picked up actively by newsletters and a few months later by Bloomberg TV and CNBC. By March 2007, it was pretty well ensconced as the biggest site for the mortgage industry itself, with everyone sending in tips and information.'

The site was fed by the industry it reported on, so Krowne was getting live, first-hand, unmediated information from hundreds of sources across the industry. What his site demonstrated was that the knowledge was out there.

'Ninety-nine per cent of the information that we got – tips from people in the companies – proved correct. People out there *knew* what was going on in their organisations. We'd get a lot of vociferous denials from management – but the angrier they got about leaks, the more true the leaks turned out to be. There were very few instances where the problem was a disgruntled employee making things up. We did all we could to verify the information, at risk to ourselves, but the information we got was usually very honest. There is a phenomenon where whistle-blowing is almost always accurate. Otherwise why take the risk?'[7]

Krowne wasn't a banking insider or a policy wonk or even an economist. He was just a guy on the ground who looked around and asked himself questions about what he saw. Being an outsider may have been an advantage, giving him a less-biased perspective on what he heard and saw. Most Cassandras are outsiders, either by accident of birth, or life, or by dint of what they see, which sets them irrevocably apart.

Heather Brooke grew up in two different places – the US and the UK, where she went to an 'absolutely terrible' school in the Wirral. When her parents divorced, she returned to the States, where she trained to be a journalist. It was there, she said, that she developed her expectations of government.

'I picked up a different attitude to the sense of entitlement people have about their leaders,' she told me. 'Americans expect to be able to find out where their taxes are going, they expect to be able to influence their local school boards. It is considered their right to get involved.'

She moved back to the UK in 1997 and found much that she relished.

'I found British people to be less blind to the world. In the US, I find that American people have total ignorance or a lack of curiosity about the world and they also have a lot of ignorance and confidence that what they are doing is right. They haven't considered other options. I have more debates here than in the US. Americans will skirt controversy where UK people are willing to get into an argument, they enjoy playing devil's advocate.'

But what Brooke did not like was the British political system, its tradition of deference and its absence of citizens' rights.

'People here are kept in their place and trying to make a change is considered rude, brash. Lobby journalists in particular have a lot to lose. They're mostly first-class people who've finagled their way into the heart of power. They're made to know that it is a privilege for them to be let in; they have no sense of entitlement. They have no confidence you can challenge authority and still get stories – any information you're given is a gift, not a statutory right. That's how Britain runs. That leads to a lot of consensus because everyone wants to agree, not be the odd person out causing trouble. I was an outsider anyway and had nothing to lose. So I didn't do things that way. It just wasn't the way that I thought about power.'

Brooke began to write her first book, *Your Right to Know*, which looked at what new rights the Freedom of Information Act (2000) might bring when it came into force in 2005. Since it was taking so long to implement, she'd assumed that it would bring massive procedural changes – but when she started making enquiries, it seemed that no one was doing much of anything to prepare. This made her suspicious, so she tested the waters by asking about MPs' expenses.

'I asked about expenses just because, when I'd been a reporter in Washington State in 1992 I had asked for a politician's expenses and that had been a big story there, so I thought I'd do the same here. But there, I'd got the information in a day! Here, the result was totally different. What they published in October 2004 was just one number – they'd just added everything up! It was a meaningless number and you couldn't tell if it was legitimate or if they'd just made it up. So I kept asking and they kept refusing and I thought that was very questionable – so I kept on.'

Brooke was well on her way to breaking one of the major political scandals of her generation but that wasn't her prime motivation. What she really wanted was to change the way that people looked at their government, the way that they thought and wrote about it.

'My motivation is a very American one, it's about civic responsibility: this is my government and I have a right to know. But it also went beyond that. I was asking these questions not as a journalist but as a campaigner. I wanted to be able to do the kind of journalism that *didn't* incur favours. I didn't want to have to owe favours and get to see reports because I'd schmoozed people. I think that's quite corrupt. What I was trying to do was to change the way journalists work here.'

But the *Daily Telegraph* ended up getting the big scoop on MPs' expenses the old-fashioned way: they just wrote a cheque. That meant that they owned the data, but what Brookes had wanted was for it to be in the public domain. For one newspaper to buy the data achieved nothing. She'd wanted all of us, as citizens, to have the right to know where our money was going and why. Brookes was thrilled by the uproar the information produced but profoundly disappointed that her more fundamental campaign – to change the relationship between people and politics – hadn't been understood.

'In the old days, the *Sunday Times* put investment into the Insight team and they were willing to challenge the authorities. And with expenses, I had done that, too. But nobody else had done anything! They put in a few Freedom of Information requests but they never followed them up. They never used the law to change the system. They took "no" for an answer. But they hadn't served the higher purpose of journalism which is to challenge authority and reveal inconvenient truths.'

Challenging authority in the interests of truth is what all Cassandras do. This makes them awkward, annoying, and difficult. Such qualities are often used in attempts to discredit them and to isolate them but it is those same qualities that drive them to persevere.

'My father was a bizarre character,' Paul Moore recalls. He's careful not to say that he is like his father, but he clearly thinks that they had a lot in common.

'He had a massive sense of integrity and won an open scholarship to Oxford when he was sixteen-and-a-half. He was an extraordinary personality – incredible integrity but also a very passive, dependent personality, who, if he didn't get the attention he wanted from Mum, would have a serious paddy. So he was an odd fellow. This comes down in the genes: thinking out of the box. He was never in the box. I guess there's quite a lot of him in me.'

Even before he was fired, Moore's position at HBOS had been contentious because he insisted on challenging and questioning CEO James Crosby's authority and strategy.

'Crosby fired me because he didn't like me as a person and he didn't like the challenges I raised to his strategies: stack 'em high and sell 'em cheap. He didn't like that I said this carried enormous risk and they needed to reconsider it. He really didn't brook any challenge to his authority and he didn't like the fact that I was always asking, was always going to be asking, difficult questions because that was my job.'

'When my relatives heard I was working at a bank, they thought I was going to be a teller!' Frank Partnoy laughs now at what he considers, nevertheless, to have been a significant advantage when he became a Wall Street investment banker.

'I grew up in Kansas and didn't have the built-in blinders that someone with more pedigree might have. My parents didn't go to Harvard or Yale. And maybe to me the stakes seemed lower. To many people, once you're at Morgan Stanley and have climbed the mountain, the idea of leaving it behind is unthinkable. For me, it wasn't such a big deal.'

In *F.I.A.S.C.O.*, Partnoy unsparingly chronicles his growing enthusiasm and then disgust with the trading world he moved in. Not being from that world helped him to see what kind of world it was — and what the costs of conformity would entail.

'Everyone I knew who had been an investment banker for a few years, including me, was an asshole. The fact that we were the richest assholes in the world didn't change the fact that we were assholes. I had known this deep down since I first began working on Wall Street. Now, for some reason, it bothered me.'

Partnoy left and wrote first about his own experiences and

then, in *Infectious Greed*, about the rampant explosion not in derivatives but in financial disasters caused by derivatives. He predicted that there would be more, and this was early, in 2003. (In 2002 he had also tried to explain to Congress that Enron had collapsed not because of a few bad men but because of derivatives, but no one really paid attention then either.) Then in 2006 he was back in Washington, warning about the structural problems inherent in credit-ratings agencies like Moody's. Apart from having a strong stomach for unpopular positions, why could he see what others did not?

'I am the sort of person who wakes up every morning, I wipe the slate clean and everything is up for grabs and I am constantly questioning everything. I think also there's something about my educational experience at Yale Law School. Those three years are so focused on questioning everything; that's what Yale Law School is by design – an institution whose constituents are trying to make the world a better place all the time. It seems to generate a lot of people who don't wear blinders and try to keep them off, almost religiously.'

Partnoy left banking to work in academia, a world, he says, where prestige, intellectual respect, is the equivalent of a bonus. You can't use prestige, he says; you can't spend it. It just makes you happy. But he's not only a professor; as well as academic papers, he also writes popular books about finance and history and he testifies before Congress. He is never exclusively wedded to one mindset, but always travelling between perspectives. It's what political theorist Hannah Arendt called 'thinking without a bannister'.

'Even within my profession, I think people climbing the ladder are constrained. So you have to make sacrifices not to be constrained. For me freeing myself from those constraints is what gives me happiness and gives me freedom. When you are a teenager, or in college, you're always re-examining your life. But when most people graduate, they stop doing that and I wonder why. Is it that it gets too draining to keep questioning your life?'

This highly unconstrained travel, between points of view, is hard work and it can be risky, not just because it can take you off well established career paths, but because it provokes questions that, as a Cambridge professor once sternly reminded me, 'one is not invited to ask'. Questions that one is not invited to ask make everyone uncomfortable, not least because they don't easily lend themselves to prepared answers. But in the intersection between perspectives, real insight can be gleaned.

For Deborah Layton, what ultimately turned her into a Cassandra was her sense of history. Layton's own background, she says, pulled her in two directions: she was both a great conformist and also a rebel.

'I'm the youngest of four kids – my siblings are ten, eight, seven years older than me. So as I grew up, I was very used to looking up to others and abiding by their rules. When they'd grown up, I was stuck at home with ancient parents. I started to rebel and get attention by doing silly things – climbing the tallest tree, smoking, not turning up at school. So needing acceptance, that made me a good follower – but being a bit of a rebel saved me.'

Layton was one of the few survivors after the Reverend Jim Jones led 918 of his followers to commit suicide at the Peoples Temple in Guyana. Layton had been an outstanding follower – life at a Yorkshire boarding school, she says, had equipped her to fit in and shut up – but throughout the seven years that she belonged to the Temple, there was never a time she didn't notice when things weren't quite what they purported to be.

'I never spoke up in the Peoples Temple. I was scared to death all the time. But I watched and I worked hard to look more loyal than anyone else because I figured if he trusted me more than others I'd have more freedom not to be watched so closely. There was always this little voice saying: Get out! Get out! And, of course most of the time I didn't get out because I was so scared. But there were other things too. Like one day, I'd been smoking secretly and Jim called me over and I thought he could read my thoughts. But he didn't ask me anything and I realised: he doesn't know everything. I held on to that for many years. And then, after I'd been made financial secretary, I knew how much money we had. So I couldn't understand, when we got to Guyana, why we had to live in such awful poverty. It just didn't make sense.'

Small incongruities kept Layton puzzled and puzzling. But what ultimately got her to escape from Guyana was a sense that she was watching history repeat itself.

'My mother had been born in Germany and my father used to tell us about her life there – the concert musicians who'd played in her home, which had been an elegant Bauhaus building. They'd had an art collection from Hamburg, fabulous paintings and a wonderful Klimt sculpture. We had an etching of Albert Einstein that he'd signed – and all of this made me realise how much my mother missed Germany. You could feel the loss, the loss of a whole life, a whole culture. In our basement there was a suitcase with canned goods – they were emergency rations. So it was already in my mind that bad things could happen and you had to be prepared.'

When Jim Jones started preaching about the enemies that the Temple faced and began to practise mass suicide drills, Layton felt an overwhelming sense of *déjà vu*.

'When Jim talked about apocalyptic events, I think to a lot of people they were just unimaginable, but they sounded real to me because, in our family, apocalyptic events did happen. Since my childhood I'd known that these things were real. I knew that thousands of people, of families, could die – and it wasn't just some abstract history lesson. It was what happened to people like me. It was exactly what happened to people like me. I knew that, if I didn't get out, I would certainly die.'

Layton did escape and tried to warn government officials of the very real danger that threatened the Jonestown population. None of them grasped the reality or the urgency of what she was saying and action came too late.

'What disturbs me now is that Jonestown isn't even in the history books. No one knows about it any more. But there are still cults. Enron was a cult. America has been cult-ified and being an individual and standing proud doesn't happen much. When I got back to California, I went to work for a stock brokerage. And I realised there were men on the trading floor who'd get million-dollar bonuses and they'd take getting yelled at and abused because they had so much at stake – spectacular homes and kids in private schools. And they couldn't stand up and say "no" because they had to keep these jobs.'

'All of us cross these lines of not speaking up on our own behalf. It's true of marriages too; people think it could never happen to me. It happens in abusive relationships – you think you love him so you don't speak out. To take true notice will change your life. But it definitely puts you on the outside. It's just the way you see things.'

Although ensconced inside an establishment newspaper – the *Financial Times* – Gillian Tett is, in her own way, an outsider too: a pretty, slight, blonde woman working in structured finance. That she has a gentle lisp and a Ph.D. in anthropology definitely set her apart from mainly male, macho bankers. In 2006, when she and her team became seriously alarmed by what they saw in structured finance, they tried to point out the dangers. It was, she says, a lonely endeavour, too boring and technical, too much nitty-gritty, and bad news to boot. But she credits some of her insight not to her outsider perspective but to her training as a social anthropologist.

'Anthropology is a brilliant background for looking at finance,' she said. 'You're trained to look at how societies or cultures operate holistically, so you look at how all the bits move together. And most people in the City don't do that. They are so specialised, so busy, that they just look at their own little silos. One of the reasons we got into the mess we are in is because everyone failed to ask hard questions: Why are credit cards so cheap? Why can I get such a big mortgage? The silence suited everyone! Who had incentives to see? No one. What was missing in banking was the wider perspective, the context. But that didn't happen in finance. It wasn't in anybody's interest to look further.'

That absence of holistic thought, Tett believes, allows us all to become narrow and deep. Buried deep at the bottom of our riverbeds, we are blind to connections and dependencies. We see only what we know and like and are lulled into a sense of mastery by our isolation from challenge. That feels comfortable, of course, until different perspectives bring unwanted and unwonted challenges.

'One of the most powerful people in the US government at the time stood up on the podium at Davos and waved my article, the article that predicted the problems at Northern Rock, as an example of scaremongering.'[8]

The fragmentation of the banking world, together with its sheer complexity, she argues, encouraged financiers to regard banking as its own world, distant and detached from the rest of society. This became very clear when she was summoned one day to Canary Wharf which is, she was at pains to point out, an island.

'So I was called to Canary Wharf by this banker who said: "I don't know why you keep saying CDOs and structured finance are opaque and murky. It's all on Bloomberg terminals; it's right there." But what, I asked him, what about the people who don't have Bloomberg terminals? He looked at me as if to say: there *are* people out there without Bloomberg terminals – and we're supposed to care about them? He had just retreated to his Bloomberg cyber village.'[9] The chain that linked a synthetic CDO of ABS, say, with a 'real' person was so convoluted it was almost impossible for anybody to fit that into a single cognitive map.[10]

Being able to draw a cognitive map requires travelling well outside our immediate knowledge and safety. It means meeting people not like ourselves, in industries and neighbourhoods far from our own and, when we're there, having the confidence and curiosity to keep asking questions. Robert Schiller, the Yale economist who so famously warned about the property bubble and impending financial collapse, says that his work is deeply informed by his wife, who is not an economist at all, but a clinical psychologist. Drawing our cognitive map calls on a breadth of experience – either from different disciplines or different life experiences.

At first sight, there's nothing remotely unconventional about Roy Spence. He's enjoyed a highly successful career running a Texas advertising agency whose clients have been some of the business greats: Sam Walton of Wal-Mart, Herb Kelleher of Southwest Airlines. He also worked on presidential campaigns with Bill Clinton, with whom he's been friends since the 1970s. Spence's company does what all ad companies do and Roy is like successful executives you meet everywhere: handsome, energetic, polite, punctilious. Just an ad guy, you might think.

But Roy was one of the few people to turn down business with Enron. And he seems to be one of those people who can tap into the *Zeitgeist* and see things that others don't. Was it being in Texas, when the rest of the ad world is based in New York, that gave him his particular take on events?

'It helps,' he agreed. 'It helps that if you come home from Manhattan with your head stuffed full of nonsense, everyone here will tell you.'

But much more important, he felt, was his experience growing up with his sister, Susan, who was born with spina bifida.

'When I used to push my sister to school, I thought I was crippled. If you come from a place that is vulnerable to start with, it's out in the open: we have something different going on here. That changes who you are and how you look at things. When you're out there, you see yourself being looked at and you become the watcher, too. You start to see how other people see. And the vulnerability of other people, too.'

He stopped for a second, remembering his sister.

'People thought my sister was different. Well, she was: she could never walk. But people couldn't see beyond that. You saw how blind they were. And it makes you think: if they're missing so much about me and about her, what am I missing about them?'

The image of the young Texan boy pushing his sister to school, scrutinising faces while trying to imagine the thoughts behind them, is striking: simultaneously he sees through his own eyes, his sister's eyes and the eyes of those watching him. The dialogue he has with himself about those different perspectives is one definition of thought.

What Roy describes is akin to empathy but goes far beyond it. He doesn't see through the eyes of power, but through the eyes of the vulnerable. This perspective is typical of Cassandras and whistleblowers.

'There was one difficult moment when we were in Bristol and our daughter Natasha was about five or six,' Steve Bolsin recalls. At the time, he was encountering a lot of resistance to the questions he kept asking about the failure rate of Bristol's paediatric cardiac surgery.

'And one night Maggie and I were discussing this – what to do about Bristol? – and Natasha came downstairs in her nightgown holding her teddy and asked what we were arguing about?

Maggie said: "Too many kids are dying and Dad doesn't know what to do." She just looked at me and said: "You have to stop them killing the children." It was quite obvious to a five-year-old that it was thoroughly reprehensible behaviour. It was so bloody obvious! It is not morally acceptable to experiment on little children. You should be looking at the individuals the system is supposed to serve, instead of seeing the whole thing as just a power game.'

It is in the nature of the power game that it blinds its players to the powerless. But the game changes entirely when that perspective alters.

'I am married to a soldier,' says Cynthia Thomas. 'But you shut your feelings down in the military to survive. They all choose to bury their heads in the sand because it is easier that way. It is drilled into your head that you have to be supportive. And you believe that the military will take care of them if something happens. So you are in this bubble where you can't really see what's going on.'

For years, Thomas says, she lived in that bubble. She took it for granted that the military would look after her husband and their family, that nothing would go wrong, that they were OK. And she was surrounded by other wives and families who did exactly the same thing. But then, as the Iraq War wore on, she started to see events from a very different perspective, the perspective of powerlessness.

'Tim was wounded in 2005 and came back on life support. In 2007, he was redeployed even though he was not supposed to be. He had brain injuries, fractures on his pelvis. His doctor said: he won't be able to save himself if gets shot at. But they didn't care, they redeployed him anyway. And then my stepson called and said he was joining the marines. The bubble popped. I thought – oh my God, after everything that happened, these wars are going to be endless and our kids will be fighting them. That moment,

I thought: if I don't do something or try to, this will go on for ever. And I was upset but I finally did something, I opened up to human beings.'

Seeing life through the eyes of young vulnerable men, in a world where most mass media only charts the progress of the powerful, showed Thomas a world of suffering she had been blind to. Thomas's mantra now is that, in war, there are no unwounded soldiers – and she has opened her coffee house to tend to all of the wounded. Anyone can come in, regardless of political opinion. It was her openness to them that allowed her to see how dangerous life was becoming for the soldiers of Fort Hood. The soldiers aren't getting the help they need, she says, because once diagnosed with post-traumatic stress disorder (PTSD) they aren't supposed to be redeployed.

'There's real pressure here not to diagnose it. We have soldiers on fifteen medications and they have an adjustment disorder, a mood disorder, you can call it anything but PTSD because they know if they have PTSD they can get a medical discharge and the government would have to pay them for being disabled and that's a lot of money. The military is a business; if your employee can't do his job, you get rid of him. So you just have this tension building, boys needing help and everyone refusing to see they need help.'[11]

At first, it was hard for Thomas to find a site for her coffee house; just having that physical presence would raise issues that most of the town preferred to overlook. Killeen, close to Fort Hood, is a tightly knit military community, many fear getting in trouble with Command; everyone hopes that trouble will pass them by. But Thomas sees what others won't because she looks with the eyes of the most vulnerable.

'Just looking around this community and seeing the cost of the war, it is so hard on a daily basis. Walking around on post and looking at really young faces – eighteen, nineteen – they're babies! Oh my God, they don't grasp the severity of it. Nobody understands. You can't describe it. We have boys coming back so young and their lives are ruined. No one knows the cost of war. They don't want to think about it. They'd have to look in the mirror and say: this is what we did.'

Cassandras all believe that if you can overcome wilful blindness, and force people to see what is happening, that that alone will bring change. They're prepared for conflict because they see it as a necessary step towards change. But, in some cases, they recognise that the facts alone won't prove powerful enough. You need the influence of public opinion.

'To be honest I am the sort of person if I have something to say I will say it,' says Margaret Haywood. To her, this is a statement of fact that she can do nothing to alter. 'I'm not purposefully hurtful but I am quite an up-front person. Safeguarding vulnerable adults is very important to me, and doing nothing was never really an option. I had to do something about it to put things right.'

A qualified nurse, Haywood first worked for the BBC's *Panorama* when she supplied back-up support to an unqualified carer going undercover to investigate how easy it was to get a job. The experience had given her a taste of how powerful such programmes can be and when *Panorama* asked her to go undercover herself, she had no qualms.

'We were acting on complaints that we'd received after that first show went out. We knew there was a problem and we knew the only way to deal with it was to go and take a look. I applied for jobs using my own qualifications; it was all above board and the first six hospitals were fine. And then as soon as I stepped on to the ward, I knew there were problems.'

At the Royal Sussex County Hospital in Brighton, Haywood found patients without care plans, with blank medical charts, left in bed most of the day without dignity or attention. One elderly woman waited over two hours for a commode; others were left afraid, ignored and without pain relief. There was, she said, no continuity of care; patients were screaming in pain, left in their own dirt and left alone to die.

'Fluid charts were not maintained so you had no way of knowing what the patients had had to eat or drink. It was absolutely awful. I went to the ward manager and her response to me was: it was more about financial constraints. I understand money but we are talking basic human needs – filling a chart in, giving medication! It doesn't take money, just time management from nurse or carer. That is what spurred me on. The fact as well that the sister on the ward was more concerned about financial implications – that worried me even more.'

Secretly she filmed many of the horrors that she witnessed. She felt she owed it to her patients and their relatives (many of whom had complained to no avail) to let the world see what was going on inside the hospital.

'Sometimes things can take too long,' Haywood explained to me. 'I knew it was controversial what I did but I reported my concerns and I tried to go through all the proper channels and nothing was taken on board. It all took such a long time and those people were at risk of further harm. What happened to me was a drop in the ocean compared to what was happening to the poor patients.'

Her empathy with her patients cost her dear. After a four-year inquiry, the Nursing and Midwifery Council's fitness-to-practise panel struck her off the nursing register. It was their toughest possible sanction, imposed, they said, because she had violated her patients' right to privacy. The public outcry was immediate and vociferous – not least because the BBC had, before the broadcast, gone to great lengths to secure the agreement of every patient's relatives, many of whom were as eager as Haywood to have the hospital's abuse revealed. Over 40,000 people signed petitions supporting her and, five months later, the High Court overturned the judgement on appeal.

'Well, of course I was delighted. Not just with the decision but with all the nurses who'd backed me. Nowadays, when I'm teaching and do a session on whistleblowing, I say: you have to live with your decision. If you do nothing, you might be keeping a vulnerable person at risk of further harm. You have to be able to sleep at night. Imagine that patient is your granddad or grandmother – would you like someone to do something about it? However hard it is, you can't lose empathy for the people around you. You have to see through their eyes. If you're blind to them, what are you doing there? To me, they are what the job is all about.'

After Hurricane Katrina, Maria Garzino felt that same commitment when she saw the people of New Orleans on television.

'The looks on their faces: that hopelessness thing,' Garzino recalled. A member of the Army Corps of Engineers, she had recently come back from Iraq and what she saw on television seemed horribly familiar.

'You look at the faces of individuals and they know they have a good chance of being dead very soon. And they're pleading for help that should be there. And you realise: it isn't coming. It didn't come. The failure was something beyond an inadequate response. It was a break in trust. When someone doesn't do their best, your trust is gone. How do you restore it? I volunteered to go down to New Orleans in any capacity because I wanted people to understand that the Army Corps cared deeply. All I could guarantee was that I would do my best. That's the only way you can restore trust.'

Garzino was experienced in emergency work and she loved it. After begging and conniving to be sent to New Orleans, she was made Pump Team Installation Leader, assigned to install new pumps that were supposed to protect the city for the next fifty years.

'Pretty quickly I realised something was wrong. Working with contractors on emergency work is very fast-paced so you need a relationship of trust. The first things that are said are: this is [a] twenty-four–seven project; we are going to help each other, that's the deal. Failure isn't an option. Forthright disclosure is essential; you have to be direct and honest. But I was noticing that contractors didn't want to say anything, they were hiding things and it was hard to get information.'

Garzino kept pressing for the information she needed and hoping for the best. But she didn't understand how the firm MWI had got the contract for pumps that appeared to be ill-suited to their task.

'My problem is: this seems to be good-old-boy network, we tell you what we need to know. This is not a good candidate for partner of the year. Delivery dates were short. We have only a few months to get the pumps in place. NOAH is predicting three or four storms that year that could hit the area, so we have to get this done. Then the schedules slipped. That was unacceptable.'

As Garzino relayed the detail of her story to me, she struggled to stay calm. Her frustration with a firm that didn't seem to care about deadlines or quality or the life-and-death nature of the job distresses her to this day.

'We started testing and the pumping systems fell apart each time we turned them on. Very concerned is an understatement. When you turn these pumps on, they blow their guts out – in very different ways. The head people would bypass me and call New Orleans and get lesser requirements. So they tried to reduce specification. Well – why even bother testing? It was so ridiculous, they never made it through testing. The final test was laughable – they just did away with testing the pump assembly and said, "Hopefully they will hold together long enough".'

Garzino finally cracked when she heard the people of New Orleans being assured that the pumps would keep them safe. She knew no such guarantee could be made. Being very careful fastidiously to follow the chain of command, in 2006 she began to press for a process of review. When she couldn't get any satisfaction, in 2007 she went to the Office of Special Counsel (the part of the Department of Justice charged with investigating whistleblower complaints by federal employees).[12] The OSC insisted the Inspector General of the Department of Defense investigate her concerns. While that report upheld many of her complaints, it none the less concluded there had been no serious violations. But Garzino would not be deterred and submitted highly detailed counter-arguments. She was emotional about her campaign but she knew it was the nitty-gritty engineering detail that proved her argument.

'Two a.m. I'm replying to emails. I have a twelve-foot-tall pile of documents on my desk. If you paid me for the work I did on this,' Garzino recalled ruefully, 'I could retire right now. Every night. Every weekend. If you realise you won't give up, then you must do the best job you can.'

The Inspector General was told to look again, but again came back saying the pumps were safe. In an unprecedented move, the OSC then decided to appoint an independent engineering expert to analyse all the available information. His report entirely vindicated the years of Garzino's effort, finding that the pumps installed in New Orleans did not protect the city adequately and that the Army Corps of Engineers could have saved $430 million in replacement costs by buying proven equipment.

'Everything I said was affirmed; it was the greatest day of my four years in this thing. It absolutely justified the pain.'

Pitting herself against the Army Corps, against a powerful contracting firm, made for a long and frightening battle. Why, I kept wondering, hadn't she given up? A passionate love of engineering (coupled with a hatred for bad engineering) was part of the answer. So too was a determination to finish what she had begun and a serious commitment to public trust. But key to Garzino's determination was her sense that someone had to stand up for the people of New Orleans who had already been so badly let down.

'There was a day we drove down to where the pumps were going to be installed. I remember there was a lot of debris around, they were changing the road to allow heavy construction traffic to get through. They raised the body of an eight-year-old girl. And no one would look. No one wanted to acknowledge what had just happened. But that is what needs to be at the forefront of your mind! Let's talk about this! But they couldn't even look that in the eye. People don't want to look at a really bad thing. One reason this stuff is allowed to happen is because people don't want to look at it and acknowledge it. There were a whole lot of people there that day but no one talked about it.'

For Garzino, seeing what everyone wanted to deny, and acting on that knowledge, was an intrinsically necessary act. She had a strong sense of duty, not just to her organisation but to what it stood for. For Joe Darby, who handed in the photographs of Abu Ghraib, the decision was just as taxing but just as clear.

'After about three days, I decided to hand the pictures in. You have to understand: I'm not the kind of guy to rat somebody out. I've kept a lot of secrets for soldiers. In the heat of the moment, in a war, things happen. You do things you regret. I have exceeded the proper use of force myself a couple times. But this crossed the line to me. I had the choice between what I knew was morally right and my loyalty to other soldiers. I couldn't have it both ways.'[13]

Darby was able to think beyond his friends and his colleagues and see that there were other people, very different from himself, who mattered.

One of the things you have to understand is the mentality
of where I grew up, in Western Maryland. It's a small town,
and there's not a lot of work. So most people are either in
the military, in the Reserves, or they're related to somebody
who is. They're good people, but I knew they weren't going
to look at the fact that these guys were beating up prisoners. They were going to look at the fact that an American
soldier put other American soldiers in prison. For *Iraqis*.
And to those people – who basically are patriotic, socially
programmed people who believe whatever they're told – the
Iraqis are the enemy, and screw whatever happens to them.
Ignorance is bliss they say but you can't stand by and let this
happen.

What Cassandras and whistleblowers show us is that the forces
that enable wilful blindness can be overcome. That this can happen
feels heroic but is rarely experienced as heroism in real life. Men
like Steve Bolsin and Joe Darby, women like Margaret Haywood
and Gayla Benefield see through the eyes of the powerless and
what they see changes who they are and what they feel is right. But
this change comes at a high cost, because their full-sightedness
explodes the status quo.

Because the confrontations between Cassandras and the rest of
the world are so profound, they are reflected back to us in stories; the conflict between a passion for truth and the desire for
illusion has been a mainstay of drama since *Oedipus*. Whether it's
Hickey, smashing the myths that sustain the bums of Harry
Hope's bar in *The Iceman Cometh*, or Gregers Werle determined
to excavate family secrets in *The Wild Duck*, or Emilia, revealing
to Othello the folly of his jealousy, the bearer of truths have to
be punished. All of these dramas of revealed truths – and they're
all tragedies – can be at times almost unbearable to watch as one
truth explodes multiple illusions. Cassandras may see the truth,

but they inspire fury because those truths were so energetically and necessarily hidden, and because their revelations demand change. We side with the truth-teller but, in the comfort of the theatre, we don't have to bear the cost.

In the real world, the cost of being a Cassandra is more ambiguous. In one study of whistleblowers, 30 per cent of them had been removed from their offices by security men carrying guns – that is how dangerous they were deemed to be.[14] Most weren't surprised to lose their jobs but were disappointed by how hard it was to find employment subsequently. Steve Bolsin moved to Australia after his friends advised him that he was a 'marked man' and would never again find a position within the NHS. Maria Garzino often found herself sitting at her desk with nothing to do. For years, Gayla Benefield had to endure the open hostility of her neighbours, while for Frank Partnoy and Cynthia Thomas perhaps the hardest part is explaining why they've stepped out of their presumed roles. Paul Moore was fired, then castigated by an internal HBOS inquiry before the bank's collapse finally vindicated him. Harry Markopolos was so frightened by Madoff's ring of influential investors that he started carrying an airweight Model 642 Smith and Wesson everywhere he went. For none of these Cassandras was their clear-sightedness untrammelled.

When he got home from Iraq, Joe Darby was excoriated by his neighbours. Once Donald Rumsfeld named him on television, he had to relocate and assume a new identity. His old friends weren't proud that he had held America to a higher standard; for him to have looked beyond them was just a form of betrayal.

'He was a rat, he was a traitor, basically he was no good,' said Colin Engelbach, commander of the Veteran of Foreign Wars post in Darby's home town. 'His actions were no good, border-line traitor. Do you put the enemy above your buddies? I wouldn't.'[15]

But not all Cassandras are punished. Though many have had to wait to see their prophecies validated and to earn respect for their foresight, courage and perseverance, they have all found themselves more powerful with the truth than without it. The mother who discovered child abuse in her family found in herself a stronger, more capable parent than she knew she was. The executive who dared to resist the power of silence in a meeting can look back at a problem fixed instead of buried. The bystander who wasn't passive, the soldier who could not obey, all take as their reward a comfort in knowing that they did what they could and did not choose to look away. Hannah Arendt says that what such individuals gain is the knowledge that, whatever else happens, they can live 'together with themselves', continuing in their minds a dialogue that is neither incriminating or soporific but dynamic and alive.

The greatest shock, for Cassandras and whistleblowers alike, is their revised view of the world. Having started as conformists and loyalists, they emerge from their experience wary of authority and sceptical of much that they see and read and hear. Seeing the truth, and then acting on it, changes their vision of life. This independence of mind can instil a profound sense of isolation. But setting themselves free from consolatory fictions can also reveal new allies and soul mates and inspire a vibrant and purposeful identity.

'I don't regret any of it,' says Joe Darby. 'I made my peace with my decision before I turned the pictures in. I knew that if people found out it was me, I wouldn't be liked. But the only time I have ever regretted it was when I was in Iraq and my family was going through a lot. Other than that, I never doubted that it was the right thing. It forced a big change in my life, but the change has been good and bad. I liked my little quiet town, but now I have a new place, with a new job and new opportunities.'

Cynthia Thomas's commitment to running the coffee house

absorbs her night and day. She used to be the one in her family who stayed in touch, brought everyone together; now she's too busy to take a day off. She says her parents are supportive – they're from the military, too – but still don't quite understand. But having seen what she's seen, she can't go back.

'I always used to say, "I don't know what I want to be when I grow up". And now I know. I found myself in this cause and I am not the same person any more.'

As for Markopolos, his testimony about the SEC proved a triumphant performance as he proudly demonstrated how much more one small, smart team could achieve than a vast Washington bureaucracy.

> The four of us did our best to do our duty as private citizens and industry experts to stop what we knew to be the most complex and sinister fraud in American history. We were probably a lot more foolish than brave to keep up our pursuit in the face of such long odds. What troubles us is that hundreds of highly knowledgeable men and women also knew that Bernard Madoff was a fraud and walked away silently, saying nothing and doing nothing. They avoided investing time, energy and money to disclose what they also felt was certain fraud. How can we go forward without assurance that others will not shirk their civic duty?[16]

Such moments of glory are few and far between. But, for all the punishment and pain they sometimes endure, those who struggle to see share a core belief that seeing the truth matters and will have an impact. The most telling quality of Cassandras is that they believe they can have an impact, that change can happen when the truth is confronted, not ignored. Nobody I've spoken to has articulated that more clearly than Sherron Watkins when she talked about meeting Coleen Rowley, who revealed the FBI's failure to act on warnings before 11 September, and Cynthia Cooper, who blew the whistle on MCI/WorldCom's accounting fraud.

'Cynthia Cooper of WorldCom, Coleen Rowley of the FBI and myself were all together because we had been on that cover of *TIME* magazine as Women of the Year. And we were talking about what made us do what we did, and did we have anything important in common. So, we are all three women. We're also first-born. We're also women of faith. We're also breadwinners for our families. But I think the most telling thing about us is that we grew up in tiny towns with less than 10,000 people. And in that small kind of town, there is the sense of: oh goodness, that tree fell down and knocked down that little shed, let's go call the city, or, there's trash in that vacant lot, better pick it up. There's that sense that your actions matter. What you do matters.'

12. SEE BETTER

Lear: Kent, on thy life, no more.
Kent: My life I never held but as a pawn
       To wage against thine enemies; nor fear to lose it,
       Thy safety being the motive.
Lear: Out of my sight!
Kent: See better, Lear . . .

King Lear, William Shakespeare

Cassandras show us that we don't have to be blind. They are inspirational individuals because they prove the possibility of change. Unafraid of conflict, they are more interested in exploring ideas than in defending them. These are people capable of a rich dialogue with themselves, who aren't isolated by power and for many of whom a sense of history delivers an enriched sense of the future. They listen carefully to silence but don't succumb to it. As such, they clearly demonstrate that, while wilful blindness may be part of the human condition, it need not define who we are.

Many people, admiring Cassandras from a distance, hesitate to step into their shoes. The role looks too demanding, the costs too high. But most of us don't wish to go through life blind either. We don't want to collude in what we know to be wrong, and however much we may enjoy the comfort of confirming friends and affirming institutions, we would also like to think we had

some influence over what we see and what we edit out. Alerted
to how insidiously wilful blindness works, we may be more
attuned to it and determine to be on our guard. But old habits
die hard; the riverbed is deep and we can't shake off millennia of
neurobiology and a lifetime of cultural comforts.

What we can do is ask the question: what are the conditions
required for wilful blindness to flourish? How far might we be
able to mitigate those conditions, to make it easier to hear the
quiet voices at the back of our minds begging for attention?
Could we develop new habits to keep us more aware?

We can start by recognising the homogeneity of our lives, our
institutions, neighbourhoods and friends, putting more effort into
reaching out to those who don't fit in and seeing positive value
in those that prove more demanding. Looking at any of our major
institutions – from parliament to corporate boards, think tanks and
churches – that homogeneity suddenly looks like a weakness and
a risk. Diversity, in this context, isn't a form of political correct-
ness but an insurance against the internally generated blindness
that leaves these institutions exposed and out of touch. The very
fact that these groups feel comfortable should ring alarm bells.

By the same token, we have to acknowledge our biases.
Whenever I discuss bias in groups of business leaders and
educators, far from being disturbed by the findings of Implicit
Association Tests, they're rather relieved. Men are glad to hear that
biases aren't all their fault; women and members of religious or
ethnic minorities feel their suspicions have been validated. Maybe
they're reassured to learn that they can't help being biased and
that it isn't personal. What those findings do mean, however, is that
once we've acknowledged the biases we bring to any group, we
have to adjust for them. A balance of bias may be the best we
can achieve.

Knowing the hard limits to our cognitive capacity and the
huge costs of long hours should not be an intractable problem to

address. We have a century of data and a roll call of the disastrous consequences that follow those who insist that heroic hours are a proof of commitment to an employer. Companies that measure work by hours could make themselves smarter by the simple act of measuring contribution by output rather than input, and celebrating those who can go home early.

Many people – and not a few companies – like to think that they can somehow stretch the cognitive limits of their minds, that doing lots of Sudoku or using programs like *Brain Trainer* will somehow enlarge their capacity. They're out of luck. The only exercise that seems to nurture, or at least protect our brains is aerobic exercise.[1] Yoga, toning and stretching may make you feel good but, in fMRI scans, only aerobic exercise seemed to have a visibly positive impact on the brain. If you want to protect your own intellectual capacity, or that of your employees, the only way to do that is to go to the gym – or go home. When Gail Rebuck assumed the chairmanship of Random House, she inherited what she calls 'an hours culture' in which everyone stayed late to impress the boss. Unwilling and unable to work this way herself, she let it be known that anyone working past six p.m. was either incompetent or had a boss who didn't understand how to manage workload. The culture shifted overnight. The sooner we associate long hours and multitasking with incompetence and carelessness the better. The next time you hear boasts of executives pulling an all-nighter or holding conference calls in their cars, be sure to offer your condolences: it's grim being stuck in sweatshops run by managers too ignorant to understand productivity and risk. Working people like this is as smart as running your factory without maintenance. In manufacturing and engineering businesses, everyone learns that the top priority is asset integrity: protecting the machinery on which the business depends. In knowledge-based economies, that machinery is the mind.

We can – and should – all learn to be extremely wary of big
ideas, the grand ideologies that appear too neatly to answer all
questions. But being wary isn't enough to combat blindness; we
need actively to seek disconfirmation. When Alice Stewart conducted her survey on childhood cancers, she worked with a
statistician named George Kneale and their partnership is a model
of how different, contentious minds can support each other.

'I couldn't have done anything without George,' Alice Stewart
told her biographer, Gayle Greene. 'I like to think he's the power
engine of our ship and that I occasionally flick the steering
wheel.'[2]

Fellow scientists described Kneale's work as outstanding, elegant and exquisite, but what's most interesting is the way that
Kneale himself thought about his job.

'It's my job to prove that Dr Stewart's theories are wrong. I am,
in effect, trying to disprove her. Hence the strength of our long
association.'[3]

In his seeking for *dis*confirmation, Stewart knew that Kneale
protected her from potential blindness in her own thinking – and
she was smart and confident enough to appreciate that challenge.
What Kneale and Stewart understood between them was that the
risk of losing their theory was outweighed by the danger of being
blind. To paraphrase Voltaire, they understood (in ways that
Greenspan could not) that, while doubt isn't a very pleasant condition, certainty is absurd.

Theirs was an elegant and inspiring collaboration between two
very different people: Stewart articulate, sociable and energetic,
Kneale withdrawn, shy, more comfortable with numbers than
people. What made them so effective was not that they were the
same but that they brought different thinking styles, questions and
challenges to a problem whose solution they both sought. They
tackled a common purpose with uncommon levels of challenge
and debate. It was precisely because Kneale kept trying to

disprove Stewart – and couldn't – that enabled her to stand up for so many years against Richard Doll and the medical establishment. If we admire what Stewart did, we might best express that admiration by adopting her methods.

The ability to endure debate and conflict requires practice and it takes protection. This can be done with humour, as when the CEO of British Airways Colin Marshall appointed Paul Birch to be the official corporate Fool. Birch had a licence to speak up and to challenge.

'One of the roles of the jester is to declare, "Just because you're the boss doesn't mean you know better,"' Birch said. 'The jester's role is to draw attention to things that are going wrong, to stir things up.'

Birch says he got the idea from *King Lear* but he used his position to get BA employees to unpack some of their conventional thinking and to approach problems in different ways. It helped, he said, to highlight customer grievances and to enable executives to see how foolish they, and the company, could be at times.

'When things go wrong,' he said, 'employees usually have a good idea of how to fix them. You need to create a state in which they've got the courage to do something. You want to build organisations where everyone sees provocation as one of their essential roles.'[4]

Writing about groupthink, Irving Janis recommended institutionalising dissent. He used the example of the Vatican, which used to appoint a Devil's Advocate to ask hard questions during the process of canonisation. When Janis was writing, there was evidence that the role had decayed into a formality, but at least it still existed. Today, it's sad (but perhaps telling) that the post has been abolished. We would do well to resurrect it within our organisations as a means of protecting dissent and encouraging argument.

'How do you know what's going on in the company?' my

CFO once asked me. It was a brilliant question because, regardless of the size of the company or the leadership, it's very hard to answer. Many executives say the numbers tell them everything, but anyone working in those organisations knows that that is wrong. In some of the organisations I've worked with, we have conducted blind audits and obedience audits, in an effort to gauge how much organisational silence, obedience and conformity we had within the organisation. The results were always startling, because they unearthed the unmentionables: the known unknowns that no one wanted to talk about. That helped us to understand what needed to be changed and, perhaps more importantly, sent a signal that silence wasn't golden, it was dangerous.

When she ran Guidant, CEO Ginger Graham instigated a form of radical honesty, designed to ensure that she, and her management team, unearthed silent truth, recognised their own biases and adjusted for them.

'Each member of the senior management team would take turns sitting on a tall stool in front of the room. One by one, their peers would bring up a shortcoming they'd observed and offer suggestions for improvement. The manager on the hot seat could only listen, not comment. As you can imagine, many a manager's first impulse was to disagree or try to explain away some of these comments. But if several people in the group mentioned the same thing, the manager would begin to understand that his or her behaviour truly needed to be addressed. As the members of the management team became more comfortable with this approach, they began to welcome more and more feedback.'

Graham acknowledged that the process sounded rather cruel but said that what it achieved was a level of honesty among colleagues she hadn't achieved any other way. The fact that she too took part in it was essential and she valued it because it allowed her to see what her biases and mental habits obscured.

'There is tremendous power in an organisation when you hear the truth said out loud. The cat is out of the bag. We can see the cat. Now, are we going to just look at it or do something about it? We had changed the frame.

'You have to decide you are going to seek disconfirmation; you just can't expect it spontaneously to emerge because it won't happen,' she told me. 'In many meetings, we would assign someone in public to be devil's advocate, to call out challenges, disagreements, identify holes, gaps and concerns. You need to be really clear about the role. The person taking it has to be thanked and rewarded for it. Another way to do the same thing is to ask two questions: what are all the reasons we are right? What are all the reasons we are wrong? It takes a lot of discipline to do this, and not to stack the deck.'

Bringing in outsiders is one way to identify the unconscious knowledge embedded within organisations and bring it to the surface. It can be startling how a little dissent, how even a few questions, can change the tenor of a discussion. Graham used coaches in her organisation a great deal, to deliver feedback to her about her own performance and to keep the dialogue within her organisation open and free-flowing. Hers was a concerted and consistent attempt to ensure she was not surrounded by ostriches, that her organisation was not silent. Critical to her success was not just having one outside voice, but having a multitude of voices and perspectives. She engineered what many leaders miss: debate.

'I wish someone had challenged me,' John Browne wrote when reviewing his mercurial career running BP. 'I wish someone had challenged me and been brave enough to say: "We need to ask more disagreeable questions."' Browne could have sought out more serious challenge, and he should have. That he did not says much about him and the organisation that Tony Hayward inherited.

'Once you are in a leadership position, no one will ever give you the inner circle you need,' says Saj-nicole Joni. 'You have to go out and find it.' Joni is a professional 'third opinion', the thinking partner who works with leaders and who, uniquely, has no agenda.

'When you are at the top of an organisation, everyone has an agenda,' she says. 'They will either be pushing forward their agenda to please you, or their own agenda to enhance themselves. That's fine; you can recognise that and that's the first opinion you'll get. Then you'll get a second opinion from a technical expert: a lawyer, accountant, software architect or strategist. But you need a third opinion which comes from someone who has nothing but your best interests, the company's best interests, at heart. That person is a thinking partner. Not someone who knows the answer but thinks alongside with you in order to find it.'

What Joni is describing is that dialogue with oneself that Arendt calls thinking – except she's suggesting it doesn't have to be done alone. It is the very best leaders, she says, who recognise that they need this dialogue and who reach out and find the people with whom they can have it.

'Most leaders in big positions live in a world where every major decision is never really clearly right or wrong. They become aware of that often through some jarring event in their life – illness, some level of fear, perhaps something that happened in their childhood. And they realise that, at the level they're playing, if they don't get countervailing voices, they are personally at risk of not meeting their obligations.'

Talking to her, it's clear why Joni is a third opinion. She works hard at thinking. She comes, she says, from a family where what she was told as a child didn't fully explain what she saw. That left her with a lifelong drive to search for the full story. In conversation, her responses don't automatically echo or affirm what's been said, but challenge it, test it, take it further. Joni believes that, in order not to be blind, two things are critical: unvarnished truth and unfettered exploration. One alone won't do.

'If you just do unfettered exploration, it wastes energy. The exploration has to have impact; it has to be mission-critical and real. Same with unvarnished truth. Leaders who don't build the networks that bring them the truth will make big mistakes. Having a small network of people who will bring you the unvarnished truth and with whom you can have unfettered exploration, they are a partial antidote to wilful blindness.

'True leaders – whether they are at the top of an organisation or within it – know that you cannot go into execution mode and retain peripheral vision. You can't focus both on the woods and the trees. So you need a network to watch out when you have your head down. There is tremendous value to being able to shut down and focus – but you put yourself at risk if you don't have people out there scouting the horizon, covering your back.'

Joni says that part of what third opinions provide, and monitor, is dissonance. They don't look to quell it; rather they look to ensure that there is appropriate dissonance around critical issues.

'It's about having the right fight. Dissonance has value but it has to be practical. Leaders have to ask: what issues are so critical that we create end-to-end line of sight and structured dissonance around them? You can't do it on everything. You have to choose where it counts and make it work, and stop nonsense everywhere else. Using your riverbed analogy: what dissonance and third opinions offer is a tributary that takes you somewhere else, gives you a different perspective. It isn't so wildly different that it's irrelevant – but it stops you sinking into a place where you cannot see what's happening around you.'

In his analysis of why smart executives fail, Sydney Finkelstein calls companies where there is no dissent 'zombie companies'.[5]

These zombie companies can still be full of energy and activity, and they may even inspire tremendous loyalty and generate a great deal of cash. But, as Pat Lewis found at Bear Stearns, that activity is blind because it can't and won't embrace the 'trouble-maker' who is on the lookout for unpredictable threats and challenges.

Outsiders – whether you call them Cassandras, devil's advocates, dissidents, troublemakers, fools or coaches – are essential to any leader's ability to see. But it's impossible for outsiders to remain outsiders for ever. At Harvard Business School, Max Bazerman has looked extensively at the forces of wilful blindness that conspire to erode the independent perspective of auditors. They may be humourless but their role is the same as the Fool's: to challenge, question, and test assumptions. The real problem, Bazerman concluded, is not that auditors are blatantly corrupted; such cases are very rare. What is more common is that, over time, the outsider's familiarity with the business biases them in its favour, or in favour of its ends and goals. This is entirely unconscious and they can't help it – which is why Bazerman recommends that auditors have defined contract periods.

'Auditors must have fixed, limited contract periods during which they cannot be terminated. All fees and other contractual details should be specified at the beginning of the contract and must be unchangeable. In addition, the client must be prohibited from rehiring the auditing firm at the end of the contract; instead, the major accounting firms would be required to rotate clients.'[6]

Current legislation doesn't make these requirements; it mandates auditor rotation but this is just defined as a change in the lead partner within the firm – not a change of firm itself. And there is nothing in current regulations to prevent a client from firing an auditor. In other words, many of the incentives to turn a blind eye to accounting detail remain firmly in place.

Bazerman also argues that clients should be prohibited from hiring auditors to come and work for them. As he points out, 'an auditor can't be impartial when he or she hopes to please a client in order to develop job options'. That Bazerman recommends such draconian steps isn't because he has some deep-seated suspicion of accountants. It is because he understands all too well the forces that conspire to make, and keep, such advisors blind. His insights could apply to any outside advisors, because that process of unconscious bias isn't specific to accounting but to being human.[7]

So we can't depend on outsiders alone. We need also to develop in ourselves two critical habits: critical thinking and courage.

I remember studying Hegel with Michael Tanner, a notorious and difficult philosophy professor, renowned for his leather jackets and a record collection – mostly Wagner – that covered most of his office floor. After reading him my analysis of Hegel's *Philosophy of History*, I looked to him for praise that I'd mastered so difficult and obscure a text. No chance. 'That's fine,' said Tanner, unimpressed. 'Now: what's wrong with Hegel?' That was the beginning of my education. What's a little worrying is that such critical thinking hadn't occurred to me until I got to university.

To be a critical thinker starts with resisting the urge to be a pleaser. Today, I'm shocked by the consistency with which my students prefer knowing the 'right' answer to the process of searching for it. 'Tell me what I need to know to get a good grade/pass the exam/get the degree' is the common student's refrain. Years of GCSE drills haven't helped, shaped as they are by a highly confined sense of what constitutes the 'right' answer. Yeats may have believed that 'education is not the filling of a bucket but the lighting of a fire' but most schools today are judged by how well they keep those buckets topped up. Their students are being taught an intellectual form of obedience so that, by the time they reach university, their idea of debate is often little more than second-guessing the instructor. When their answer is the same as mine, they believe they're right – and they stop thinking just when they most need to start.

In medical schools, this is a well-understood and studied phenomenon. Medical students themselves say that they tend to be conventional, obedient 'good' kids, not likely to challenge what they're told. And the 'hidden curriculum' of their training demonstrably exacerbates those tendencies.[8] But such behaviours aren't unique to medicine. The combination of fewer university places, together with reduced job opportunities and rising costs, has produced a generation of deeply compliant, submissive students intimidated by the competition and lack of opportunity that they know awaits them on graduation. When business-school leaders start wondering whether they should teach critical thinking, you have to wonder what they've been teaching heretofore – *uncritical* thinking? Is that thinking at all – or just a style of informed obedience that carries on, uninterrupted, into employment?

'Jail is full of pleasers,' says Justin Paperny. He's one of Pavlo's protégées, another young man who made the wrong choices in financial services and ended up in jail. Today, inspired by Pavlo, he shares his experiences with college students, trying to warn them of the dangers he so blithely overlooked.

'The other day, I was doing a talk at the University of Southern California, and I asked: "How many of you are pleasers?" Three-quarters of the hands go up. And I said to them, "How you are today in the classroom is how you will be at work. I was a pleaser. If you will do anything for an A, then you will do anything for your boss."

'I wanted to please my professor. Thinking back to high school, I think of people who were not afraid to be different, to think their own way. Sometimes they were ostracised and people

made fun of them – but lots of people secretly admired them! I
never had their courage. I wanted to fit in and not be different.
And I look at those people now and they have wonderful lives!
They're their own people, living their own lives.'

Their own people, living their own lives: that is what we
should aspire to in the schools that we build and the teaching that
we deliver. Not compliant, obedient conformists but individuals
who insist on thinking for themselves.

That aspiration lies at the heart of programmes developed by
the psychologist Philip Zimbardo. Having learned from his
Stanford Prison Experiment just how powerfully the dynamics of
a situation can blind us to who we are and the moral impact of
our actions, Zimbardo has devoted a distinguished career to interrogating many of the behaviours which that early experiment
showed him: how do we raise and educate individuals so that
they will think for themselves, challenge what they see, be prepared to turn their assumptions upside down and examine them?
In particular, how do we teach them to resist the influence of the
situations in which they find themselves?

'One of the things we used to do,' Zimbardo recalled, 'was
something I called "deviant for a day". It was just a little exercise in trying to step outside yourself, violate your own image
and see what happens. Sometimes it was no more than just
putting a dot on your head and walking around like that all day.
The world responds to you differently – so you see the world
differently.'

The exercise, Zimbardo told me, made the students aware of
just how responsive they were to what their friends expected of
them. They came to appreciate just how easily and unwittingly
they conformed to others' expectations of them. They got used
to being pleasers because that's what everyone else was doing,
too.

'Their friends want them to be their expectation, for them to behave as they're "supposed" to behave. But at the end, they all say that the experience of bucking that expectation is so liberating – breaking these bonds. It's tremendously important to learn that you do not have to be, and you do not have to think, what everyone else expects or wants you to be or to think. That you can be your own person.'

Zimbardo was creating for his students the experience that Roy Spence had with his sister: learning how to think about what other people are seeing and what they themselves might be missing. Such critical thinking is pointless and frustrating however, without the courage to act on it.

That's the aim of Ervin Staub's programme for teaching children how to deal with bullies: the development of interventionists who have the courage and expertise not to be passive but who gain the experience of standing up for others. The same thinking underlies Zimbardo's newest venture, the Heroic Imagination Project, which aims to find, train and celebrate ordinary men and women who see and seize the opportunity to reach beyond their own narrow purview to become what he calls 'ordinary heroes'.

'We are currently pilot-testing a full-scale hero curriculum for fifth-graders in Michigan and Wisconsin and we want to transfer it to summer camps and clubs,' Zimbardo told me. 'We also are hoping to bring it to the UK. The goal is to change people's patterns of understanding, altering their thinking from "me" to "we". We do think anyone can be a hero but it's about compassion, altruism, empathy and moral courage to empower people to take positive action during crucial moments in their lives.'

When Zimbardo talked about his Project to a group of some 600 sixth-formers gathered to hear him in London, their enthusiasm was palpable. They had an instant, visceral response to the idea that they did not have to be passive, that their dissonant perspectives could be positive, constructive, even heroic.

All of these programmes confront that fear of conflict that so often leaves us paralysed, preferring not to see. Their emphasis on rehearsal – practising and acting out different kinds of response – is based on the premise that this is how we can change the way our minds are comfortable behaving. Their big promise is that they teach generations of individuals not to be bystanders. Crimes like the poisoning of Libby, Montana, aren't perpetrated by a few bad people but by large numbers of individuals who don't blow the whistle, don't stand up and say 'no'.

Changing the game can require surprisingly little: a simple question – Do we mean this? Did I understand correctly? – can turn the tide. The French sociologist, Serge Moscovici, found that just the existence of a minority opinion can have a huge impact on the direction discussions take. Subsequent researchers have found that just knowing that there is a dissenting voice is enough to induce different cognitive processes that yield better judgements.[9] Each one of us needs to develop the courage to be that voice when we are worried by what we see.

Context counts. Undoubtedly there are organisational constructs and cultures that create more favourable conditions for wilful blindness than others. Heroic leadership styles, companies highly focused on the power and influence of a single individual, provoke the kind of second-guessing among executives that stops them thinking or analysing what they know to be true. It is always intrinsically difficult for leaders to know what is going on in their organisations, but never more so than when their personalities or egos quash debate or dissent. That so many recent corporate and institutional failures have occurred inside organisations with strong leaders should make us all wonder whether the celebrity of magazine covers and guru status is good for anyone. Whether CEOs are celebrated for being a 'Sun King', 'the most aggressive CEO in America' or whiz-kids, you can be sure that the more elevated their status, the less likely it is that anyone will dare to articulate an uncomfortable truth. Power is dangerous, a bubble and a barrier. Wise leaders would do well to see it as a handicap, not a reward – unless there is a profound level of discontinuity built into the environment already.

'In India, it is just impossible to escape contradiction,' says Ajit Nayak. He's been studying the emergence of Indian businesses and business leaders over the last decade. 'India, as a nation, is still under construction – so no matter how successful you are, it is impossible to keep life out. You can't escape people. You can go on the train and you're looking out the window and you will never see the landscape without people in it. So even if you're very wealthy and you're very successful, the contradictions of poverty and disease and just the sheer difficulty of getting things done – they're always right there in front of you. You cannot be cut-off; you can't sanitise your experience. The contradictions are everywhere.'

He's particularly intrigued by Ratan Tata, who runs the largest business and is the largest employer in India. Tata lives alone in a small flat; his lifestyle is striking only for its lack of flamboyance.

'If you take someone like Ratan Tata,' says Nayak, 'he sits in the front of his car with his driver. He can't sit in the back and read the paper because it's too bumpy. There are so many pot-holes in the road that it's just physically impossible to read! So he knows when his driver's child is sick and what he needs to do because they talk. He has no choice; they have to engage.'

However uncomfortable they may be, the potholes of Indian roads help to keep Tata connected. The discontinuities of life in India, says Nayak, are so endemic that the bubble of power into which the wealthy and successful disappear in the West simply doesn't exist.

'It's very paradoxical because Indian companies are very hier-archical so you will be surrounded by yes men. But at the same time, the country itself is so unpredictable that you can build a company – as Sunil Mittal did, importing generators – and then have it taken away from you. So you know you just have to keep interrogating everything you see. Because the one thing you know is that you cannot control what will happen.'

That a discontinuous environment might constitute a competitive advantage is an interesting thought. But Tata's motto – question the unquestionable – suggests that his perspective isn't merely passive but deliberate. Is it possible to engineer this kind of discontinuity? Perhaps. Two psychologists – one from California, one from Canada – did it just by asking their students to read an absurd short story by Kafka, 'The Country Doctor'.[10] The story is full of contradictory or apparently senseless details. Its non-linear untraditional story is uncomfortable; it won't fit our expectation and that, it turns out, can be quite a good challenge for our brains.

'People feel uncomfortable when their expected associations are violated,' said Travis Proulx, one of the study's authors. 'That creates an unconscious desire to make sense of their surroundings. That feeling of discomfort may come from a surreal story, or from contemplating their own contradictory behaviours, but, either way, they're motivated to learn new patterns.'

After reading the short story, Proulx's volunteers were both more motivated to look for different patterns – and more successful in finding them. In other words, they could see more. Proulx was at pains to point out that merely assailing your mind with Kafka, Lewis Carroll or a David Lynch movie won't suddenly enhance your performance; it is the unexpectedness of the experience that counts.

'What is critical here is that our participants were not expecting to encounter this bizarre story [he continued]. If you expect that you'll encounter something strange or out of the ordinary, you won't experience the same sense of alienation. You may be disturbed by it, but you won't show the same learning ability.

The key to our study is that our participants were surprised by the series of unexpected events, and they had no way to make sense of them. Hence, they strived to make sense of something else.'[11]

Although this is what many an offsite tries to achieve, many leaders would balk at artificially injecting discontinuity into their working environment, arguing that the economic environment is quite disturbing enough as it is. But what Proulx's experiment aimed at − jolting us out of blinkered thinking and obedient behaviour − can be achieved in less dramatic ways.

Perplexed by the findings of his own groupthink hypothesis, Irving Janis proposed that leaderless meetings might free participants to explore a wider array of information and solutions. That bad habit of second-guessing doesn't disappear even after college; however vigilant leaders can be, in suppressing their own thoughts and preferences, opinion and debate often flow more freely in their absence. Once anyone has a hint of a desired outcome − and smart people infer some hints from nothing more than a word or two − the desire to please the boss can eliminate a whole range of options.

My best memory of my management team captures a moment in the history of our company when we needed to confront major, operational issues on the east coast at the same time that I had to be on the west coast. I tried phoning in for a while but it was clear the team could talk to me or talk to each other. The decisions they made that day without me were some of the smartest we made.

The value of my absence was that it allowed people to change position without feeling that they were losing face. One of the reasons groups become so polarised is because participants feel that, having laid out their position, changing it appears weak. That nervousness is exacerbated when the boss is present. Discussions and creative dissonance, though, aren't about defending but about exploring positions – and that's easier when no one feels that changing their mind looks indecisive.

Similarly, setting several different teams to solve the same problem sends a clear message that there are no right answers; what matters is to find as wide an array of possible answers as possible. One of the best chief executives I've ever seen in action, Carol Vallone of WebCT, used to require her department heads to change roles when debating strategy. That way, she said, they had to abandon their silos and adopt different perspectives.

History is a different perspective, albeit one that is strikingly absent from most business thinking and education. The commercial world's love affair with novelty, innovation and revolution is so pronounced as to blind it to longer-term trends and patterns. As eager as every pundit and politician was to castigate BP during its Deepwater Horizon disaster, what no one wanted to know about was the 'heroic' leadership style of John Browne and its long-term impact on the firm he had built. The excitement and heat around the event focused on the here and now, not on any of the harder, deeper lessons that might have been derived from a longer view. It was easier to castigate Tony Hayward's poor decisions than to reflect on the origins of a company apparently unable to fix itself.

When I discussed the lack of history in the business community with Frank Partnoy, who has himself so wryly chronicled wild examples of Wall Street malfeasance, he was aghast.

'Certain aspects of history just tend to disappear. We hear it but don't want to hear it – so it goes away. And then we have to learn all those important lessons anew. Many of my students haven't heard of Ken Lay or Michael Milken or Ivar Kreuger. There are kids graduating now who know nothing about Enron. I sometimes think the only way around this is to make desk calendars to keep those memories in front of you: Frank Partnoy's financial-fraud desk calendar!'

We talked about Alfred Chandler, who had, virtually single-handedly, invented deep, analytic business history and had lived long enough (until 2007 when he died at the age of eighty-eight) to remember much of it personally. But today, Partnoy reckoned, Chandler wouldn't even get tenure. Business schools prefer to teach instead the live case study, always in the present, with no past at all. There is a special narcissism in the belief that we, and our times, are special, that we have nothing to learn from the past – even about who we are. This extreme bias for the present leaves us blind to the patterns and trends developing all around us.

One of the benefits of a sense of history is that it can alert us to trends, and sensitise us to weak signals. If we paid attention – for more than a few weeks – to Steve Bolsin's experience in Bristol, doctors in the NHS might know how well they're performing and whether they're more likely than their colleagues to kill or cure their patients. The challenge of weak signals, or near misses, is knowing when to take them seriously and when to dismiss them. Most people aren't seers; they can't immediately tell the difference.

Weak signals acquire meaning when you bring them together to map trends. That's what Steve Bolsin was trying to do when he began to collect data about the children's heart operations in Bristol. When he got to Australia, he took that idea one stage further and conducted an experiment in which anaesthesiology clinicians, covering more than 26,000 cases in 100 hospitals, carried personal digital assistants (PDAs) to collect three kinds of data: logbook data (keeping track of hours and kinds of work undertaken), personal performance data (such as success or failure in arterial-line or catheter insertions) and incident reporting (which are basically errors and mistakes). The data was then automatically analysed before being returned to the clinician, who then got a clear, objective report of their own performance. What Bolsin says this generated is 'the "near miss" incident data, which has been the "holy grail" of health care safety experts'.[12]

Bolsin's experiment was tremendously successful: a documented 98 per cent recording rate among trainees appeared to reverse the effects of their 'hidden curriculum'. But two very interesting features emerged from the study. First, participants took part in it because they wanted to improve their own performance – and the simple PDA helped them to monitor their own patterns. It allowed them to see how they were doing, without the interference of their own biases. Second, although there was no requirement for publication or sharing of individual performance data, some specialists actually wanted to use their performance charts to demonstrate the likely risks of complications to patients. The data depersonalised some of the hard decisions they were facing and made it easier for everyone to see what their choices were.

Perhaps most important of all, Bolsin's study demonstrated that it is possible, even easy, to collect performance data that is useful, relevant and current. It's also, potentially, very powerful.

'If they had just collected mortality data for general practices in the UK,' Bolsin told me, 'they could have picked up Harold Shipman before he had killed one hundred patients [and he may have killed as many as four hundred]. At eighty patients, he would have been detected as an outlier. It would have been the same at Bristol. Just ten deaths would have made the department an outlier – but over sixty children died. Data will help us if we are prepared to do it.'

Tracking weak signals also tests hypotheses, wild guesses that may, or may not, turn out to be prescient. After all, how do you know anything has changed if you are still collecting the same data from the same people in the same way?

That was the question Herb Meyer asked himself when, in the

early 1980s, he began to forecast the collapse of the Soviet
Union. Meyer's a contentious figure, then and now. Deceptively
understated, he describes himself as running a small independent
publishing business in Washington State. What that doesn't tell
you is that, under Reagan, he served as Special Assistant to the
Director of Central Intelligence, and Vice Chairman of the CIA's
National Intelligence Council. In that capacity, he managed the
production of the US National Intelligence Estimates – which
meant that, in the face of derision from the political and intelligence communities, he could test his hypothesis that the USSR
was on the verge of collapse.

'Everyone was telling us the Soviet Union was fine. Our spies
would bring us information about how many bombs, how many
tanks. They would bring us all the data they'd always brought us.
So we kept thinking what we'd always been thinking. Ask the
same questions of the same people, of course you're going to get
the same answers.

'So I decided to do something different. I made a list of everything I might expect to find if my hypothesis was right. If the
Soviet economy was collapsing, what would you see? If it *wasn't*
collapsing, what would you see? And then – this is the critical
part – I made sure all that information went to one guy. Just one
guy. Then, if nothing comes in, you have your answer. And it
doesn't get lost in all the noise.'

One of the pieces of information that came in, Meyer told me,
was news that a weekly meat train had been hijacked and all the
meat stolen. The army had come out – but then the Politburo
had told the army to back off but tell no one. Let the people have
the meat.

'Well, that's not what happens when everything in the
economy's just fine, is it? You don't have people stealing meat and
you don't have the army letting them get away with it. So that
started to tell us something. And then there was more like that.

What's important is that, without the hypothesis, that piece of information would never *ever* have been picked up. That's what didn't happen in 9/11: we weren't looking for what we couldn't see.'

What Meyer was doing was accumulating weak signals to see if they added up to a meaningful trend. He might have been wrong. But if he had been wrong, he would at least have known that.

Doesn't all of this require a great deal of time and patience? Yes it does. But the best decisions require testing, painful discussion, dialogue, thinking without banisters. In his memoirs, the diplomat George Kennan described one of the greatest and boldest decisions ever made, which was the creation of the Marshall Plan by the US government at the end of the Second World War.

You say: 'This should not be so difficult. Why don't we tell these people to draw up a plan for the reconstruction of their economic life and we'll see whether we can support it?'

Someone says, 'That's no good. They are too tired to draw up a plan. We have to do it for them.'

Then someone says: 'Maybe what we need isn't a plan at all. Maybe we just haven't given them enough in the past. If we just give them more, things will work out all right.'

Another then says: 'That's probably true but we've got to figure out how the money is going to be spent.'

Then somebody says: 'That's right, we need a program but it would be a mistake for us to try to draw this program up all by ourselves.'

Then someone says: 'That's absolutely right. The thing for us to do is to tell these Europeans to draw up a plan and submit it . . .'[13]

Kennan describes being driven to tears of agony and frustration by the endless critical debate and evaluation that eventually produced the plan – and yet it was he who insisted from the outset that this kind of open debate was needed.

Essential issues aren't going to be resolved quickly. Who ever imagined global warming was going to be solved in one week? If the issue is so vital, isn't it worth spending time on it? We should remember the patience and pain that the Marshall Plan required, and be prepared to stay until we are resolved. If one of the symptoms of blindness is comfort, so one of the indicators of critical thinking may be discomfort. That's why unanimous decisions are intrinsically suspicious. Were there no options? No alternatives? Unanimous decisions are incomplete decisions, made when there is too much power in the room, too much obedience and too much conformity. If only one solution is visible, look again.

The sheer complexity of many decisions makes blindness all the more tempting. Can't these things be simplified? Can't we leave it to the experts?

'The banking world became very siloed in part because it all looked so complicated and geeky and boring,' says Gillian Tett, one of the few journalists who was willing to work through banking's complexity to see what was going on. 'But there are lots of issues that are like that – like global warming and poverty and science – and these are really going to affect our lives! We can't afford to delegate knowledge of these things to experts because that's how those silos get built. And not just in businesses but in our lives, in our society.'

Her point is well made. As long as we back away from subjects we find too complex or too complicated, we keep ourselves blind, abdicating responsibility. The banking collapse could happen, Tett argues, because we let it happen by our decision not to question financial instruments we did not understand. 'You need cultural translators – journalists, academics, thinkers who can interpret a lot of technical information,' Tett concedes. 'You need them to make these subjects accessible, so that we are *all* thinking about them. We have to ask ourselves: how many silos are there that I am shutting my eyes to? We need constant monitoring of those silos and a lot of checks and balances so they cannot get so isolated.'

In Libby, Montana, Andrew Schneider was one of those cultural translators. Had he not written his story for the *Seattle Post-Intelligencer*, Libby's children might still be playing in contaminated playgrounds. But that newspaper published its last print edition on 17 March 2009. It still exists online and Schneider now publishes his own investigative journalism online (www.coldtruth.com). But the time and money that must be invested to uncover stories like Libby are increasingly hard to find.

As newspaper revenues decline, they have fewer reporters but more stories. That means the capacity to commit time and people to long-term investigations has almost disappeared. The American journalist Heather Brooke was a cultural translator, fighting her Freedom of Information battle for years, trying to get public insight into the expenses of Members of Parliament. She had the help of a barrister working *pro bono* but no British newspaper was up for the challenge. In the US, when Harry Markopolos tried to warn investors about Bernard Madoff, he worked with a *Wall Street Journal* journalist, John Wilke, for *three years* but Wilke never had time to write the story. He had all the information – Markopolos had done the work – but the paper had too many stories, too few reporters. Had the paper unmasked Madoff earlier they might have caught him before all his investors' money was gone.

Investigative reporting, whether in newspapers or television, has a grand but fading tradition of asking hard questions and unveiling awkward truths. It is an expensive business, because it takes time, effort and legal protection and it will ultimately disappear if our desire to be entertained cripples our need to be informed.

'We need to keep having discussions about what is important to an open society,' Heather Brooke argues. 'The public needs to understand that, if the media are considered just to be business operations, and if they abdicate their responsibility by reading *OK!* and celebrity gossip all day, then they can't expect the government to be upstanding or to be held to account. It is up to everyone to be involved, keep an eye out and be aware of what is going on and to be outraged when their trust is abused. But if people just sit around reading *Heat* or *Hello!* and don't stay engaged, then they have to accept a corrupt government. A corrupt banking system. And scientists who lie. If you can't be bothered to know what is going on, you have no right to complain. It comes down to whether you think of yourself as a child and a victim or as an adult who can make change.'

It is in this context that new ventures, like ProPublica and Wikileaks, take on crucial importance. Both were set up to counter the waning of investigative journalism, albeit they address the challenge in quite different ways. ProPublica focuses on stories 'with moral force', aiming to produce journalism that 'shines a light on the exploitation of the weak by the strong and on the failures of those with power to vindicate the trust placed in them'.

'We won't lobby. We won't ally with politicians or advocacy groups. We look hard at the critical functions of business and of government, the two biggest centers of power, in areas ranging from product safety to securities fraud, from flaws in our system of criminal justice to practices that undermine fair elections. But we also focus on such institutions as unions, universities, hospitals, foundations and on the media when they constitute the strong exploiting or oppressing the weak, or when they are abusing the public trust.'

In 2009, the website's first full year of publication, ProPublica won the Pulitzer Prize for Investigative Reporting, the George Polk

Award for environmental reporting, the National Magazine Award for Reporting, the Selden Ring Award for 'investigative reporting that has brought results' from the Annenberg School of the University of Southern California, both the Magazine Award and the Online Award from Investigative Reporters and Editors, the Overseas Press Club Online Journalism Award, the Sigma Delta Chi Award for online investigative reporting, the Edward R. Murrow Award for Media Entrepreneurship, the Dart Award for Excellence in Coverage of Trauma and the James Aronson Award for Social Justice Journalism. Funding for the site depends entirely on charitable donations.

In conjunction with PBS's *Frontline* programme, ProPublica conducted a lengthy investigation into BP's safety and environmental record. What was so striking was their commitment to this project long after Deepwater Horizon had disappeared from from pages around the world.*

Also funded by donations, Wikileaks operates a different model, providing a publishing platform for leaked information which is classified, confidential, censored or otherwise withheld from the public and which must be deemed 'of political, diplomatic, ethical or historic significance' by its board. Since launching in December 2006, the site has posted leaked documents on everything from Somali execution plans to the Iraq War, scientology and Russian oil field explosions. It exists explicitly as an outlet for whistleblowers whom it goes to great technical lengths to protect. Its servers are distributed over multiple international jurisdictions and the servers do not keep logs, so that no records of their access can be seized. Anonymisation is built into the Wikileaks network so that no one – neither the organisation itself nor any government or enforcement agency – can know who has accessed the site. In addition, the organisation

* The Spill, PBS *Frontline*, transmitted 28 Oct, 2010

provides instructions on how to submit material by post and from netcafés and wireless hotspots, so that, were WikiLeaks to be infiltrated by a government intelligence agency, leakers could not be traced. All of this is designed to make it safe to surface and expose the information which others might prefer we remain blind to.

In July 2010, Wikileaks was widely criticised when it published over 90,000 pages of documents concerning the Iraq War. Publishing the documents, military leaders argued, put the lives of informants and collaborators at risk. But at the heart of Wikileak's mission is the belief, as articulated by the Supreme Court when ruling on the Pentagon Papers, that 'only a free and unrestrained press can effectively expose deception in government'.

According to the site, 'It is easy to perceive the connection between publication and the complaints people make about publication. But this generates a perception bias, because it overlooks the vastness of the invisible. It overlooks the unintended consequences of failing to publish and it overlooks all those who are emancipated by a climate of free speech.'

In other words, the organisation is using a combination of technology and international legal jurisdictions to try to ensure that citizens and media outlets can no longer say that they were blind, that they did not and could not know what was being done in their name. What is less clear is whether people will make the effort to look. While the public appetite for 90,000 pages of confidential government memos may be limited, for impact, Wikileaks still needed traditional media to make sense of it.

When you make the effort to look, to do the critical thinking, what you come up with are a lot of critical questions. And in the course of writing this book, several have stuck with me.

As I've watched BP wrestle with its operational issues, I've begun to wonder whether we now have organisations that are simply too complex to manage. There's a whole army of complexity consultants who seem to revel in the sheer difficulty we have created for ourselves. After John Browne left BP and the company sat down to try to analyse what had gone so horribly wrong, one of the culprits they identified was their love of complexity. In their intellectual hubris, the company leaders believed that their ability to manage internal complexity was a source of competitive advantage. This is Daedalus gone mad. Instead of worshipping complexity, we need to challenge it.

But BP is not unique in its love affair with complexity. Many organisations view their own impenetrability as a feat of fantastic intellectual virtuosity. They pride themselves on how hard their businesses are to understand. In reality, it's a huge cause of blindness and explains why, when such companies get into trouble, they can't find their way out of it. Aren't we in danger of building monstrosities we can't run? Never mind too big to fail – haven't we built corporations that, in their size, complexity and impact, are simply too dangerous?

If they are too complex to grasp, either we need to change, or they do. Gillian Tett's argument – that banking products became too complex for anyone to understand – should make us highly wary of that complexity. It's a great defence and goes some way towards explaining the public funk and legislative paralysis that has followed the banking crisis. If no one is prepared to understand derivatives or credit swaps or CDOs, then everyone is easily bamboozled by lobbyists, flattery and deliberate obfuscation. Such blindness is incapacitating; we can't have the robust public debate that we need. This may, of course, be what complexity is for – to keep debate and the power of regulation firmly at bay. But complexity will persist unless, like the child in 'The Emperor's New Clothes', someone is prepared to stand up and say: I don't believe what I'm told. There isn't anything inherently brilliant about complexity or any reason why the failure to untangle it should be a source of pride.

The questions concerning the safety of banks that are too big to fail apply to any vast corporation: are they not only too big to manage but too big to police? As a society are we comfortable with companies who put their employees' lives in danger? Isn't there a limit to the number of people any corporation can kill before they're no longer allowed to trade? In the same way that we have to acknowledge the cognitive limits of our minds, we need to accept the effective limits of organisations and, when they get too big to manage, break them up.

If we lack the legislative or regulatory muscle to control such businesses, we place ourselves in the position where we have to be blind to their actions. Inevitably we make ourselves bystanders – because there's nothing we can do about them. What that means is that we seem prepared to treat very large complex organisations the same way that we treated banking and financial services: despair of their opacity and walk away. Their sheer size isolates them from critical dissent. But what these companies do matters too much. We cannot afford to abdicate, handing over control of them to others who may not know any better.

The model that the manufacturing company W. L. Gore has adopted – in which no business unit can be larger than 100 people – is intriguing. Many would argue that true global industries simply can't be effective on such a scale, but we need to challenge this orthodoxy and have the debate. I'd go further and argue that complexity fails until or unless we can prove our mastery of it.

We could know, and we should know, when these businesses are simply beyond us. What we do know is that hierarchies exacerbate blindness and obedience. That means we need either to find ways to tease the obedience out of these organisations or to

change their structures. Every business is a community and they
need to become places where, as Sherron Watkins says, what you
do matters.

We need to ask some hard questions too of the way we educate and train our children. To what extent are we bringing them
up to be 'good soldiers', compliant and well conformed? In a
straitened economy, the perceived risks of being outspoken and
the implied rewards of obedience are immense. Yes I can hear a
thousand teachers despairing at the prospect of more argument
but it's the silent classrooms that scare me.

The psychotherapist Pamela Stewart works with a startling array
of patients, from middle-class professionals to convicted murder-
ers. She once observed to me that there was one significant
similarity among her patients: their childhoods were invariably
silent. That silence, she said, was about fear: fear of conflict primarily, a fear that a debate, once started, could only end with the
family's destruction. That silence becomes self-perpetuating: without conflict, everyone remains afraid and blind. The only way to
break that cycle is to be willing to endure the noise.

But we also need to celebrate those that make the noise, heroes
more inspiring than talent-contest winners and drunken movie
stars.

'We have monuments for people who have displayed physical
courage in war,' Lieutenant Colonel Krawchuk mused. 'But
where are the monuments to people who said no, we won't do
this because it's a bad or wrong or unethical decision?'

It's a good question and one that pertains well beyond the military. How can we celebrate the dissenters, the debaters, the
Cassandras? Where is the statue to Hugh Thompson, who inter-
vened in the My Lai massacre? To Joe Darby or Steve Bolsin?
Their heroic dissent sets a standard for critical thinking that is
more inspiring than scepticism, and richer than doubt. Generations of lawyers had their worldview informed by Atticus Finch

when they read *To Kill a Mockingbird*; generations of doctors will go into medicine inspired by the work of Paul Farmer, journalists by *All the President's Men* and around the world new voices entered politics because of Nelson Mandela. We need to celebrate the Darbys, Benefields, Haywoods and Bolsins, the ordinary people who would not be blind, who should know and did know what to do. The most important thing to remember about Cassandras and whistleblowers is that they are ordinary people. They show us our own capacity to see and to act on what we see.

When we are wilfully blind, there is information we could know, and should know, but don't know because it makes us feel better not to know. Neuroscience shows us how some of this occurs, offering a tangible reality to experiences that, heretofore, felt entirely abstract. But in the course of writing this book, I've started to wonder how far the science encourages us to see our brains as separate entities, grand machines of which we are the passive agents. How long will we wait, I wonder, before a murderer pleads innocent on the grounds that 'my brain made me do it'? Could the science encourage us to believe that our blindness is hard-wired, inevitable, inescapable – not wilful at all?

The most crucial learning that has emerged from this science is the recognition that we continue to change right up to the moment we die. Every experience and encounter, each piece of new learning, relationship or reassessment alters how our minds work. And no two experiences are the same. In his work on the human genome, the Nobel laureate Sydney Brenner reminds us that even identical twins will have different experiences in different environments and that that makes them fundamentally different beings. Identical twins develop different immune systems. Mental practice alone can change how our brains operate.[14] The plasticity and responsiveness of our minds is what makes each of us most remarkable.

In other words, however determinist the brain science may appear, we all handle our experiences in unique ways. We aren't automata serving the master computer in our heads and our capacity for change can never be underestimated. The parents and children who emerge from abusive families full of new hope and the conventional student whose college experience exposes him to dissent have a stronger sense of their own capacity because of what they've seen and been able to overcome. Towns like Libby are not weaker but stronger because of the power to change that they discovered in themselves. Scientists are stronger when they confront disconfirmation than when they hide from it, and companies only regain confidence and value when they stop defending the past and can conceive of a different future.

We make ourselves powerless when we choose not to know. But we give ourselves hope when we insist on looking. The very fact that wilful blindness is willed, that it is a product of a rich mix of experience, knowledge, thinking, neurons and neuroses, is what gives us the capacity to change it. Like Lear, we can learn to see better, not just because our brain changes but because we do. As all wisdom does, seeing starts with simple questions: what could I know, should I know, that I don't know? Just what am I missing here?

NOTES

Introduction

1 This comes from the transcript of the court case, United States of America vs Kenneth L. Lay in the United States District Court for the Southern District of Texas, Houston Division, May 2006.

2 Model Penal Code Section 2.02(7) and Wilful Blindness Author(s), Jonathan L. Marcus Source: *Yale Law Journal*, Vol. 102, No. 8, Symposium: Economic Competitiveness and the Law (Jun., 1993), pp. 2231–2257.

1. Affinity and Beyond

1 Luo, S. and E.C. Klohnen (2005), 'Assortative Mating and Marital Quality in Newlyweds: A Couple-Centered Approach', *Journal of Personality and Social Psychology* 88(2): 304.
Hitsch, G.J., A. Hortacsu, et al. (2009), 'Matching and Sorting in Online Dating', *American Economic Review* 10(1): 130–63.

2 He is referring to the year ending March 2007, which is the most recent data. Nearly one-fifth of Americans and Europeans use online dating sites.

3 A Wall Street journalist queried the statistics emerging from online dating sites match.com, PlentyofFish.com and eHarmony and concluded that of these only the eHarmony statistics were convincing. *Marriage-Maker Claims are Tied in Knots* by Carl Bialik, *Wall Street Journal*, 29 July 2009.

4 Chandler, J., T.M. Griffin, et al. (2008), 'In the "I" of the storm: Shared initials increase disaster donations', *Judgment and Decision Making* 3(5): 404–10.

5 Brendl, C.M., A. Chattopadhyay, et al. (2005), 'Name Letter

Branding: Valence Transfers When Product Specific Needs Are Active', *Journal of Consumer Research* 32: 405–15.

6   Moreland, R.L. and R.B. Zajonc (1982), 'Exposure Effects in Person Perception: Familiarity, Similarity, and Attraction', *Journal of Experimental Social Psychology* 18: 395–415.

7   See *The Music Instinct: How Music Works and Why We Can't Do Without It* by Philip Ball, Bodley Head, 2010.

8   Matthew 7: 3.

9   Pronin, E., T. Gilovich, et al. (2004), 'Objectivity in the Eye of the Beholder: Divergent Perceptions of Bias in Self Versus Others', *Psychological Review* 111(3): 781–99.

10 There are two excellent websites where you can find out about the different areas in which the IAT is relevant and where you can take the tests yourself: http://www.projectimplicit.net/general-info.php and https://implicit.harvard.edu/implicit/

11 Macrae, C. Neil, Alan B. Milne, and Galen V. Bodenhausen (1994), 'Stereotypes as Energy-Saving Devices: A Peek Inside the Cognitive Toolbox', *Journal of Personality and Social Psychology* Vol. 66, No. 1, 37–47.

12 Email to author from William Osborne, Friday 30 October 2009.

13 William Osborne keeps track of these issues on his website, http://www.osborne-conant.org/articles.htm

14 Bishop, B., *The Big Sort: Why the Clustering of Like-Minded America Is Tearing Us Apart*, Boston, Houghton Mifflin, 2008.

15 Ibid, p. 5.

16 *Going to Extremes: How Like Minds Unite and Divide*, Oxford University Press, 2009.

17 Dolores Albarracin, *Psychological Bulletin* Vol. 153, No. 4.

18 'The News about the Internet' by Michael Massing, *New York Review of Books*, 13 August 2009.

2. Love Is Blind

1   S.L. Murray, J.G. Holmes, et al. (1996) 'The Self-Fulfilling Nature of Positive Illusions in Romantic Relationships: Love is Not Blind but Prescient' *Journal of Personality and Social Psychology* 7(6): 1155–1180.

2   Daniel Kahneman, *Judgement under Uncertainty: Heuristics and Biases*, Cambridge, Cambridge University Press, 1982.

3   One Plus One: Relationships Today: Infidelity. http://www.one-plusone.org.uk/publications/informationsheets/sexualinfidelity.pdf and http://www.savemarriage.co.uk/extramarital-fact-fantasy-the-truth-about-affairs/

4   Araton, Harvey, 'Apologizing, Woods Sets No Date for Return to Golf', *New York Times*, 20 February 2010.

5   Author interview.

6   Florian, V., M. Mikulincer, et al. (2002), 'The anxiety-buffering function of close relationships: Evidence that relationship commitment acts as a terror management mechanism', *Journal of Personality and Social Psychology* 82(4): 527.

7   Bartels, A. and S. Zeki (2004), 'The neural correlates of maternal and romantic love', *NeuroImage* 21(3): 1155–66.

8   O'Gorman, C. *Beyond Belief*, London, Hodder and Stoughton, 2009.

9   McGreevy, Ronan, 'Most people no longer trust the Church, Government or banks', *Irish Times*, 29 April 2010, p. 3.

10 Author interview.

11 Author interview.

12 Sereny, G., *Albert Speer: His Battle with Truth*, London, Picador, 1996, pp. 102–3.

13 Ibid. p. 106.

14 Author interview.

15 Sereny, *Albert Speer*, p. 115.

16 Ibid. p. 368.

17 Ibid. p. 405.

3. Dangerous Convictions

1   http://www.sightline.org/research/sust_toolkit/communications-strategy/drewwestenresearch

2   Westen, D., *The Political Brain: The Role of Emotion in Deciding the Fate of the Nation*, New York, Public Affairs, 2007.

3   Greene, G., *The Woman Who Knew Too Much: Alice Stewart and the secrets of radiation*, Ann Arbor, University of Michigan Press, 1999, p. 57.

4   Ibid. p. 73.

5   BMJ video: http://www.youtube.com/watch?v=proyrn2AAMA

6   Greene, *The Woman Who Knew Too Much*, p. 82.

7   Author interview, 26 November 2009.

8   *Lancet*, 23 January 1897: 289.

9   Lowe, J.J., inventor, *Method and means for visually determining the fit of footwear*, US patent 1,614,988, Washington, DC: United States Patent Office: 1927.

10 *When Prophecy Fails* by Leon Festinger, Henry W. Riecken and Stanley Schachter, first published by the University of Minnesota Press 1956 and republished by Pinter and Martin in 2008, p. 56.

11 Ibid. p. 138.

12 Ibid. p. 88.

13 Ibid. p. 108.

14 Ibid. p. 110.

15 Ibid. p. 161.

16 Ibid. p. 171.

17 Greenwald, A.G. (1980), 'The Totalitarian Ego: Fabrication and Revision of Personal History', *American Psychologist* 35(7): 603–18.

18 *The Deflationist: How Paul Krugman found politics* by Larissa MacFarquhar, *New Yorker*, 1 March 2010.

19 Interview with Mike Wallace, 1959. www.youtube.com/watch?v=pMTDaVpBPRO

20 Alan Greenspan, *The Age of Turbulence,* Allen Lane, 2007, pp. 51–2.

21 Testimony before Congress THE FINANCIAL CRISIS AND THE ROLE OF FEDERAL REGULATORS, Thursday 23 October 2008, House of Representatives, Committee on Oversight and Government Reform, Washington, DC.

22 Partnoy, F. (2003), *Infectious Greed: How Deceit and Risk Corrupted the Financial Markets*, London, Profile Books, p. 114.

23 Ibid. p. 406.

24 Speaking at Bath Literature Festival, 27 February 2010.

25 Stanford alumni magazine, March/April 2009, p. 46.

26 Kirk, Michael, 'The Warning', Frontline, PBS, airdate: 20 October 2009. http://www.pbs.org/wgbh/pages/frontline/warning/ view/

28 US Senate Hearing on the Collapse of Enron Corporation: first hearing 18 December 2001.

29 Testimony before Congress THE FINANCIAL CRISIS AND THE ROLE OF FEDERAL REGULATORS, Thursday 23 October 2008, and Government Reform, Washington, DC, p. 37.

4. The Limits of Your Mind

1   Quotes and descriptions taken from author interviews, the TELOS report commissioned by BP before the incident and the Chemical Standard Board's report following the incident. Telos Group, *BP Texas City Site Report of Findings: Texas City's Protection Performance, Behaviors, Culture, Management and Leadership*, 21 January 2005.

US Chemical Safety and Hazard Investigation Board, *Investigation Report: Refinery Explosion and Fire (15 Killed, 180 Injured) BP Texas City, March 23, 2005. Report No. 2005-04-I-TX*, March 2007. Available online: http://www.csb.gov/assets/document/CSBFinalReportBP.pdf

2   From the CSB investigation report.

3   2004 Annual Report, available online: http://www.bp.com/live-assets/bp_internet/globalbp/STAGING/global_assets/downloads/B/bp_ara_2004_annual_review.pdf

4   'EA: The Human Story' was nominated for Joel Spolsky's *Best Software Essays of 2004*.

5   The collected works of Ernst Abbe can be found via the Gutenberg Project: http://www.gutenberg.org/etext/19755

6   If you are interested in more technical detail, there's an interesting analysis of how productivity declines throughout the day: http://www.worklessparty.org/timework/chapman.htm

7   Tomasi, D., R.L. Wang, F. Telang, V. Boronikolas, M.C. Jayne et al., 'Impairment of Attentional Networks after One Night of Sleep Deprivation' *Cereb. Cortex* Vol. 19, No. 1, 233-40, 2009.

8   University of California, Berkeley: Human Factors Curriculum for Refinery Workers.

9   Belenky, G.M.D., 'Managing Sleep and Circadian Rhythms to Sustain Operational Performance', Powerpoint presentation given to the ALPA 52nd Air Safety Forum.

10   Some researchers speculate that the epidemic of obesity in the US and elsewhere may be related to chronic sleep loss. Fryer, B. (2006), 'Sleep Deficit: The Performance Killer', *Harvard Business Review* 84(10): 53-9.

11   Ibid. Ref. 34.

'Brain activity is Visibly altered following Sleep Deprivation', *Nature* (news release), 2002.

Tomasi, D., R.L. Wang, et al. (2009), 'Impairment of Attentional Networks after one Night of Sleep Deprivation', *Cereb. Cortex* 19(1): 233–40.

National Safety Foundation (2009), '2009 Asleep in America: Poll Highlight and Findings'.

12 Czeisler, Charles (2006), 'Sleep Deficit: the performance killer'. A conversation with Harvard Medical School Professor Charles A. Czeisler, *Harvard Business Review* Vol. 84 (10) 53–9.

13 Author interview in Urbana, Illinois.

14 Chris Chabris and Dan Simons have written an extended riff on their theme in a new book that explores the many ways in which we make cognitive and visual errors: Chabris, Christopher, and Daniel Simons, *The Invisible Gorilla*, New York, Crown Books, 2010.

15 Jason McCarley, 'Elements of Human Performance in Baggage X-Ray Screening', paper presented at the Fourth Annual Aviation Security Technology Symposium, Washington, DC, 29 November 2006.

16 Simons, D.J. (2007), 'Inattentional Blindness', *Scholarpedia* 2(5): 3244; Horrey, W.J., D.J. Simons, et al. (2006), 'Assessing Interference from Mental Workload Using a Naturalistic Simulated Driving Task: A Pilot Study', *Proceedings of the Human Factors and Ergonomics Society, 50th Annual Meeting*: 2003–6.

Ambinder, M.S. and D.J. Simons (2005), 'Attention Capture: The Interplay of Expectations, Attention and Awareness', *Neurobiology of Attention* Chapter 12: 69–75.

17 Strayer, D.L., F.A. Drews, et al. (2006), 'A Comparison of the Cell Phone Driver and the Drunk Driver', *Human Factors* 48(2): 381–91.

18 http://www.rospa.com/roadsafety/info/mobile_phone_report.pdf

19 Email from Department for Transport. Also http://www.dft.gov.uk/excel/173025/221412/221549/227755/503336/article4.xls

20 'Driven to Distraction', *New York Times*, 7 January 2010.

21 Ibid.

22 NVIDIA press release: http://www.nvidia.com/object/io_1262839759949.html

23 Grimes, T. (1991), 'Mild auditory-visual dissonance in television news may exceed viewer attentional capacity', *Human Communication Research*, 18(2), 268–98.

24 http://www.stanford.edu/group/multitasking/memos/Bergen_
    MultitaskingMemo.pdf

25 Kahneman, Daniel, *Attention and Effort,* New York, Prentice Hall,
    1973.
    Kahneman, D., & Treisman, A., (1984), 'Changing views of atten-
    tion and automaticity' in R. Parasuraman and R. Davies (eds)
    Varieties of Attention, New York, Academic Press.

26 Gilbert, D.T. (1991), 'How Mental Systems Believe', *American
    Psychologist* 46(2): 107–19.

27 Gilbert, D.T., R.W. Tafarodi, et al. (1993), 'You can't not believe
    everything you read', *Journal of Personality and Social Psychology*
    65(2): 221.

28 Most of the leading investment banks have worked hard to ensure
    that their intake of new recruits is evenly balanced, fifty/fifty men
    and women. But they mostly fail to maintain this balance because
    the women leave, recognising that this kind of work schedule is
    not conducive to family life – or any kind of life. But when I have
    confronted partners on this issue, they point out that more
    employees would dilute the bonus pool.

29 Finkelstein, S., *Why Smart Executives Fail,* New York, Portfolio, 2003.

30 Milgram, S. (1970), 'The Experience of Living in Cities', *Science,*
    167.

31 Not his real name; he asked to remain anonymous.

32 Zimbardo, P.G., *The Lucifer Effect: How good people turn evil,* New
    York, Random House, 2007.

33 Zimbardo has written about the SPE extensively. Among the
    many accounts, perhaps the best is the most recent in his book *The
    Lucifer Effect.* There is also an excellent video of the experiment on
    his website: http://www.prisonexp.org/

34 Zimbardo, *The Lucifer Effect,* p. 344.

5. The Ostrich Instruction

1 *Daily Mail,* 3 October 2009.

2 British Association of Dermatologists website, launching their Sun
   Awareness programme.

3 American Academy of Dermatology: http://www.skincarephysicians.
   com/skincancernet/whatis.html

4 Author interview.

5   http://www.dailymail.co.uk/news/article-466395/Tanorexic-
    young-mother-dies-skin-cancer-seven-years-sunbeds.html#ixzz0
    YRAwzhRd

6   American Academy of Dermatologists, Indoor Tanning Fact
    Sheet.

7   Luborsky, L. and B. Blinder (1965), 'Looking, Recalling and GSR
    as a Function of Defense', *Journal of Abnormal Psychology* 70(4):
    270–80.

8   Hammond, John S., L. Keeney Ralph, et al. (2006), 'The Hidden
    Traps in Decision Making', *Harvard Business Review* 84(1): 118–26.

9   http://www.rgemonitor.com/blog/roubini/142759/

10 Author interview.

11 Author interview 18 November 2009; Kelly, K., *Street Fighters:
    The last 72 hours of Bear Stearns, the toughest firm on Wall Street*, New
    York, Porfolio, 2009.

12 Milliken, Frances J., Morrison, Elizabeth,W. et al. (2003), 'An
    exploratory study of employee silence: Issues that employees don't
    communicate upward and why', *Journal of Management Studies*
    40(6): 1453–76.

13 Schneider, A. and D. McCumber, *An Air That Kills: How the
    asbestos poisoning of Libby, Montana uncovered a national scandal*, New
    York, G.P. Putnam's Sons, 2004, p. 87.

14 Ibid. p. 105.

15 Ibid. p. 8.

6. Just Following Orders

1   Seligman, M.E.P., *Authentic Happiness*, London, Nicholas Brealey
    Publishing, 2003.

2   Milgram, S., *Obedience to Authority*, New York, Harper Perennial,
    1974, Preface p. xiii.

3   Ibid. p. 31.

4   According to John Darley in author interview, Princeton, Sep-
    tember 2009.

5   Milgram, *Obedience to Authority*, p. 188.

6   Although much has been written about this experiment, there is
    no substitute for the first-hand account, which is lucid, accessible
    and thought-provoking.

7   Sheridan, Charles and Richard G. King, 'Obedience to Authority

with an Authentic victim' (1972) *Proceedings of the 80th Annual Convention of the American Psychological Association'* 165–166.

8   Pronin, E., T. Gilovich, et al. (2004), 'Objectivity in the Eye of the Beholder: Divergent Perceptions of Bias in Self Versus Others', *Psychological Review* 111(3): 781–99.

9   Blass, T. (1999), 'The Milgram Paradigm After 35 Years: Some Things We Now Know about Obedience to Authority', *Journal of Applied Social Psychology* 29(5): 955–78.

10   Burger, J.M. (2009), 'Would People Still Obey Today?' *American Psychologist* 64(1): 1–12.

11   The show was done with a live audience that shouted, 'Punishment! Punishment!' One participant, whose grandparents had died in the Holocaust, said she regretted taking part; another Romanian participant said that her experience under Ceaucescu had given her the strength to say 'no'.

12   Milgram, *Obedience to Authority*, p. 8.

13   Hofling, C.K., E. Brotzman, et al. (1966), 'An Experimental Study in Nurse-Physician Relationships', *Journal of Nervous and Mental Disease* 143(2): 171–80.

14   Pavlo's account of his career at MCI is told in full in *Stolen Without a Gun* by Walt Pavlo and Neil Weinberg, published by Etika LLC, 2007.

15   Declassified evidence available at www.texascityexplosion.com

16   US Chemical Safety and Hazard Investigation Board, *Investigation Report: Refinery Explosion and Fire (15 Killed, 180 Injured) BP Texas City, March 23, 2005. Report No. 2005-04-I-TX*, March 2007, p. 142.

17   Email dated 26 August 2004.

18   Telos Group, *BP Texas City Site Report of Findings: Texas City's Protection Performance, Behaviors, Culture, Management and Leadership*, 21 January 2005, p. 32.

19   See Morris, Erroll (2008), *Standard Operating Procedure*, USA, Sony Pictures: 111 minutes.

20   Eugen Tarnow, 'Self Destructive Obedience in the Airplane Cockpit and the Concept of Obedience Optimization' published in *Obedience to Authority: Current Perspectives on the Milgram Paradigm*, edited by Thomas Blass, Erlbaum Associates, New Jersey, 2000.

21 Martin, J., B. Lobb, G. Chapman, and R. Spillane, (1976) 'Obedience under conditions demanding self-immolation', *Human Relations*, 29, 345–56.

22 Mark Osiel, *Obeying Orders: Atrocity, Military Discipline and the Law of War*, Transaction Publishers, 2002, p. 8.

23 Ibid.

7. The Cult of Cultures

1 Author interview, Washington, DC, September 2009.

2 Milgram, S., *Obedience to Authority*, New York, Harper Perennial, 1974, p. 114.

3 Asch, S.E. (1955), 'Opinions and Social Pressure', *Scientific American* 193(5): 3–5.

4 Larsen, K.S., J.S. Triplett, et al. (1979), 'Collaborator Status, Subject Characteristics and Conformity in the Asch Paradigm', *Journal of Social Psychology* 108: 259–63.

5 Ibid.
Berns, G.S., J. Chappelow, et al. (2005), 'Neurobiological Correlates of Social Conformity and Independence During Mental Rotation', *Journal of Biological Psychiatry* 58: 245–53.

6 Larsen, K. S., J. S. Triplett, et al. (1979), 'Collaborator Status, Subject Characteristics and Conformity in the Asch Paradigm', *Journal of Social Psychology* 108: 259–263.

7 See James Surowiecki, *The Wisdom of Crowds*, Doubleday, New York, 2004. Also Grofman, B., S.L. Feld (1988), 'Rousseau's general will: A Condorcetian perspective', *American Political Science Review* 82: 567–76.

8 'Bubbleology: Wall Street goofed on the last bubble. Now it sees new ones forming everywhere', CNNMoney, 24 June 2003.

9 http://www.bristol-inquiry.org.uk/final_report/bristol_story.pdf – p. 119.

10 http://www.bristol-inquiry.org.uk/final_report/bristol_story.pdf – p. 145.

11 Panksepp, J., S.M. Siviy, and L.A. Normansell (1985), 'Brain opioids and social emotions', in M. Reite, and T. Field (eds), *The Psychobiology of Attachment and Separation*, New York: Academic Press, pp. 3–49.

12 Panksepp, J. (2003), 'NEUROSCIENCE: Feeling the Pain of Social Loss', *Science* 302(5643): 237–9.
    Baumeister, R.F., and M.R. Leary (1995), 'The Need to Belong: Desire for Interpersonal Attachments as a Fundamental Human Motivation', *Psychological Bulletin* 117(3): 497–529.

13 Stillman, T.F., R.F. Baumeister, et al. (2009), 'Alone and without purpose: Life loses meaning following social exclusion', *Journal of Experimental Social Psychology* 45(4): 686–94.

14 Partnoy, F., *F.I.A.S.C.O.: Blood in the water on Wall Street*, New York, W.W. Norton, 1997, 2009.

15 Ibid. pp. 95–6.

16 Goldie, J., L. Schwartz, et al. (2003), 'Students' attitudes and potential behaviour with regard to whistle blowing as they pass through a modern medical curriculum', *Medical Education* 37: 368–75.
    Wolf, T.M., P.M. Balson, J.M. Faucett, and H.M. Randall (1989), 'A retrospective study of attitude change during medical education', *Medical Education* 23: 19–23; and Hundert, E.M., D. Douglas-Steele, J. Bickel (1996), 'Context in medical education: the informal ethics curriculum', *Medical Education* 30: 353–64.

17 Berns, G.S., J. Chappelow, et al. (2005), 'Neurobiological Correlates of Social Conformity and Independence During Mental Rotation', *Journal of Biological Psychiatry* 58: 245–53.

18 Ibid.

19 Janis, I.L., *Victims of Groupthink: A psychological study of foreign-policy decisions and fiascoes*, Boston, Houghton Mifflin, 1972, p. 13.

20 Kelly, K., *Street Fighters: The last 72 hours of Bear Stearns, the toughest firm on Wall Street*, New York, Porfolio, 2009, pp. 152–3, 160–1.

21 O'Neill, Paul, *The Price of Loyalty: George W. Bush, the White House, and the Education of Paul O'Neill*, New York, Simon and Schuster, 2004.
    McClellan, S., *What Happened: Inside the Bush White House and Washington's Culture of Deceptions*, New York, Public Affairs, 2008.

22 McClellan, *What Happened*.

8. Bystanders

1 Morris, Erroll (2008), *Standard Operating Procedure*, USA, Sony Pictures: 111 minutes.

2 Darley, J., and B. Latane (1968), 'Bystander Intervention in Emergencies: Diffusion of Responsibility', *Journal of Personality and Social Psychology*, 8(4):377–83.

3 Ibid.

4 Latane, B., and S. Nida (1981), 'Ten Years of Research on Group Size and Helping', *Psychological Bulletin* 89(2): 308–24.

5 'Joint enterprise law means even bystanders can get life', Frances Gibb, *The Times*, 9 July 2009.

6 Cornblatt, J. (30 October 2009), 'Bystanders No More: Teaching Kids to Respond to Violent Crime', http://www.newsweek.com/blogs/the-human-condition/2009/10/30/bystanders-no-more-teaching-kids-to-respond-to-violent-crime.html

7 'Murder, She Read', *New York* 31(18) 38–41.

8 Blenkinsopp, J., and M.S. Edwards (2008), 'On Not Blowing the Whistle: Quiescent Silence as an Emotion Episode', *Research on Emotion in Organizations* 4: 181–206.

9 http://www.ellsberg.net/bio

10 Brewer, L., *Confessions of an Enron Executive*, Bloomington, Author House, 2004.

11 Swartz, M., and S. Watkins, *Power Failure: The inside story of the collapse of Enron*, New York, Doubleday, 2003, p. 121.

12 US Department of Justice, Office of Community Oriented Policing report on Bullying in Schools, www.cops.doj.gov

13 http://www.thenationalsurvey.co.uk/

14 Keith E. Stanovich, and Richard F. West (2000), 'Individual differences in reasoning: Implications for the rationality debate?' *Behavioral and Brain Sciences*, 23, pp. 645–66.

15 Quoted in Horwitz, G.J., *In the Shadow of Death: Living outside the gates of Mauthausen*, London, I.B.Tauris & Co, 1991.

9. Out of Sight, Out of Mind

1 Telos Group, *BP Texas City Site Report of Findings: Texas City's Protection Performance, Behaviors, Culture, Management and Leadership*, 21 January 2005.

US Chemical Safety and Hazard Investigation Board, Investigation

Report: Refinery Explosion and Fire (15 Killed, 180 Injured) BP Texas City, March 23, 2005. Report No. 2005-04-I-TX, March 2007. Available online: http://www.csb.gov/assets/document/CSB FinalReportBP.pdf

2   CSB report p. 193.

3   http://texascityexplosion.com/ctc/broadcast/files/ev5/DEPO— Manzoni,%20John.pdf

4   Milgram, S., *Obedience to Authority*, New York, Harper Perennial, 1974, p. 38.

5   Darley, J., A. Teger, et al. (1973), 'Do Groups Always Inhibit Individuals' Responses to Potential Emergencies?' *Journal of Personality and Social Psychology* 26(3): 395–3.

6   Dixon, N.F., *On the Psychology of Military Incompetence*, New York, Futura Publications, 1976.

7   Dixon, N.F., *Our Own Worst Enemy*, London, Jonathan Cape, 1987.

8   Goodwin, S.A., A. Gubin, et al. (2000), 'Power Can Bias Impression Processes: Stereotyping Subordinates by Default and by Design', *Group Processes and Intergroup Relations* 3(3): 227–56.

9   http://i.a.cnn.net/cnn/2005/images/11/03/brown.emails.pdf

10   Interview with Ted Koppel, 2 September 2005. http://espanol. video.yahoo.com/watch/223063/786068

11   http://i.a.cnn.net/cnn/2005/images/11/03/brown.emails.pdf 2 September 2005.

12   One of the most remarkable examples of this is done by Rush Trucking, which trucks car components into Native American reservations, where they are assembled before being trucked out again to the US.

13   Note made by Wilhelm Bonse as part of his internal inquiry into the Texas City explosion: Management Accountability Project, Texas City Isomerization Explosion, Final Report, 26 June 2006.

14   Testimony of Dr David Graham to the Senate Finance Committee, November 2004: http://finance.senate.gov/hearings/testimony/ 2004test/111804dgtest.pdf

15   'UK's Vioxx users call for justice', *The Times*, 31 August 2009. http://www.timesonline.co.uk/tol/life_and_style/health/features/ article6813991.ece

16   'London lawyers Linklaters accused of helping to hide Lehman

billions' by Phillip Inman and Jill Treanor, *Guardian*, 13 March 2010, and 'Auditor could face liability in Lehman Case' by Michael J. de la Merced, *New York Times*, 14 March 2010.

17 Feynman, R.P., *What Do You care What Other People Think? Further adventures of a curious character*. London, Unwin Paperbacks, 1988.

18 http://lightgreenstairs.com/green-choices/sigg-not-taking-responsibility/

19 'Outsourcing the Fight' by Peter W. Singer, Director, 21st Century Defense Initiative, Brookings Institute. http://www.brookings. edu/opinions/2008/0605_military_contractors_singer.aspx

20 Other examples of this phenomenon: the BBC reported children sewing footballs in Uttar Pradesh in 1998 for Nike; Channel 4 alleged child labour in Tesco's supply chain in Bangladesh in 2006; and Gap ran into controversy in 2007 over child labour used by subcontractors of its suppliers. More recently, Apple has come under fire for the low wages paid to workers manufacturing its iPhone.

21 Sandell, Michael, *The Reith Lectures*, transcript available: http:// www.bbc.co.uk/programmes/b00kt7sh

22 Testimony before Congress THE FINANCIAL CRISIS AND THE ROLE OF FEDERAL REGULATORS Thursday 23 October 2008, House of Representatives, Committee on Oversight and Government Reform, Washington, D.C. http://oversight.house. gov/images/ stories/documents/20081024163819.pdf

10. DE-moralising Work

1 Schwab, R.S., 'Motivation in measurements of fatigue', in *Fatigue*, ed.
    W.F. Floyd, and A. T. Welford, Lewis, London, 1953, pp. 143–8.

 2 Vohs, Kathleen, D. (2008), 'Merely Activating the Concept of Money Changes Personal and Interpersonal Behavior', *Current Directions in Psychological Science* 17(3): 208–12.

 3 Adcock, R.A., A. Thangavel, et al. (2006), 'Reward-Motivated Learning: Mesolimbic Activation Precedes Memory Formation', *Neuron* 50(3): 507–17.

 4 Pessiglione, M., L. Schmidt, et al. (2007), 'How the Brain Translates Money into Force: A Neuroimaging Study of Subliminal Motivation', *Science* 316(5826): 904–6.

5   Pink, Daniel H., *Drive: The Surprising Truth about What Motivates Us*, Canongate, New York, 2009.

6   Zhou, X., Vohs, Kathleen D., et al. (2009), 'The Symbolic Power of Money: Reminders of Money Alter Social Distress and Physical Pain', *Psychological Science* 20(6): 700–6.

7   Author interview.

8   Vohs, K.D., N.L. Mead, et al. (2006), 'The Psychological Consequences of Money', *Science* 314(5802): 1154–6.

9   Vohs, 'Merely Activating the Concept of Money Changes Personal and Interpersonal Behavior'.

10 Finch, J. (2010), 'I save tax by never visiting my family, says tycoon Hands', *Guardian*, 6 February 2010.

11 Paul Moore's testimony to the House of Commons Select Committee: http://ftalphaville.ft.com/blog/2009/02/11/52320/hbos-the-moore-memo/

12 The Riskminds Risk Managers Survey 2009.

13 Frey, B., S. and F. Oberholzer-Gee (1997), 'The Cost of Price Incentives: An Empirical Analysis of Motivation Crowding-Out', *American Economic Review* 87(4): 746–55.

14 Ibid.

15 Gneezy, U., and A. Rustichini (2000), 'A Fine Is a Price', *Journal of Legal Studies* 29(1): 1–17.

16 Bowles, S. (2008), 'Policies Designed for Self-Interested Citizens May Undermine "The Moral Sentiments": Evidence from Economic Experiments', *Science* 320(5883): 1605–9.

17 Greene, J.D., R.B. Sommerville, et al. (2001), 'An fMRI Investigation of Emotional Engagement in Moral Judgment', *Science* 293(5537): 2105–8.
    Robertson, D., J. Snarey, et al. (2007), 'The neural processing of moral sensitivity to issues of justice and care', *Neuropsychologia* 45(4): 755–66.

18 Lewis, Michael, *The Big Short: Inside the Doomsday Machine*, New York, W.W. Norton and Co., 2010.

19 Court document.

20 Author interview; also Groopman, J. (2009), 'Diagnosis: What Doctors Are Missing', *New York Review of Books*.

21 Gingrich, N., *To Renew America*, New York, Harper Collins, 1995. Quoted in Bandura, Albert, 'Impeding ecological sustain-

ability through selective moral disengagement', *International Journal of Innovation and Sustainable Development* Vol. 2, No. 1, 2007.

22 Ibid.

11. Cassandra

1   Miceli, M.P., and J.P. Near (2005), 'Standing Up or Standing By: What Predicts Blowing the Whistle on Organizational Wrong-doing?' *Research in Personnel and Human Resources Management* 24: 93–136.

2   Written testimony of Harry Markopolos, Chartered Financial Analyst, Certified Fraud Examiner before the US Senate Banking, Housing and Urban Affairs Committee, Thursday 10 September 2009.

3   Author interview.

4   Markopolos, H., *No One Would Listen: A True Financial Thriller*, Hoboken, New Jersey, Wiley & Sons, 2010.

5   Hansen, J., D. Johnson, A. Lacis, S. Lebedeff, P. Lee, D. Rind, and G. Russell (1981), 'Climate impact of increasing atmospheric carbon dioxide', *Science* 213, 957–66, doi:10.1126/science.213.4511.957.

6   Lizza, R., 'The Contrarian', *New Yorker*, 2009.

7   Author interview.

8   Barton, L., 'On the money', *Guardian*, 31 October 2008.

9   Interview, 27 February 2010.

10 Tett, G., *Fool's Gold: How unrestrained greed corrupted a dream, shattered global markets and unleashed a catastrophe*, London, Little, Brown, 2009, p. 299.

11 A twelve-year study published in the June 2007 issue of the journal *Epidemiology and Health* clearly demonstrated that the risk of suicide among male US veterans is more than two times greater than that of the general population after adjusting for a host of potentially compounding factors, including age, time of service and health status. A report released this past May 2010 by the VA Inspector General noted that 'veterans returning from Iraq and Afghanistan are at increased risk for suicide because not all VA clinics have 24-hour mental care available . . . and many lack properly trained workers'.

Media reports of suicide deaths and suicide attempts among active duty OEF and OIF soldiers and veterans began to surface back in 2003 after a spate of suicides in Iraq during the first months of the war. Since then, both the military and the VA have stumbled and fumbled in their attempts to answer questions about the severity of this malady. For example, while all the military services maintain suicide prevention programmes, the Army in its August 2007 Army Suicide Event Report acknowledged that soldiers committed suicide last year at the highest rate in twenty-six years, and more than a quarter did so while serving in Iraq and Afghanistan. The report noted 'a significant relationship between suicide attempts and number of days deployed in Iraq, Afghanistan or nearby countries where troops are participating in the war effort'. The report added that there also 'was limited evidence to support the view that multiple deployments are a risk factor for suicide behaviors'. It might be noted here that this report was released only after an FOIA request. From the Vietnam Veterans of America: http://www.vva.org/who.html

12   www.osc.gov

13   *GQ*, September 2006. http://www.gq.com/news-politics/news-makers/200608/joe-darby-abu-ghraib?currentPage=2

14   Alford, C.F., *Whistleblowers: Broken Lives and Organizational Power*, Ithaca, Cornell University Press, 2001.

15   CBS, *Sixty Minutes*, 25 January 2007. http://www.cbsnews.com/video/watch/?id=2972689n&tag=related;photovideo

16   Testimony of Harry Markopolos, CFA, CFE, before the US House of Representatives Committee on Financial Services, 9.30 a.m. Wednesday 4 February 2009.

12. See Better

1   Hillman, C.H., K.I. Erickson, et al. (2008), 'Be smart, exercise your heart: exercise effects on brain and cognition', *Nature Reviews Neuroscience* 9: 58–65.

2   Greene, p. 223.

3   Greene, p. 244.

4   'He's No Fool (But He Plays One inside Companies)' by Curtis Sittenfeld, *Fast Company*, 31 October 1998. http://www.fast-company.com/magazine/19/nofool.html

5   Finkelstein, Sydney, *Why Smart Executives Fail and what you can learn from their mistakes,* Portfolio, 2003.

6 Bazerman, Max H., G. Loewenstein, et al. (2002), 'Why good accountants do bad audits', *Harvard Business Review* 80(11): 96–102.

7 Ibid.

8 Bolsin, S.N., T. Faunce, et al. (2005), 'Using portable digital technology for clinical care and critical incidents: a new model', *Australian Health Review* 29(3): 297–305.

9 Nemeth, Charles, Ofra Mayseless, Jeffrey Sherman, and Yvonne Brown (1990), 'Exposure to Dissent and Recall of Information', *Journal of Personality and Social Psychology* Vol. 58, No. 3, 429–37.

10 'Connections from Kafka: Exposure to Meaning Threats Improves Implicit Learning of an Artificial Grammar', Travis Proulx and Steven J. Heine, *Psychological Science*, Vol. 20, Issue 9, p. 1125–31.

11 http://biblioklept.org/2009/09/16/reading-kafka-and-watching-lynch-will-make-you-smarter/

12 Ref. 250.

13 Kennan, G.F., *Memoirs*, Pantheon, 1983.

14 Pascual-Leonoe, A., N. Dang, et al. (1995), 'Modulation of Muscle Responses Evoked by Transcranial Magnetic Stimulation During the Acquisition of New Fine Motor Skills', *Journal of Neurophysiology* 74(3): 1037–45.

BIBLIOGRAPHY

Abagnale, Frank. *Catch Me If You Can: The Amazing True Story of the Most Extraordinary Liar in the History of Fun and Profit*, New York: Broadway Books, 1980.

Adcock, R. Alison, Arul Thangavel, Susan Whitfield-Gabriel, Brian Knutson, and John D.E. Gabriele. 'Reward-Motivated Learning: Mesolimbic Activation Precedes Memory Formation', *Neuron* Vol. 50, No. 3, 507–17, 2006.

Addley, Esther. 'How Britain Fell in Love with the Tan', *Guardian*, 1 August 2009.

Akerlof, George A., and Robert J. Shiller. *Animal Spirits: How Human Psychology Drives the Economy, and Why It Matters for Global Capitalism*, Princeton University Press, 2009.

Aleccia, JoNel. 'Hospital Bullies Take a Toll on Patient Safety', *MSNBC.com*, July 9, 2008.

Alford, C. Fred. *Whistleblowers: Broken Lives and Organizational Power*, Ithaca, NY: Cornell University Press, 2001.

Ambinder, Michael S., and Daniel J. Simons. 'Attention Capture: The Interplay of Expectations, Attention and Awareness', *Neurobiology of Attention* Vol. 12, 69–75, 2005.

Anderson, Cameron, and Jennifer L. Berdahl. 'The Experience of Power: Examining the Effects of Power on Approach and Inhibition Tendencies', *Journal of Personality and Social Psychology* Vol. 83, No. 6, 1362, 2002.

Anderson, Cameron, and Adam D. Galinsky. 'Power, Optimism and Risk Taking', *European Journal of Social Psychology* Vol. 36, 511–36, 2006.

Arendt, Hannah. 'Personal Responsibility under Dictatorship', in

Jerome Kohn (ed.), *Responsibility and Judgment*, New York: Schocken Books, 2003.

———. *The Jewish Writings*, New York: Schocken Books, 2007.

Ariely, Dan. *Predictably Irrational: The Hidden Forces That Shape Our Decisions*, New York: Harper Collins, 2008.

Aron, Arthur, Elain N. Aron, Michael Tudor, and Greg Nelson. 'Close Relationships as Including Other in the Self', *Journal of Personality and Social Psychology* Vol. 60, No. 2, 241–53, 1991.

Aronson, Elliott. 'Back to the Future: Retrospective Review of Leon Festinger's *A Theory of Cognitive Dissonance*', *American Journal of Psychology* Vol. 110, No. 1, 127–157, 1997.

Asch, Solomon E. 'Opinions and Social Pressure', *Scientific American* Vol. 193, No. 5, 31–5, 1955.

Asthana, Anushka. 'Report Reveals How Britons Were Lured into Spiral of Debt', *Observer*, 7 February 2010.

Auletta, Ken. *Three Blind Mice: How the TV Networks Lost Their Way*, Vintage Books, 1991.

Baaars, Bernard J., William P. Banks, and James B. Newman (eds). *Essential Sources in the Scientific Study of Consciousness*, Cambridge: MIT Press, 2003.

Banaji, Mahzarin R. 'Foreward: The Moral Obligation to Be Intelligent', in Eugene Borgida and Susan T. Fiske (eds), *Beyond Common Sense: Psychological Science in the Courtroom*, Wiley-Blackwell, 2007.

Banaji, Mahzarin R., Max H. Bazerman, and Dolly Chugh. 'How (Un)Ethical Are You?', *Harvard Business Review*, 56–64, 2003.

Banaji, Mahzarin R., Curtis Hardin, and Alexander J. Rothman. 'Implicit Stereotyping in Person Judgment', *Journal of Personality and Social Psychology* Vol. 65, No. 2, 272, 1993.

Bandura, Albert. 'Social Cognitive Theory of Moral Thought and Action', in William M. Kurtines and Jacob L. Gewirtz (eds), *Handbook of Moral Behavior and Development*, Hillsdale, New Jersey, Lawrence Erlbaum Associates, 1991.

———. 'Moral Disengagement in the Perpetration of Inhumanities', *Personality and Social Psychology Review* Vol. 3, 193–209, 1999.

———. 'Impeding Ecological Sustainability through Selective Moral Disengagement', *International journal of Innovation and Sustainable Development* Vol. 2, No. 1, 8–32, 2007.

————. 'The Reconstrual of "Free Will" from the Agentic Perspective of Social Cognitive Theory', in J. Baer, J.G. Kaufman and R.F. Baumeister (eds), *Are We Free? Psychology and Freewill*, Oxford University Press, 2008.

————. 'Social Cognitive Theory Goes Global', *British Psychological Society* Vol. 22, No. 6, 504–6, 2009.

Bandura, Albert, Gian-Vittorio Caprara, and Laszlo Zsolnai. 'Corporate Transgressions through Moral Disengagement', *Journal of Human Values* Vol. 6, No. 1, 57–64, 2000.

Barnes, Brooks. 'Studios' Quest for Life after DVDs', *New York Times*, 25 October 2009.

Bartels, Andreas, and Semir Zeki. 'The Neural Correlates of Maternal and Romantic Love', *NeuroImage* Vol. 21, No. 3, 1155–66, 2004.

Barton, Laura. 'On the Money', *Guardian*, 31 October 2008.

Baumeister, Roy, C. Nathan DeWall, Nicole Mead, and Kathleen Vohs. 'Social Rejection Can Reduce Pain and Increase Spending: Further Evidence That Money, Pain, and Belongingness Are Interrelated', *Psychological Inquiry* Vol. 19, No. 3–4, 145–7, 2008.

Baumeister, Roy F., and Kenneth J. Cairns. 'Repression and Self-Presentation: When Audiences Interfere with Self-Deceptive Strategies', *Journal of Personality and Social Psychology* Vol. 62, No. 5, 851–62, 1992.

Baumeister, Roy F., and Mark R. Leary. 'The Need to Belong: Desire for Interpersonal Attachments as a Fundamental Human Motivation', *Psychological Bulletin* Vol. 117, No. 3, 497–529, 1995.

Baumgardner, Ann H. 'To Know Oneself Is to Like Oneself: Self-Certainty and Self-Affect', *Journal of Personality and Social Psychology* Vol. 58, No. 6, 1062–72, 1990.

Bazerman, Max H. *Negotiating Rationally*, New York: Free Press, 1993.

————. *Judgment in Managerial Decision-Making*, Wiley, 2002.

Bazerman, Max H., and Mahzarin R. Banaji. 'The Social Psychology of Ordinary Ethical Failures', *Social Justice Research* Vol. 17, No. 2, 111–15, 2004.

Bazerman Max, H., and Dolly Chugh. 'Decisions without Blinders', *Harvard Business Review* Vol. 84, No. 1, 88–97, 2006.

Bazerman Max, H., George Loewenstein, and A. Moore Don. 'Why Good Accountants Do Bad Audits', *Harvard Business Review* Vol. 80, No. 11, 96–102, 2002.

Begley, Sharon. 'Adventures in Good and Evil', *Newsweek* Vol. 153, No. 18, 46–9, 2009.

Belenky, Gregory M.D., 'Managing Sleep and Circadian Rhythms to Sustain Operational Performance', Powerpoint presentation to the ALPA 52nd Air Safety Forum.

Berns, Gregory S., Jonathan Chappelow, Caroline F. Zink, Giuseppe Pagnoni, Megan E. Martin-Skursk, and Jim Richards. 'Neuro-biological Correlates of Social Conformity and Independence during Mental Rotation', *Journal of Biological Psychiatry* Vol. 58, 245–53, 2005.

Bishop, Bill. *The Big Sort: Why the Clustering of Like-Minded America Is Tearing Us Apart*, Boston: Houghton Mifflin, 2008.

Blakeslee, Sandra. 'What Other People Say May Change What You See', *New York Times*, 28 June 2005.

Blanchflower, David. 'My Time at Threadneedle Street Certainly Wasn't Boring', *Guardian*, 8 June 2009.

Blanford, Nicholas. 'The Admiral Ordered "Turn" and the Ships Collided', *The Times*, 2 September 2004.

Blass, Thomas. 'The Milgram Paradigm after 35 Years: Some Things We Now Know About Obedience to Authority', *Journal of Applied Social Psychology* Vol. 29, No. 5, 955–78, 1999.

Blenkinsopp, John, and Marissa S. Edwards. 'On Not Blowing the Whistle: Quiescent Silence as an Emotion Episode', *Research on Emotion in Organizations* Vol. 4, 181–206, 2008.

Bolsin, Stephen N., Tom Faunce, and Mark Colson. 'Using Portable Digital Technology for Clinical Care and Critical Incidents: A New Model', *Australian Health Review* Vol. 29, No. 3, 297–305, 2005.

Bowen, Frances, and Kate Blackmon. 'Spirals of Silence: The Dynamic Effects of Diversity on Organizational Voice', *The Journal of Management Studies* Vol. 40, No. 6, 1393–1417, 2003.

Bowles, Samuel. 'Policies Designed for Self-Interested Citizens May Undermine "The Moral Sentiments": Evidence from Economic Experiments', *Science* Vol. 320, No. 5883, 1605–9, 2008.

BP. 'Cost Benefit Analysis of the Three Little Pigs', Powerpoint slide produced in evidence by BP, date unknown.

Brendl, C. Miguel, Amitaa Chattopadhyay, Brett W. Pelham, and Mauricio Carvallo. 'Name Letter Branding: Valence Transfers

354 WILFUL BLINDNESS

When Product Specific Needs Are Active', *Journal of Consumer Research* Vol. 32, 405–15, 2005.

Brewer, Lynn. *Confessions of an Enron Executive*, Author House, 2004.

Brooke, Heather. 'Promises of More Open Government Have Been Made Before', *The Times*, 11 June 2009.

———. 'Unsung Hero', *Guardian*, 15 May 2009.

Brown, David K. *Warrior to Dreadnought: Warship Development 1860–1905*, Chatham Publishing, 1997.

Brown, Jim. 'New Federal Whistleblower Office Off to Slow Start in First Year on the Job', *Canadian Press*, 2 May 2008.

Browne, John. *Beyond Business: An Inspirational Memoir from a Visionary Leader*, Weidenfeld & Nicolson, 2009.

Bruno, S. Frey. 'A Constitution for Knaves Crowds out Civic Virtues', *Economic Journal* Vol. 107, No. 443, 1043–53, 1997.

Burger, Jerry M. 'Would People Still Obey Today?', *American Psychologist* Vol. 64, No. 1, 1–12, 2009.

Burkin, Kevin, and Brian H. Kleiner. 'Protecting the Whistleblower: Preventing Retaliation Following a Report of Patient Abuse in Health-Care Institutions', *Health Manpower Management* Vol. 24, No. 3, 119–24, 1998.

Burton, Robert A. *On Being Certain: Believing You Are Right Even When You're Not*, St Martin's Griffin, 2008.

'Bystanders Can Stop Bullying'. http://myhighplains.com/fulltext?nxd_id=64841.

Cacioppo, John T., Richard E. Petty, and Mary E. Losch. 'Attributions of Responsibility for Helping and Doing Harm: Evidence for Confusion of Responsibility', *Journal of Personality and Social Psychology* Vol. 50, No. 1, 100, 1986.

Canada Safety Council. 'Don't Just Stand There – Do Something', 2004.

Cannon, M.D., and A.C. Edmondson. 'Failing to Learn and Learning to Fail (Intelligently)', *Long Range Planning* Vol. 38, No. 3, 299–319, 2005.

Carey, John. 'The Unwisdom of Crowds', *BusinessWeek*, 7 May 2009.

Carozza, Dick. 'Chasing Madoff: An Interview with Harry Markopolos', *Fraud* Vol. 23, No. 3, 2009.

Carr, Drury Gunn, and Doug Hawes-Davis. *Libby, Montana*, a film produced by High Plains Films and distributed by Typecast Releasing, 2006.

Carville, James, and Mary Matalin. *All's Fair: Love, War and Running for President*, New York: Random House, 1994.

Cassidy, John. 'After the Blowup', *New Yorker*, 11 January 2010, pp. 28–33.

Chandler, Jesse, Tiffany M. Griffin, and Nicholas Sorensen. 'Improving Decision Making by Means of Dissent', *Journal of Applied Social Psychology* Vol. 31, 48–58, 2001.

———. 'In the "I" of the Storm: Shared Initials Increase Disaster Donations', *Judgment and Decision Making* Vol. 3, No. 5, 404–10, 2008.

Channel 4 Television (UK), 'Would You Save a Stranger', April 2, 2009. Available online: http://channel4.com/programmes/would-you-save-a-stranger

Chugh, Dolly, and Max H. Bazerman. 'Bounded Awareness: What You Fail to See Can Hurt You', *Mind and Society* Vol. 6, No. 1, 1–18, 2007.

Chugh, D, Bazerman, M.H., and M.R. Banaji. 'Bounded Ethicality as a Psychological Barrier to Recognizing Conflicts of Interest', to appear in Moore, D., D. Cain, G. Loewenstein, and M.H. Bazerman (eds), *Conflicts of Interest: Problems and Solutions from Law, Medicine and Organizational Settings*, London: Cambridge University Press.

Cohen, Stanley. *States of Denial: Knowing About Atrocities and Suffering*, London: Polity, 2001.

Cornblatt, Johannah. 'Bystanders No More: Teaching Kids to Respond to Violent Crime', *Newsweek*, 30 October 2009.

Creed, W.E. Douglas. 'Voice Lessons: Tempered Radicalism and the Use of Voice and Silence', *Journal of Management Studies* Vol. 40, No. 6, 1503–36, 2003.

'Criminal Law–Willful Blindness–Ninth Circuit Holds That Motive Is Not an Element of Willful Blindness'. *Harvard Law Review* Vol. 121, No. 4, 1245–53, 2008.

Crozier, W. Ray. *Shyness and Embarrassment: Perspectives from Social Psychology*, Cambridge University Press, 1990.

Darley, John M. 'Social Organization for the Production of Evil', *Psychological Inquiry* Vol. 3, No. 2, 199–218, 1992.

Darley, John M., and C. Daniel Batson. '"From Jerusalem to Jericho": A Study of Situational and Dispositional Variables in Helping

Behavior', *Journal of Personality and Social Psychology* Vol. 27, No. 1, 100–8, 1973.

Darley, John M., and B. Latane. 'Bystander Intervention in Emergencies: Diffusion of Responsibility', *Journal of Personality and Social Psychology* Vol. 8, No. 4, 377–383, 1968.

Darley, John M., Allan Teger, and Lawrence D. Lewis. 'Do Groups Always Inhibit Individuals' Responses to Potential Emergencies?', *Journal of Personality and Social Psychology* Vol. 26, No. 3, 395–9, 1973.

DiMaggio, Paul. 'Culture and Cognition', *Annual Review of Sociology*, 1997.

Dixon, Norman F. *On the Psychology of Military Incompetence*, London: Futura Publications, 1976.

Dixon, Norman F. *Our Own Worst Enemy*, London: Jonathan Cape, 1987.

Dorsey, David. *The Force*, New York: Random House, 1994.

Eastwick, Paul W., Jennifer A. Richeson, Deborah Son, and Eli J. Finkely. 'Is Love Colorblind? Political Orientation and Interracial Romantic Desire', *Personality and Social Psychology Bulletin* Vol. 35, No. 9, 1258–68, 2009.

Economics, London School of. 'Letter to the Queen in Response to Her Question:Why Had Nobody Noticed That the Credit Crunch Was on Its Way?', 2009. Available online: http://media.ft.com/cms/3e3b6ca8-7a08-llde-b86f-00144feabdc0.pdf

Edelman, Aida. 'A Double Agent, That's What I Was', *Guardian*, 14 November 2009.

Edmondson Amy, C. 'Speaking up in the Operating Room: How Team Leaders Promote Learning in Interdisciplinary Action Teams', *Journal of Management Studies* Vol. 40, No. 6, 1419–52, 2003.

Edmondson, Vickie Cox, and George Munchus. 'Managing the Unwanted Truth: A Framework for Dissent Strategy', *Journal of Organizational Change Management* Vol. 20, No. 6, 747–60, 2007.

Ehrlinger, Joyce, Thomas Gilovich, and Lee Ross. 'Peering into the Bias Blind Spot: People's Assessments of Bias in Themselves and Others', *Personality and Social Psychology Bulletin* Vol. 31, No. 5, 680–92, 2005.

Eichenwald, Kurt. *Serpent on the Rock:* New York: Broadway Books, 1995.

Engelmann, Jan B., C. Monica Capra, Charles Noussair, and Gregory S. Berns. 'Expert Financial Advice Neurobiologically "Offloads" Financial Decision-Making under Risk', *Public Library of Science*, 2009.

Epley, Nicholas, and Thomas Gilovich. 'Just Going Along: Non-conscious Priming and Conformity to Social Pressure, *Journal of Experimental Social Psychology* Vol. 35, No. 6, 578–89, 1999.

Evans, Rob. 'The Lonely Life of a Construction Industry Whistle-blower', *Guardian*, 15 May 2009.

Felblinger, Dianne M. 'Incivility and Bullying in the Workplace and Nurses' Shame Responses', *Journal of Obstetric, Gynaecologic and Neonatal Nursing* Vol. 37, 234–42, 2008.

Festinger, Leon, and James M. Carlsmith. 'Cognitive Consequences of Forced Compliance', *Journal of Abnormal and Social Psychology* Vol. 58, 203–10, 1959.

Festinger, Leon, and Nathan Maccoby. 'On Resistance to Persuasive Communications', *Journal of Abnormal and Social Psychology* Vol. 68, No. 4, 359–66, 1964.

Festinger, Leon, Henry W. Riecken, and Stanley Schachter. *When Prophecy Fails: A Social and Psychological Study of a Modern Group That Predicted the Destruction of the World*, Harper Torch Books, 1956.

Feynman, Richard P. *What Do You Care What Other People Think? Further Adventures of a Curious Character*, Unwin Paperbacks, 1988.

Finch, Julia. 'I Save Tax by Never Visiting My Family, Says Tycoon Hands', *Guardian*, 6 February 2010.

Fincher, Richard D. 'Mediating Whistleblow Disputes', *Dispute Resolution Journal*, February/April 2009.

Fine, Cordelia. *A Mind of Its Own: How Your Brain Distorts and Deceives*, W.W. Norton, 2006.

Finkelstein, Sydney. *Why Smart Executives Fail*, New York: Portfolio, 2003.

Fitzgerald, C.C. Penrose. *The Life of Vice-Admiral Sir George Tryon K.C.B.*, William Blackwood and Sons, 1897.

Florian, Victor, Mario Mikulincer, and Gilad Hirschberger. 'The Anxiety-Buffering Function of Close Relationships: Evidence That Relationship Commitment Acts as a Terror Management Mechanism', *Journal of Personality and Social Psychology* Vol. 82, No. 4, 527, 2002.

Fohrman, Donald W. 'Champaign Couple Heartened by Pending Texting Law', http://www.illinoispersonalinjurylawyerblog.com/2009/08/champaign_couple_heartened_by.html, 2009.

Forster, Sophie, and Nilli Lavie. 'Harnessing the Wandering Mind: The Role of Perceptual Load', Cognition Vol. 111, 345–55, 2009.

Freedman, Jonathan L., and Scott C. Fraser. 'Compliance without Pressure: The Foot-in-the-Door Technique', Journal of Personality and Social Psychology Vol. 4, No. 2, 195–202, 1966.

Frey, Bruno, S., and Felix Oberholzer-Gee. 'The Cost of Price Incentives: An Empirical Analysis of Motivation Crowding-Out', The American Economic Review Vol. 87, No. 4, 746–55, 1997.

Fryer, Bronwyn. 'Sleep Deficit: The Performance Killer', Harvard Business Review Vol. 84, No. 10, 53–9, 2006.

Gabor, Thomas. Everybody Does It! Crime by the Public, University of Toronto Press, 1994.

Garcia, Stephen M., Kim Weaver, Gordon B. Moskowitz, and John M. Darley. 'Crowded Minds: The Implicit Bystander Effect', Journal of Personality and Social Psychology Vol. 83, No. 4, 843, 2002.

Gentile, Mary. 'Giving Voice to Values', Aspen Institute. https://caseplace.org/d.asp?d=3371

Gerstein, Marc. Flirting with Disaster, New York: Union Square Press, 2008.

Gerstein, Marc S., and Robert B. Shaw. 'Organizational Bystanders', People & Strategy Vol. 31, No. 1, 47–54.

Gibb, Frances. 'Joint Enterprise Law Means Even Bystanders May Get Life', The Times, 2009.

Gilbert, Daniel T. 'How Mental Systems Believe', American Psychologist Vol. 46, No. 2, 107–19, 1991.

Gilbert, Daniel T., and Randall E. Osborne. 'Thinking Backward: Some Curable and Incurable Consequences of Cognitive Busyness', Journal of Personality and Social Psychology Vol. 57, No. 6, 940, 1989.

Gilbert, Daniel T., Brett W. Pelham, and Douglas S. Krull. 'On Cognitive Busyness: When Person Perceivers Meet Persons Perceived', Journal of Personality and Social Psychology Vol. 54, No. 5, 733–40, 1988.

Gilbert, Daniel T., Romin W. Tafarodi, and Patrick S. Malone. 'You Can't Not Believe Everything You Read', *Journal of Personality and Social Psychology* Vol. 65, No. 2, 221, 1993.

Gilovich, Thomas. *How We Know What Isn't So: The Fallibility of Human Reason in Everyday Life*, New York: Free Press, 1991.

Glazer, Myron Peretz, and Penina Migdal Glazer. *Whistleblowers: Exposing Corruption in Government and Industry*, Basic Books, 1989.

Gneezy, Uri, and Aldo Rustichini. 'A Fine Is a Price', *Journal of Legal Studies* Vol. 29, No. 1, 1–17, 2000.

Goldfarb, Zachary A. 'Staffer at Sec Had Warned of Madoff', *Washington Post*, 2 July 2009.

Goldie, John, Schwartz, Alex McConachie, and Jillian Morrison. 'Students' Attitudes and Potential Behaviour with Regard to Whistle Blowing as They Pass through a Modern Medical Curriculum', *Medical Education* Vol. 37, 368–75, 2003.

Goleman, Daniel. *Vital Lies, Simple Truths: The Psychology of Self-Deception*, New York: Simon and Schuster, 1985.

Goodman, Michael J., Julie A. Barker, and Christopher A. Monk. 'A Bibliography of Research Related to the Use of Wireless Communications Devices from Vehicles', *National Highway Traffic Safety Administration*, 2005.

Goodwin, Stephanie A., Alexandra Gubin, Susan T. Fiske, and Vincent Y. Qzerbt. 'Power Can Bias Impression Processes: Stereotyping Subordinates by Default and by Design', *Group Processes and Intergroup Relations* Vol. 3, No. 3, 227–56, 2000.

Goodwin, Stephanie A., Don Operario, and Susan T. Fiske. 'Empirical Approaches to Understanding Intergroup Conflict Situational Power and Interpersonal Dominance Facilitate Bias and Inequality', *Journal of Social Issues* Vol. 54, No. 4, 677–98, 1998.

Gordon, Andrew. *The Rules of the Game: Jutland and British Naval Command*, Naval Institute Press, 2000.

Government Accountability Project, 'Internal World Bank Report Finds Staff Fear Reprisal; Corruption Inadequately Addressed', 22 April 2009. www.whistleblower.org

Gray, Judy H., and Iain L. Densten. 'How Leaders Woo Followers in the Romance of Leadership', *Applied Psychology: An International Review* Vol. 56, No. 4, 558–81, 2007.

Green, Stephen. *Good Value: Reflections on Money, Morality and an Uncertain World*, London: Allen Lane, 2009.

Greene, Gayle. *The Woman Who Knew Too Much: Alice Stewart and the Secrets of Radiation*, Ann Arbor: University of Michigan Press, 1999.

Greene, Joshua D., R. Brian Sommerville, Leigh E. Nystrom, John M. Darley, and Jonathan D. Cohen. 'An fMRI Investigation of Emotional Engagement in Moral Judgment', *Science* Vol. 293, No. 5537, 2105–8, 2001.

Greenspan, Alan. *The Age of Turbulence*, Allen Lane, 2007.

Greenwald, Anthony G. 'The Totalitarian Ego: Fabrication and Revision of Personal History', *American Psychologist* Vol. 35, No. 7, 603–18, 1980.

Greenwald, Anthony G., and Mahzarin R. Banaji. 'Implicit Social Cognition: Attitudes, Self-Esteem and Stereotypes', *Psychological Review* Vol. 102, No. 1, 4–27, 1995.

Groopman, Jerome. 'Diagnosis: What Doctors Are Missing', *New York Review of Books*, 5 November 2009.

Grover, Steen L., and Chun Hui. 'How Job Pressures and Extrinsic Rewards Affect Lying Behavior', *International Journal of Conflict Management* Vol. 16, No. 3, 287–300, 2005.

Gruenfeld, Deborah H. 'Status, Ideology and Integrative Complexity on the Supreme Court: Rethinking the Politics of Political Decision Making', *Journal of Personality and Social Psychology* Vol. 68, No. 1, 5–20, 1995.

Hammond John, S., L. Keeney Ralph, and Howard Raiffa. 'The Hidden Traps in Decision Making', *Harvard Business Review* Vol. 84, No. 1, 118–26, 2006.

Hansen, J., D. Johnson, A. Lacis, S. Lebedeff, P. Lee, D. Rind, and G. Russell. 'Climate Impact of Increasing Atmospheric Carbon Dioxide', *Science* Vol. 213, No. 4511, 957–66, 1981.

Harris, Gardiner. 'Prosecutors Plan Crackdown on Doctors Who Accept Kickback', *New York Times*, 4 March 2009.

Hawkins, Peter. 'Organizational Culture: Sailing between Evangelism and Complexity', *Human Relations* Vol. 50, No. 4, 417–40, 1997.

Henriksen, Kerm, and Elizabeth Dayton. 'Organizational Silence and Hidden Threats to Patient Safety', *Health Services Research* Vol. 41, No. 4 p2, 1539, 2006.

Hester, Robert and Garavan, Hugh. 'Working Memory and Executive Function: The Influence of Content and Load on the Control of Attention', *Memory & Cognition* Vol. 33, No. 2, 221–33, 2005.

Heyman, James, and Dan Ariely. 'Effort for Payment', *Psychological Science* Vol. 15, No. 11, 787–93, 2004.

Hilberg, Raul. *Perpetrators, Victims, Bystanders: The Jewish Catastrophe 1933–1945*, New York: Harper Collins, 1992.

Hillman, Charles H., Kirk I. Erickson, and Arthur F. Kramer. 'Be Smart, Exercise Your Heart: Exercise Effects on Brain and Cognition', *Nature Reviews Neuroscience* Vol. 9, 58-65, 2008.

Hills, Stuart L. (ed). *Corporate Violence: Injury and Death for Profit*, Lanham, Maryland, Rowman and Littlefield, 1987.

Hitsch, Gunter J., Ali Hortacsu, and Dan Ariely. 'Matching and Sorting in Online Dating', *American Economic Review* Vol. 10, No. 1, 130–63, 2009.

Hofling, Charles K., Eveline Brotzman, Sarah Dalrymple, Nancy Graves, and Chester M. Pierce. 'An Experimental Study in Nurse–Physician Relationships', *Journal of Nervous and Mental Disease* Vol. 143, No. 2, 171–80, 1966.

Hogan, Linda. 'Confronting the Truth: Conscience in the Catholic Tradition', Lahwah, New Jersey, Paulist Press, 2000.

Horrey, William J., Daniel J. Simons, Evan G. Buschmann, and Kevin M. Zinter. 'Assessing Interference from Mental Workload Using a Naturalistic Simulated Driving Task: A Pilot Study', *Proceedings of the Human Factors and Ergonomics Society, 50th Annual Meeting*, 2006.

Horwitz, Gordon J. *In the Shadow of Death: Living Outside the Gates of Mauthausen*, London: I.B. Tauris & Co., 1991.

Hough, Richard. *Admirals in Collision*, London: Hamish Hamilton, 1959.

Howard, John W., and Myron Rothbard. 'Social Categorization and Memory for in-Group and out-Group Behavior', *Journal of Personality and Social Psychology* Vol. 38, No. 2, 301–10, 1980.

'Info Overload Can Kill'. *The Star-Ledger News*, 1 October 2006.

Jackson, Maggie. *Distracted: The Erosion of Attention and the Coming Dark Age*, Prometheus Books, 2008.

Janis, Irving L. *Victims of Groupthink: A Psychological Study of Foreign-Policy Decisions and Fiascoes*, Boston: Houghton Mifflin, 1972.

————. *Crucial Decisions: Leadership in Policymaking and Crisis Management*, Free Press, 1989.

Janis, Irving L., and Robert F. Terwilliger. 'An Experimental Study of Psychological Resistances to Fear Arousing Communications', *Journal of Abnormal and Social Psychology* Vol. 65, No. 6, 403–10, 1962.

Joint Commission, 'Behaviors That Undermine a Culture of Safety', *Joint Commission*, 2008.

Kahneman, Daniel, Alan B. Krueger, David Schkade, Norbert Schwarz, and Arthur A. Stone. 'Would You Be Happier If You Were Richer? A Focusing Illusion', *Science* Vol. 312, No. 5782, 1908–10, 2006.

Kahneman, Daniel, Paul Slovic and Amos Tversky, *Judgement under Uncertainty: Heuristics and Biases*, Cambridge University Press, 1982.

Karabell, Zachary. 'The One Who Saw It Coming', *Newsweek*, 19 January 2009.

Kegan, Robert, and Lisa Laskow Lahey. 'The Real Reason People Won't Change', *Harvard Business Review*, 85–92, 2001.

————. *Immunity to Change: How to Overcome It and Unlock Potential in Yourself and Your Organisation*, Harvard Business Press, 2009.

Kelly, Kate. *Street Fighters: The Last 72 Hours Of Bear Stearns, the Toughest Firm on Wall Street*, New York: Portfolio, 2009.

Kerber, Ross. 'The Whistleblower: Dogged Pursuer of Madoff Wary of Fame', *Boston.com*, 8 January 2009.

Kida, Thomas. *Don't Believe Everything You Think: The 6 Basic Mistakes We Make in Thinking*, Prometheus Books, 2006.

Knutson, Brian, Andrew Westdorp, Erica Kaiser, and Daniel Hommer. 'Fmri Visualization of Brain Activity During a Monetary Incentive Delay Task', *NeuroImage* Vol. 12, 20–7, 2000.

Kohn, Nicholas W., and Steven M. Smith. 'Collaborative Fixation: Effects of Others' Ideas on Brainstorming', *Applied Cognitive Psychology* Vol. DOI: 10.1.1002/acp.1699, 2010.

Kolb, Bryan, and Ian Q. Whishaw. 'Brain Plasticity and Behavior', *Annual Review of Psychology*, No. 49, 43–64, 1998.

Kolbert, Elizabeth. 'The Catastrophist', *New Yorker*, 2009.

Krackow, Annamarie, and Thomas Blass. 'When Nurses Obey or Defy Inappropriate Physician Orders: Attributional Differences', *Journal of Social Behavior and Personality* Vol. 10, No. 3, 585–94, 1995.

Krugman, Paul. 'How Did Economists Get It So Wrong?', *New York Times*, 6 September 2009.

Kunda, Ziva. 'The Case for Motivated Reasoning', *Psychological Bulletin* Vol. 108, No. 3, 480–98, 1990.

Kunst-Wilson, William Raft, and R.B. Zajonc. 'Affective Discrimination of Stimuli That Cannot Be Recognized', *Science* Vol. 207, 557–8, 1980.

Larsen, Knud S., Jeff S. Triplett, William D. Brant, and Don Langenberg. 'Collaborator Status, Subject Characteristics and Conformity in the Asch Paradigm', *Journal of Social Psychology* Vol. 108, 259–63, 1979.

Latane, Bibb, and John Darley. 'Group Inhibition of Bystander Intervention in Emergencies', *Journal of Personality and Social Psychology* Vol. 10, No. 3, 215–21, 1968.

———. 'Apathy', *American Scientist* Vol. 57, 244–68, 1969.

Latane, B., and Steve Nida. 'Ten Years of Research on Group Size and Helping', *Psychological Bulletin* Vol. 89, No. 2, 308–24, 1981.

Latane, B., and J. Rodin. 'A Lady in Distress: Inhibiting Effects of Friends and Strangers on Bystander Intervention', *Journal of Experimental Social Psychology* Vol. 5, No. 2, 189–202, 1969.

Layton, Deborah. *Seductive Poison: A Jonestown Survivor's Story of Life and Death in the Peoples Temple*, Aurum Press, 1999.

Lazear, Edward P. 'Performance Pay and Productivity', *American Economic Review* Vol. 90, No. 5, 1346–61, 2000.

Lea, Stephen E.G., and Paul Webley. 'Money as Tool, Money as Drug: The Biological Psychology of a Strong Incentive', *Behavioral and Brain Sciences* Vol. 29, 161–209, 2006.

Lee Hamilton, V., and Joseph Sanders. 'Personality and Social Psychology Review', *Personality and Social Psychology Review* Vol. 3, 222–233, 1999.

Liu, James H., and Bibb Latane. 'Extremization of Attitudes: Does Thought- and Discussion-Induced Polarization Cumulate?', *Basic and Applied Social Psychology* Vol. 20, No. 2, 103–10, 1998.

Lizza, Ryan. 'The Contrarian', *New Yorker*, 6 & 13 July 2009.

Long, Jennifer. 'Testimony at the Oversight Hearing on the Internal Revenue Service', *US Senate Committee on Finance*, 1997.

Luborsky, Lester, and Barton Blinder. 'Looking, Recalling and GSR as a Function of Defense', *Journal of Abnormal Psychology* Vol. 70, No. 4, 270–80, 1965.

Lundberg, George D. 'How Will Changes in Physician Payment by Medicare Influence Laboratory Testing?', *Journal of the American Medical Association* Vol. 258, No. 6, 803–9, 1987.

Luo, Shanhong, and Eva C. Klohnen. 'Assortative Mating and Marital Quality in Newlyweds: A Couple-Centered Approach', *Journal of Personality and Social Psychology* Vol. 88, No. 2, 304, 2005.

Mack, Arien. 'Inattentional Blindness: Looking without Seeing', *Current Directions in Psychological Science* Vol. 12, No. 5, 180–4, 2003.

Macrae, C. Neil, Alan B. Milne, and Galen V. Bodenhausen. 'Stereotypes as Energy-Saving Devices: A Peek inside the Cognitive Toolbox', *Journal of Personality and Social Psychology* Vol. 66, No. 1, 37, 1994.

Manz, Charles C., Vikas Anand, Mahendra Joshi, and Karen P. Manz. 'Emerging Paradoxes in Executive Leadership: A Theoretical Interpretation between Corruption and Virtuous Values', *Leadership Quarterly*, No. 19, 385–92, 2008.

Marcus, Jonathan L. 'Model Penal Code Section 2.02(7) and Willful Blindness', *Yale Law Journal* Vol. 102, No. 8, 2231–57, 1993.

Markey, P. M. 'Bystander Intervention in Computer-Mediated Communication', *Computers in Human Behavior* Vol. 16, No. 2, 183–8, 2000.

Markopolos, Harry. *No One Would Listen: A True Financial Thriller*, Hoboken, New Jersey, Wiley & Sons, 2010.

Marsh, Jason. 'We Are All Bystanders', *Greater Good*, Fall/Winter, 2006.

Marsh, Stefanie, and Bojan Pancevski. *The Crimes of Josef Fritzl: Uncovering the Truth*, London: Harper Element, 2009.

Martz, John M., Julie Verette, Ximena B. Arriaga, Linda F. Slovik, Chante L. Cox, and Caryl Rusbult. 'Positive Illusion in Close Relationships', *Personal Relationships* Vol. 5, 159–81, 1998.

Maslach, Christina, and Michael P. Leiter. *The Truth About Burnout: How Organizations Cause Personal Stress and What to Do About It*, Jossey-Bass, 1997.

Massing, Michael. 'The News About the Internet', *New York Review of Books*, 29–32, 13 August 2009.

McClellan, Scott. *What Happened: Inside the Bush White House and Washington's Culture of Deceptions*, New York: Public Affairs, 2008.

McLaughlin, Brian P., and Amelie Oksenberg Rorty (eds). *Perspectives on Self-Deception*, University of California Press, 1988.

McTague, Jim. 'Looking at Greenspan's Long-Lost Thesis', *Barron's*, 28 April 2008.

Mead, Nicole L., Roy F. Baumeister, Francesca Gino, Maurice E. Schweitzer, and Dan Ariely. 'Too Tired to Tell the Truth: Self-Control Resource Depletion and Dishonesty', *Journal of Experimental Social Psychology* Vol. 45, No. 3, 594–7, 2009.

Mele, Alfred R. *Self-Deception Unmasked*, Princeton University Press, 2001.

Mendelson, Sarah E., and Theodore P. Gerber. 'Failing the Stalin Test', *Foreign Affairs* Vol. 85, No. 1, 2006.

Mesmer-Magnus, Jessica, Chockalingam Viswesvaran, Jacob Joseph, and Satish P. Deshpande. 'The Role of Emotional Intelligence in Integrity and Ethics Perceptions', *Emotions, Ethics and Decision-Making: Research on Emotion in Organization* Vol. 4, 225–39, 2008.

Miceli, Marcia P., and Janet P. Near. 'Standing up or Standing By: What Predicts Blowing the Whistle on Organizational Wrong-doing?', *Research in Personnel and Human Resources Management* Vol. 24, 93–136, 2005.

Milgram, Stanley. 'The Experience of Living in Cities', *Science* Vol. 167, 1970.

———. *Obedience to Authority*, Harper Perennial, 1974.

Milkman, Katherine L., Dolly Chugh, and Max H. Bazerman. 'How Can Decision Making Be Improved?', *Perspectives on Psychological Science* Vol. 4, No. 4, 379–83, 2009.

Miller, Dale T., and Cathy McFarland. 'Pluralistic Ignorance: When Similarity Is Interpreted as Dissimilarity', *Journal of Personality and Social Psychology* Vol. 53, No. 2, 298–305, 1987.

Miller, Rowland S. *Embarrassment: Poise and Peril in Everyday Life*, Guilford Press, 1996.

Milliken, Charles S., Jennifer L. Auchterlonie, and Charles W. Hoge. 'Longitudinal Assessment of Mental Health Problems among Active and Reserve Component Soldiers Returning from the Iraq War', *Journal of the American Medical Association* Vol. 298, No. 18, 2141–8, 2007.

Milliken, Frances, J., and Elizabeth Wolfe Morrison. 'Shades of Silence: Emerging Themes and Future Directions for Research on Silence in Organizations', *Journal of Management Studies* Vol. 40, No. 6, 1563–8, 2003.

Milliken Frances, J., Elizabeth W. Morrison, and Patricia F. Hewlin. 'An Exploratory Study of Employee Silence: Issues That Employees Don't Communicate Upward and Why', *Journal of Management Studies* Vol. 40, No. 6, 1453–76, 2003.

Moll, Jorge, Frank Krueger, Roland Zahn, Matteo Pardini, Ricardo de Oliveira-Souza, and Jordan Grafman. 'Human Fronto, Äìmesolimbic Networks Guide Decisions About Charitable Donation', *Proceedings of the National Academy of Sciences* Vol. 103, No. 42, 15623–8, 2006.

Moore, Don A., and George Loewenstein. 'Self-Interest, Automaticity, and the Psychology of Conflict of Interest', *Social Justice Research* Vol. 17, No. 2, 189–202, 2004.

Moreland, Richard L., and Robert B. Zajonc. 'Exposure Effects in Person Perception: Familiarity, Similarity, and Attraction', *Journal of Experimental Social Psychology* Vol. 18, 395–415, 1982.

Morewedge, Carey K., Daniel T. Gilbert, and Timothy D. Wilson. 'The Least Likely of Times', *Psychological Science* Vol. 16, No. 8, 626–30, 2005.

Morris, Errol. *Standard Operating Procedure*, Sony Pictures, 2008.

Morrison Elizabeth, W., Sara L. Wheeler-Smith, and Dishan Kamdar. 'Speaking up in Groups: A Cross-Level Study of Group Voice Climate', *Journal of Applied Psychology* (read under review), 2009.

Moscovici, Serge, and Marisa Zavalloni. 'The Group as a Polarizer of Attitudes', *Journal of Personality and Social Psychology* Vol. 12, No. 2, 125–35, 1969.

Murray, Sandra L., John G. Holmes, Gina Bellavia, Dale W. Griffin, and Dan Dolderman. 'Kindred Spirits? The Benefits of Egocentrism in Close Relationships', *Journal of Personality and Social Psychology* Vol. 82, No. 4, 2002.

Murray, Sandra L., John G. Holmes, and Dale W. Griffin. 'The Self-Fulfilling Nature of Positive Illusions in Romantic Relationships: Love Is Not Blind, but Prescient', *Journal of Personality and Social Psychology* Vol. 7, No. 6, 1155–80, 1996.

National Safety Council, 'National Safety Council Calls for Nation-wide Ban on Cell Phone Use While Driving' Press Release, 12 January 2009.

National Sleep Foundation, '2009 Asleep in America: Poll Highlight and Findings', 2 March 2009.

Nedd, Council A. II. 'When the Solution Is the Problem: A Brief History of the Shoe Fluoroscope', *American Journal of Roentgenology* Vol. 158, 1270, 1992.

Newrx.com. 'Women Whistleblowers Suffer More Discrimination Informs-Published Study Suggests', *Integrity International website*, 28 May 2008.

Nobuyuki, Chikudate. 'Collective Myopia and Disciplinary Power Behind the Scenes of Unethical Practices: A Diagnostic Theory on Japanese Organization', *Journal of Management Studies* Vol. 39, No. 3, 289–307, 2002.

Norton, Michael I., Jeana H. Frost, and Dan Ariely. 'Less Is More: The Lure of Ambiguity, or Why Familiarity Breeds Contempt', *Journal of Personality and Social Psychology* Vol. 92, No. 1, 97–105, 2007.

Norton, Michael I., Benoit Monin, Joel Cooper, and Michael A. Hogg. 'Vicarious Dissonance: Attitude Change from the Inconsistency of Others', *Journal of Personality and Social Psychology* Vol. 85, No. 1, 47–62, 2003.

O'Gorman, Colm. *Beyond Belief*, Hodder and Stoughton, 2009.

Obedience to Authority: Current Perspectives on the Milgram Paradigm. Lawrence Erlbaum, 2000.

Osborne, William. 'Blind Auditions and Moral Myopia: The Gender/ Racial Ideologies of the Vienna Philharmonic and the Employment Practices That Allow Them to Continue', http://www.osborne-conant.org/posts/blind.htm

Osiel, Mark J. *Obeying Orders: Atrocity, Military Discipline and the Law of War*, New Brunswick, New Jersey, Transaction Publishers, 2002.

Panksepp, Jaak. 'Neuroscience: Feeling the Pain of Social Loss', *Science* Vol. 302, No. 5643, 237–9, 2003.

Panksepp, Jaak. *Affective Neuroscience: The Foundations of Human and Animal Emotions*, Oxford University Press, 1998.

Paperny, Justin M. *Lessons from Prison: Bear Stearns, UBS Stockbroker Muses on Ethics and Provides Guide through Criminal Justice System*, APS Publishing, 2009.

Parker-Pope, Tara. 'A Problem of the Brain, Not the Hands: Group Urges Phone Ban for Drivers', *New York Times*, 2009.

Partnoy, Frank. *Infectious Greed: How Deceit and Risk Corrupted the Financial Markets*, Profile Books, 2003.

———. 'The Case against Alan Greenspan', *Euromoney* Vol. 36, No. 437, 90–6, 2005.

———. *F.I.A.S.C.O.: Blood in the Water on Wall Street*, W.W. Norton, 1997, 2009.

Pascual-Leonoe, Alvaro, Nguyet Dang, Leonardo G. Cohen, Joaquim P. Brasil-Neto, Angel Cammarota, and Mark Hallett. 'Modulation of Muscle Responses Evoked by Transcranial Magnetic Stimulation During the Acquisition of New Fine Motor Skills', *Journal of Neurophysiology* Vol. 74, No. 3, 1037–45, 1995.

Pavlo, Walter Jr., and Neil Weinberg. *Stolen without a Gun*, Tampa, Florida, Etika LLC, 2007.

PBS, Frontline. *The Warning*, produced by Michael Kirk, first aired 20 October 2009.

Pelham, Brett W., Matthew C. Mirenberg, and John T. Jones. 'Why Susie Sells Seashells by the Seashore: Implicit Egotism and Major Life Decisions', *Journal of Personality and Social Psychology* Vol. 82, No. 4, 469, 2002.

Pennebaker, Ruth. 'The Mediocre Multitasker', *New York Times*, 30 August 2009.

Perry, David L. 'Why Hearts and Minds Matter', *Armed Forces Journal*, September 2006. http:www.afji.com/2006/09/2002037

Pessiglione, Mathias, Liane Schmidt, Bogdan Draganski, Raffael Kalisch, Hakwan Lau, Ray J. Dolan, and Chris D. Frith. 'How the Brain Translates Money into Force: A Neuroimaging Study of Subliminal Motivation', *Science* Vol. 316, No. 5826, 904–6, 2007.

Petty, Richard E., Gary L. Wells, and Timothy C. Brock. 'Distraction Can Enhance or Reduce Yielding to Propaganda: Thought Disruption Versus Effort Justification', *Journal of Personality and Social Psychology* Vol. 34, No. 5, 874–84, 1976.

Phillips, Katherine W., and Robert B. Jr. Lount. 'The Affective Consequences of Diversity and Homogeneity in Groups', *Affect and Groups: Research on Managing Groups and Teams* Vol. 10, 1–20, 2007.

Piderit, Sandy Kristin, and Susan J. Ashford. 'Breaking Silence: Tactical

Choices Women Managers Make in Speaking up About Gender-Equity Issues', *Journal of Management Studies* Vol. 40, No. 6, 1477–1502, 2003.

Premeaux Sonya, Fontenot, and G. Bedeian Arthur. 'Breaking the Silence: The Moderating Effects of Self-Monitoring in Predicting Speaking up in the Workplace', *Journal of Management Studies* Vol. 40, No. 6, 1537–62, 2003.

Prentice, Deborah A., and Dale T. Miller. 'Pluralistic Ignorance and Alcohol Use on Campus: Some Consequences of Misperceiving the Social Norm', *Journal of Personality and Social Psychology* Vol. 64, No. 2, 243, 1993.

Proctor, Robert N., and London (eds.) Schiebinger. *Agnotology: The Making and Unmaking of Ignorance*, Stanford University Press, 2008.

Pronin, Emily, Thomas Gilovich, and Lee Ross. 'Objectivity in the Eye of the Beholder: Divergent Perceptions of Bias in Self Versus Others', *Psychological Review* Vol. 111, No. 3, 781–99, 2004.

Proulx, Travis, and J. Heine Steven. 'Connections from Kafka: Exposure to Meaning Threats Improves Implicit Learning of an Artificial Grammar', *Psychological Science* Vol. 20, No. 9, 1125–31, 2009.

Reite, M., and T. Field (eds). *The Psychobiology of Attachment and Separation*, New York: Academic Press, 1985.

Richtel, Matt. 'U.S. Withheld Data on Risks of Distracted Driving', *New York Times*, 21 July 2009.

Robertson, Diana, John Snarey, Opal Ousley, Keith Harenski, F. DuBois Bowman, Rick Gilkey, and Clinton Kilts. 'The Neural Processing of Moral Sensitivity to Issues of Justice and Care', *Neuropsychologia* Vol. 45, No. 4, 755–66, 2007.

Robinson, Evan. 'Why Crunch Mode Doesn't Work: 6 Lessons', *International Game Developers Association*, 2005.

Rosenhan, D.L. 'On Being Sane in Insane Places', *Science* Vol. 179, No. 4070, 250–8, 1973.

Rosin, Hanna. 'When Joseph Comes Marching Home: In a Western Maryland Town, Ambivalence About the Son Who Blew the Whistle at Abu Ghraib', *Washington Post*, 17 May 2004.

Rost, Peter. *The Whistleblower: Confessions of a Healthcare Hitman*, Soft Skull Press, 2006.

Rothschild, Jeffrey M., Carol A. Keohane, Selwyn Rogers, and Charles

A. Czeisler. 'Risks of Complications by Attending Physicians after Performing Nighttime Procedures', *Journal of the American Medical Association* Vol. 302, No. 14, 1565–72, 2009.

Roubini, Nouriel. '"The Biggest Slump in US Housing In the Last 40 Years" . . . Or 53 Years?', *RGE Monitor*, 23 August 2006. www. roubini.com/roubini-monitor/142759/the_biggest_slump_ in_US_housing_in_the_last_40_years_or_53_years

Rowe, Mary. 'Dealing with – or Reporting – "Unacceptable" Behavior (with additional thoughts about the "Bystander Effect")', *Journal of the International Ombudsman Association* Vol. 2, No. 1, 2009.

Sanders, William Gerard, and Donald C. Hambrick. 'The Effects of CEO Incentive Compensation on Subsequent Firm Investments and Performance' (unpublished).

Sands, Phillips 'Polished, Assured . . . But Was He Persuasive? No', *Guardian*, 28 January 2010.

Schmitt, Rick. 'Prophet and Loss', *Stanford*, 2009.

Schneider, Andrew, and David McCumber. *An Air That Kills: How the Asbestos Poisoning of Libby, Montana Uncovered a National Scandal*, G.P. Putnam's Sons, 2004.

Schwartz, Barry. 'Incentives, Choice, Education and Well-Being', *Oxford Review of Education* Vol. 35, No. 3, 391–403, 2009.

Seager, Ashley. 'Method of Inflation Targeting Was Wrong', *Guardian*, 2009.

Seligman, Martin E.P. *Authentic Happiness*, Nicholas Brealey Publishing, 2003.

Sereny, Gitta. *Albert Speer: His Battle with Truth*, Picador, 1996.

———. *The German Trauma: Experiences and Reflections 1938–2001*, Penguin, 2001.

Sheridan, Charles L., and Richard G. King. 'Obedience to Authority with an Authentic Victim', *Proceedings, 80th Annual Convention, APA*, 165–6, 1972.

Shermer, Michael. 'The Political Brain', *Scientific American*, 26 June 2006.

Simons, Daniel J. 'Inattentional Blindness', *Scholarpedia* Vol. 2, No. 5, 3244, 2007.

Simons, Daniel J., and Christopher F. Chabris. 'Gorillas in Our Midst: Sustained Inattentional Blindness for Dynamic Events', *Perception* Vol. 28, 1059–74, 1999.

Smith, J. Walker, Ann Clurman, and Craig Wood. *Coming to Concurrence: Addressable Attitudes and the New Model for Marketing Productivity*, Racom Communications, 2005.

Sophocles. *The Theban Plays*, Penguin, 1947.

Sorkin, Andrew Ross. *Too Big to Fail: Inside the Battle to Save Wall Street*, Allen Lane, 2010.

Stanovich, Keith E., and Richard F. West. 'Individual Differences in Reasoning: Implications for the Rationality Debate?', *Behavioral and Brain Sciences* Vol. 23, 645–726, 2000.

Staub, Ervin. 'The Roots of Evil: Social Conditions, Culture, Personality, and Basic Human Needs', *Personality and Social Psychology Review* Vol. 3, 179–92, 1999.

Staub, Ervin. *The Psychology of Good and Evil: Why Children, Adults, and Groups Help and Harm Others*, Cambridge University Press, 2003.

Stewart, Alice, Josefine Webb, and David Hewitt. 'A Survey of Childhood Malignancies', *British Medical Journal*, 1495–508, 1958.

Stillman, T.F., R.F. Baumeister, N.M. Lambert, A.W. Crescioni, C.N. DeWall, and F.D. Fincham. 'Alone and without Purpose: Life Loses Meaning Following Social Exclusion', *Journal of Experimental Social Psychology* Vol. 45, No. 4, 686–94, 2009.

Stone, Jeff, and Joel Cooper. 'A Self-Standards Model of Cognitive Dissonance', *Journal of Experimental Social Psychology* Vol. 37, 228–43, 2001.

Strayer, David L., Frank A. Drews, and Dennis J. Crouch. 'A Comparison of the Cell Phone Driver and the Drunk Driver', *Human Factors* Vol. 48, No. 2, 381–91, 2006.

Sunstein, Cass R. *Going to Extremes: How Like Minds Unite and Divide*, Oxford University Press, 2009.

Swartz, Mimi, and Sherron Watkins. *Power Failure: The Inside Story of the Collapse of Enron*, Doubleday, 2003.

Taleb, Nassim Nicholas. 'David, You're Right', *Observer*, 16 August 2009.

Tangirala, Subrahmaniam, and Rangaraj Ramanujam. 'Employee Silence on Critical Work Issues: The Cross Level Effects of Procedural Justice Climate', *Personnel Psychology* Vol. 61, 37–68, 2008.

Tangney, June Price. *Self-Conscious Emotions: The Psychology of Shame, Guilt, Embarrassment and Pride*, Guilford Press, 1995.

Tavris, Carol, and Elliot Aronson. *Mistakes Were Made (But Not by Me): Why We Justify Foolish Beliefs, Bad Decisions and Hurtful Acts*, Harcourt Inc., 2007.

Tedlow Richard, S. 'Leaders in Denial', *Harvard Business Review* Vol. 86, No. 7–8, 18–19, 2008.

Tedlow, Richard S., and David Ruben. 'The Dangers of Wishful Thinking', *American*, 86–90, 2008.

Tenbrunsel, Ann E., Kristina A. Diekmann, Kimberly A. Wade-Benzoni, and Max H. Bazerman. 'The Ethical Mirage: A Temporal Explanation as to Why We Aren't as Ethical as We Think We Are', *Harvard Business School Working Paper 08–12*, 2007.

Tenbrunsel, Ann E., and David M. Messick. 'Ethical Fading: The Role of Self-Deception in Unethical Behavior', *Social Justice Research* Vol. 17, No. 2, 223–36, 2004.

Tett, Gillian. *Fool's Gold: How Unrestrained Greed Corrupted a Dream, Shattered Global Markets and Unleashed a Catastrophe*, London: Little, Brown, 2009.

Thaler, Richard H. 'From Homo Economicus to Homo Sapiens', *Journal of Economic Perspectives* Vol. 14, No. 1, 133–41, 2000.

Thompson, Courtenay. 'Willful Blindness', *Internal Auditor*, 71–3, June 2003.

Thornberg, Robert. 'A Classmate in Distress: Schoolchildren as Bystanders and Their Reasons for How They Act', *Social Psychology of Education* Vol. 10, 5–28, 2007.

Tierney, John. 'How to Concentrate in a World of Distractions', *New York Times*, 31 May 2009.

Tomasi, D., R.L. Wang, F. Telang, V. Boronikolas, M.C. Jayne, G.-J. Wang, J.S. Fowler, and N.D. Volkow. 'Impairment of Attentional Networks after 1 Night of Sleep Deprivation', *Cereb. Cortex* Vol. 19, No. 1, 233–40, 2009.

Treanor, Jill. 'Bankers Admit They Got It Wrong', *Guardian*, 11 February 2009.

———. 'Shown the Door – Brown's Banker Falls Victim to the Whistleblower', *Guardian*, 12 February 2009.

Van Dyne, Linn, Soon Ang, and C. Botero Isabel. 'Conceptualizing Employee Silence and Employee Voice as Multidimensional Constructs', *Journal of Management Studies* Vol. 40, No. 6, 1359–92, 2003.

van Straaten, Ischa, Rutger C.M.E. Engels, Catrin Finkenauer, and Rob W. Holland. 'Meeting Your Match: How Attractiveness Similarity Affects Approach Behavior in Mixed-Sex Dyads', *Personality & Social Psychology Bulletin*. Vol. 35, No. 6, 685–97, 2009.

van Veen, Vincent, Marie K. Krug, Jonathan W. Schooler, and Cameron S. Carter. 'Neural Activity Predicts Attitude Change in Cognitive Dissonance', *Nature Neuroscience* Vol. 12, No. 11, 1469–74, 2009.

Vermeulen, Freek. 'Why Stock Options Are a Bad Option', *Harvard Business Review* (website), 21 April 2009.

Vohs, Kathleen, D. 'Merely Activating the Concept of Money Changes Personal and Interpersonal Behavior', *Current Directions in Psychological Science* Vol. 17, No. 3, 208–12, 2008.

Vohs, Kathleen D., Nicole L. Mead, and Miranda R. Goode. 'The Psychological Consequences of Money', *Science* Vol. 314, No. 5802, 1154–6, 2006.

Walker Report, 'Psychological and Behavioural Elements in Board Performance'. Vol. Annex 4, 2009.

Webb, Tim. 'Sun King Reveals His Darker Side', *Guardian*, 9 February 2010.

Webb, Tim, Robert Booth, Justin McCurry, and Paul Harris. 'How World's Biggest Carmaker Managed to Veer So Far Off Course', *Observer*, 7 February 2010.

Weinberger, Joel, and Drew Westen. 'Rats, We Should Have Used Clinton: Subliminal Priming in Political Campaigns', *Political Psychology* Vol. 29, No. 5, 631–51, 2008.

Weisbuch, Max, Stacey A. Sinclair, and Jeanine L. Skorinko. 'Self-Esteem Depends on the Beholder: Effects of a Subtle Social Value Cue', *Journal of Experimental Social Psychology* Vol. 45, No. 1, 143–9, 2009.

Werner, Anna. 'Oakland Bank's Lending Sparks Ex-Employee Lawsuit', *CBS.com*, 21 May 2008.

Wertz, Adam T., Joseph M. Ronda, and Charles A. Czeisler. 'Effects of Sleep Inertia on Cognition', Vol. 295, No. 2, 2006.

Westen, Drew. *The Political Brain: The Role of Emotion in Deciding the Fate of the Nation*, New York: Public Affairs, 2007.

Westen, Drew, Pavel S. Blagov, Keith Harenski, Clint Kilts, and

Stephan Hamann. 'Neural Bases of Motivated Reasoning: An Fmri Study of Emotional Constraints on Partisan Political Judgment in the 2004 U.S. Presidential Election', *Journal of Cognitive Neuroscience* Vol. 18, No. 11, 1947–58, 2006.

White, Jenny, Albert Bandura, and Lisa A. Bero. 'Moral Disengagement in the Corporate World', *Accountability in Research* Vol. 16, No. 1, 41–74, 2009.

Wispe, Lauren. *Altruism, Sympathy and Helping: Psychological and Sociological Principles*, Academic Press, 1978.

Woodward, Bob. *Maestro: Greenspan's Fed and the American Boom*, Simon and Schuster, 2000.

———. *State of Denial: Bush at War, Part III*, Simon and Schuster, 2006.

Young-Bruehl. *Hannah Arendt: For Love of the World*, New Haven: Yale University Press, 1982.

Zerubavel, Eviatar. *The Elephant in the Room: Silence and Denial in Everyday Life*, Oxford: Oxford University Press, 2006.

Zhou, Xinyue, Cong Feng, Lingnan He, and Ding-Guo Gao. 'Toward an Integrated Understanding of Love and Money: Intrinsic and Extrinsic Pain Management Mechanisms', *Psychological Inquiry* Vol. 19, 208–20, 2008.

Zhou, Xinyue, Kathleen D. Vohs, and Roy F. Baumeister. 'The Symbolic Power of Money: Reminders of Money Alter Social Distress and Physical Pain', *Psychological Science* Vol. 20, No. 6, 700–6, 2009.

Zimbardo, Philip G., 'Discontinuity Theory: Cognitive and Social Searches for Rationality and Normality May Lead to Madness', *Advances in Experimental Social Psychology* Vol. 31, 345–413, 1991.

Zimbardo, Philip G. *The Lucifer Effect: How Good People Turn Evil*, Random House, 2007.

Zimbardo, Philip G. 'The Heroic Imagination Project', Planning documents, 2009.

INDEX

ACKNOWLEDGEMENTS

The idea for this book derived from two plays that I wrote for the BBC about Enron; had it not been for the commissioning courage of Jeremy Howe, Clare McGinn and Sara Davies, I would never have found myself submerged in the transcript of Ken Lay's trial. Encountering the legal doctrine of wilful blindness felt like introducing a magnet to a mess of iron filings. Without Fiona Wilson, I would not have had access to that transcript and without a timely conversation with Joelle Delbourgo, my ensuing thoughts might have gone nowhere. If it weren't for Alan Weber and Claire Alexander, I might not be writing at all.

One of the glories of American academic life is the openness and enthusiasm with which scholars generously share their work and insights with curious investigators. I am immensely grateful to all of those who appear in this book, who gave their time generously and were always prepared to engage with my questions and challenges. If their work is imperfectly articulated, that is my fault, not theirs. I'd also like to thank Beth Edwards for guiding me through the legal nuances of wilful blindness, a tremendous act of generosity while she still defended the state of California. In Texas, the attorneys Brent Coon and Eric Newell were thoughtful and generous in sharing with me their years of insight into the workings of BP. They will, alas, be at work for many years to come.

I would also like to thank the people of Libby, Montana, who were open, hospitable and generous. Their character is more impressive even than the stunning surroundings in which they live.

In the United Kingdom, I am especially grateful to the London Library and the library at the University of Bath, without whose resources I would have been blind indeed. I've also been grateful for stimulating and provocative colleagues, especially Glynis Breakwell, Ajit Nayak, Michael Meyer, Sarah Dixon and Svenja Tams. I'm indebted to Ian Stockley for his insights into the world of digital direct marketing and its relationship to big ideas. I would also like to thank Don Honeyman and Gitta Sereny for being prepared to share their memories of Speer after all these years. I owe a great deal to Donna Banks and Nancy Coveney whose obsessive fact-checking has made me a more fastidious writer. I'd also like to thank David Carter and Andrew Dyckhoff of Merryck & Co. for encouraging me to share some of my thinking with their executives at an early stage. The feedback I received was encouraging and helpful.

In tracking down a strange array of experts, fraudsters and Cassandras, Isobel Eaton proved fearless and determined, regardless of time zone. While crossing the United States in what sometimes felt like a tour of industrial disasters, I was hugely encouraged and energised by the hospitality, generosity and kindness of Paul Muldoon, Jean Hanff Korelitz, Rob and Fiona Wilson, Tatiana Lanning, Cindy Solomon, David and Denise Nicholson, and Beth and Chuck Finkle. They provided sustenance in more ways than one and stopped my own blind spots from being bigger and more numerous. I'd also like to thank Nick Bicat and Philip Ridley for writing, in *Lie to Me*, the wilful blindness theme song.

I'm indebted to Mike Jones and Natasha Fairweather for their wonderful mixture of patience, punctiliousness and enthusiasm;

it's a tremendous privilege to have such quality collaborators. Their steady support and wise encouragement meant more than they can imagine.

If at times writing this book made me wilfully blind to the needs and wants of my two children, Felix and Leonora Nicholson, I hope it's also left me more appreciative of their stamina and self-sufficiency. More impressive still has been the patience and forbearance of my husband, Lindsay Nicholson. He put up with my gross intrusions into the world of neuroscience, regularly identified new cases of wilful blindness and demonstrated yet again his tremendous capacity for the perfect probing question. My trip into the land of wilful blindness was a long one and it's good to be home.

Finally I'd like to pay tribute to my sister, Pamela Stewart, who has seen wilful blindness and its costs at close quarters. She has always been prepared to articulate difficult truths and her example has been a model and an inspiration throughout my life.